Harvard
Dissertations in
Philosophy ——

Edited by

Robert Nozick

**Arthur Kingsley
Porter Professor of
Philosophy
Harvard University**

A Garland Series

Morality as Rationality

A Study of Kant's Ethics

Barbara Herman

GARLAND PUBLISHING
NEW YORK & LONDON
1990

Library of Congress Cataloging-in-Publication Data

Herman, Barbara.
Morality as rationality: a study of Kant's ethics / Barbara
Herman.
p.   cm. — (Harvard dissertations in philosophy)
Thesis (Ph.D.)—Harvard University, 1976.
Includes bibliographical references.
ISBN 0-8240-3205-5
1. Kant, Immanuel, 1724–1804.—Ethics. 2. Ethics. 3.
Reason. I. Title. II. Series.
B2799.E8H53   1990
170—dc20   89-49388

All volumes printed on acid-free, 250-year-life paper
Manufactured in the United States of America

Design by Julie Threlkeld

Preface (1989)

When I began work on this thesis, Kant's moral theory was a somewhat marginal topic in contemporary moral philosophy. Interpretations of Kant were pretty much fixed,[1] and seemingly decisive criticisms of the theory were well-entrenched. In the past fifteen years, the situation has changed dramatically. There has been a revival of interest in Kantian ethics (encouraged in part by the Kantian claims in John Rawls' *Theory of Justice*) both as an under-appreciated body of work and as a viable alternative to consequentialist thinking. The old criticisms have been shown to be based on erroneous interpretations of Kant; new interpretations make better sense of the text and suggest the range and power of the theory. This thesis was written as this process began.

The ambition of the thesis was to show that the way to understand the central claims of Kant's ethics is to accept the idea that morality is a distinctive form of rationality; that the moral "ought" belongs to a *system* of imperatives based in practical reason; and that moral judgment, therefore, is a species of rational assessment of agents' actions. It argues, in effect, that you cannot understand Kant's views about morality if you read him with Humean assumptions about rationality.

Appreciation of these facts focuses attention on "maxims": the subjective principles of action Kant uses as the objects of moral judgment. Difficulties in specifying maxims—the "action description problem"—led many commentators to doubt that maxims could be used this way. But Kant does not offer maxims as a general answer to the problem of action description. Rather he sees maxims (and the description of action that belongs in a maxim) as a way of presenting an action for a specific purpose: assessment by the norms of practical rationality. So if the purpose is the assessment of action by norms of rationality, one must look to those norms to elicit the elements of action-description needed for maxims. The thesis elaborates this idea, arguing that there is *a* maxim of an action which contains the description of the action *as-it-is-willed*, i.e., as it is part of the purposive enterprise of an agent who would act rationally.

The thesis develops its account of maxims by working with an array of cases and the non-moral Hypothetical Imperative. The requirements drawn from the norms of technical and prudential rationality dispel most of the traditional difficulties in fixing a level of generality of action description in maxims (the "tailoring" problem), difficulties that had been thought to undermine the usefulness of maxims and thus the possibility of using a moral norm (the Categorical Imperative) that depended on them. In later work[2] I extend this project to include the special requirements on action description that are to be drawn from the Categorical Imperative.

Apart from the chapters on maxims, the most useful discussions in the thesis are contained in its last chapter. Two are particularly important. In response to some possible objections it is argued that the Categorical Imperative is part of a hierarchically ordered set of moral norms. Thus the rationality of morality, while regulative, is not independent of ordinary rationality. The second is a set of speculative suggestions about what follows from the fact that the Categorical Imperative assesses maxims. If maxims contain action descriptions that reflect particular agent's willings, then there will inevitably be a subject-relative aspect to moral judgment. Different agents in similar circumstances could receive different reports from the Categorical Imperative as to what they are permitted to do—depending on the maxim each brings to the Categorical Imperative for assessment. There is reason to see this less as a difficulty for Kantian theory than as an opportunity for reflection on alternate conditions of objectivity in ethics.

—**Barbara Herman**

Notes

1.   The exceptions were the generallly ignored second half of Marcus Singer's *Generalization in Ethics*, Allen Wood's *Kant's Moral Religion*, a small set of articles by Tom Hill, Jr., and Onora (Nell) O'Neill's *Acting on Principle*.

2.   Cf. "The Practice of Moral Judgment" (1985) and "Moral Deliberation and the Derivation of Duties" (forthcoming).

Bibliography

Recent work that is related to topics of this thesis:

Buchanan, Allen. "Categorical Imperatives and Moral Principles," *Philosophical Studies* 31 (1977).

Herman, Barbara. "Integrity and Impartiality," *Monist* 66 (April 1983).

"Murder and Mayhem: Violence and Kantian Casuistry," *Monist* 72 (July 1989).

"Mutual Aid and Respect for Persons," *Ethics* 94 (July 1984).

"On the Value of Acting from the Motive of Duty," *Philosophical Review* 90 (July 1981).

"The Practice of Moral Judgment," *Journal of Philosophy* 82 (August 1985).

"Rules, Motives, and Helping Actions," *Philosophical Studies* 45 (May 1984).

Hill, Thomas, E., Jr., "Humanity as an End in Itself," *Ethics* 91 (1980).

"The Hypothetical Imperative," *Philosophical Review* 82 (October 1973).

"Kant on Imperfect Duty and Supererogation," *Kant-Studien* 62 (1971).

"Kant's Argument for the Rationality of Moral Conduct," *Pacific Philosophical Quarterly* 66 (January/April 1985).

Korsgaard, Christine M., "Kant's Formula of Humanity," *Kant-Studien* (April 1986).

"Kant's Formula of Universal Law," *Pacific Philosophical Quarterly* 66 (January/April 1985).

"The Right to Lie: Kant on Dealing with Evil," *Philosophy and Public Affairs* 15 (Fall 1986).

"Skepticism about Practical Reason," *Journal of Philosophy* 83 (January 1986).

"Two Distinctions in Goodness," *Philosophical Review* 92 (April 1983).

O'Neill, Onora (Nell). *Acting on Principle: An Essay on Kantian Ethics*: Columbia University Press, 1975.

"Consistency in Action," in Potter and Timmons, *Morality and Universality*: D. Reidel, 1987.

Rawls, John., "Kantian Constructivism in Moral Theory," *Journal of Philosophy* 77 (September 1980).

Table of Contents

Preface

I am concerned in this thesis with the Kantian claim that morality is a form (perhaps the highest form) of rationality. That is to say, in acting morally we are acting rationally _and_ there are norms of rationality that require us to act morally—in so far as we are or would be rational. The latter claim is the distinctively Kantian one, and the position in greatest need of careful statement and elaboration if it is not to seem either counter-intuitive or demonstrably false or based on some piece of archaic metaphysics.

One source of the traditional failure simply to see what Kant is saying when he claims to show the essential rationality of moral principles and conduct is in a commitment to a model of practical rationality whose sole governing norm is the means-end relation of prudential reasoning. A clear statement of this view can be found in the conclusion of Mrs. Foot's "Morality as a System of Hypothetical Imperatives" where she moves from the position that there is no special rational constraint to act morally to the claim that 'morality' itself depends upon a particular set of interests and wants (that an individual may or may not have) that we call moral or virtuous, because of their importance to us, etc. _If_, according to Mrs. Foot, a person has these moral wants, in acting morally such a person _is_ acting rationally, because acting in accordance with what one wants just is what it is to act rationally. When no such wants are present, then there is _no reason_ to act morally[1]— that is, it is in no way irrational for such a person not to act morally.

The intent of this essay is not to deny the importance of the employment of reason in the pursuit of our various contingent ends, but to suggest that a commitment to even a rather sophisticated version of such a view can prevent one from seeing that and how Kant is arguing against just this idea of a single, univocal norm of practical reason. One cannot simply assert that "irrational actions are those in which a man in some way defeats his own purposes, doing what is calculated to be disadvantageous or to frustrate his ends",[2] and then use this as the basis for the contention that there are no grounds for claiming that there is anything necessarily irrational in the amoral person's rejection of morality. The question is, why should we agree at the start that there is only one form of practical rationality? and further, that while prudential considerations always give reasons for action, moral considerations do not? (According to Mrs. Foot, it may be perfectly rational to ask 'immoral—so what?' but never 'imprudent—so what?')[3]

Overall, the aim of this work is two-fold: to make out what Kant takes the relationship between morality and rationality to be, and to make both the relationship and the resulting moral theory appear plausible and largely resistant to the standard objections. Such objections have been taken so much for granted that they often stand as an excuse for not working with the theory as it was intended or, in any case, as it was written. It is my hope that the work that follows will show the value of reading the texts with care and attentiveness. I also read them with some sympathy; it will be clear where that was necessary.

A word, then, needs to be said about the way in which I have worked with the texts. The goal of understanding the central Kantian claim has been the principle arbiter of which aspects of Kant's ethics are the focus of this study. Hence the emphasis on maxims, imperatives as principles of rational action, and the characterization of rational willing in the formulae of the Categorical Imperative. In addition to making no claim to being a comprehensive account of Kant's ethics (or even of all the main themes), this thesis is not intended to be a work of historical scholarship. I have not canvassed all the relevant texts for everything Kant has to say about the topics under consideration, although I do believe I am working with the most important. I am not concerned with particular textual or, sometimes, even theoretical inconsistencies that can be found in Kant's ethical theory unless they are found to be a barrier to advancing understanding. I at times offer analyses of central notions even when it is impossible to establish that they are precisely what Kant had in mind, and even in the face of (some) conflicting evidence. If the account rests on good textual evidence, if it enables one to use the notion fruitfully and in a fashion consistent with Kant's procedures, and there is no other, better, account that does the job as well, I take it to be well-founded and in need of no further defense.

It has been my experience that unless one adopts such a procedure, the difficulties internal to each and among the relevant texts overwhelm the interpretive effort. The only criterion of adequacy there can be for such interpretation is whether it 'opens' the text by illuminating difficult concepts or passages, and thereby advances understanding of the whole. The danger inherent in this procedure is plain—one will inevitably be tempted to force the argument or to ignore as irrelevant passages which are manifestly central to Kant's exposition. This danger is not a reason not to proceed; it is a reason to be careful. It is also one of the reasons I pay so much attention to a single text—the Groundwork of the Metaphysics of Morals—for it is harder to stray inadvertently from Kant's intentions if one is bound by the internal transitions of the argument of a text.

Something more should be said about the emphasis in what follows on the Groundwork. It is well known as the text with the greatest surface clarity; something is said in it about almost all of Kant's major ethical doctrines; it has received more attention from commentators and critics than any of the other ethical writings. While these facts are not a matter of indifference, they are not the ground of the strong emphasis on the Groundwork here. In the end, I suppose, it was that the Groundwork convinced me. I found I could move from ordinary moral conceptions to the metaphysics of morals through the theory of imperatives—as Kant claimed it was possible to do. Then again, it is in the Groundwork that the nature of action is emphasized and the forms of practical rationality and judgment introduced through a general account of imperatives founded on ordinary intuition.

Part of what I hope to show in the early chapters is just how close to intuition the general theory of imperatives is, and how it is possible to generate most of the technical apparatus Kant employs out of our standard and ordinary judgments about cases. Indeed, one of the things I hope to show is that the theory of maxims (maxims of action) actually aids us in understanding what we are doing when we assess the rationality of our own and others' conduct. In short, the Groundwork—with its emphasis on volition, imperatives, principles of judgment (for assessing the rationality of actions)—is the central text for the effort

to come to terms with Kant's controversial claim that moral principles
are a distinct species of principles of practical reason.

In the end, it is the richness, the endless fertility and continu-
ally surprising depth of insight of Kant's ethical writings that prompt
the effort to join with them neither as a historian, simply, nor merely
as a philosophical critic. To a degree, the enterprise requires an act
of faith: that there is something, perhaps a great deal, to be gained
from engaging with these texts as sympathetically and as constructively
as one is able. That others may, working from the same materials, read
them as saying something different, but also of interest, I take to be
more a confirmation of this conviction than a potential challenge to the
legitimacy of what I will have to say of them here.

Citations of Kant's works are given in the text of this essay, using
the following abbreviations:

G	Groundwork of the Metaphysics of Morals
CrPrR	Critique of Practical Reason
DV	Doctrine of Virtue
DJ	The Metaphysical Elements of Justice (Doctrine of Justice)
Religion	Religion Within the Limits of Reason Alone
CrPuR	Critique of Pure Reason

In references to the Groundwork, the Critique of Practical Reason, the
Doctrine of Virtue and the Doctrine of Justice, the first page number
given is from the English translation, the second from the Prussian
Academy edition of Kant's collected works. (References to and quota-
tions from the Groundwork are primarily from the Paton translation; when
the Beck translation is used, it is so indicated, and only the page number of the translation is given.) Page references to Religion Within

the <u>Limits</u> <u>of</u> <u>Reason</u> <u>Alone</u> are to the English translation; references to the <u>Critique</u> <u>of</u> <u>Pure</u> <u>Reason</u> are to the first edition (A) and the second edition (B) as is customary.

Notes

1. Mrs. Foot correctly discounts the case where there are other non-moral reasons which would be sufficient to produce morally correct action.

2. P. Foot, "Morality as a System of Hypothetical Imperatives", p. 310.

3. Ibid.

Chapter One: Introduction

We know it is the fundamental claim of Kant's ethics that moral
principles (if they are not 'illusory') must be principles of practical
reason. What we need to see is what this claim amounts to. We also know
that a basic tenet of his ethical system is that the principles of the
three types of imperative—technical, pragmatic, categorical—exhaust
the principles of practical reason. If there is to be a special relation
between rationality and morality, it ought to be perspicuous in the nature of the different forms of imperative. Imperatives, however, are
objective or normative principles of rational willing. That is, for
Kant, practical rationality is exhibited in volition—in willing (G 80;
412-13). What we need to do then, and this will be the primary task of
this first chapter, is start at the bottom with an account of Kant's
theory of volition.

The account of volition we give will not be complete; it is designed
to introduce the idea of imperatives as objective or normative principles
of willing: the different types of imperative will be described and
their general relation to the will indicated. The procedure will be to
present the elements of volition Kant uses and then to show how they can
be regarded in a natural and inutitive way. In a similar fashion we will
try to develop a natural rendering of imperatives—leaving aside, in this
chapter, problems special to the categorical imperative. This general
strategy will be followed throughout the essay. Some technical notion
will be introduced and defined; then considerable effort will be given to
presenting persuasive considerations drawn from simple examples to

motivate and explain Kant's formal analytical vocabulary. As this project develops we should find that we become able to use Kant's terminology with ease and insight. In the first two chapters we will consider
Kant's account of volition, paying particular attention in chapter two to
the notion of the **maxim** of an action—since it is the formal device
through which actions, willings, etc. are evaluated. Chapters three
through six will examine in detail the criteria Kant presents for assessing the rationality of particular maxims—the imperatives. In this chapter we will begin by exhibiting Kant's account of the general nature of
willing. We will show how the nature of the concept of willing Kant uses
leads to that of the imperatives as norms of the will's rationality. Our
goal is to reach an understanding of why Kant takes willing to be a
necessary component in assessments of the rationality of action.

Every 'willing', every act of volition, has three constitutive components: a motive or determining ground (Bestimmungsgrund, Bewegungsgrund)
an end (Zweck) or object (Object, Gegenstand), and a principle or law according to which an agent (a rational being) determines himself to act.[1]
Animals or subrational beings could be said to have ends and motives as
well: their activity can be described both as having a purpose (e.g., to
kill the prey) and as being motivated (by, e.g., hunger). But animals do
not, according to Kant (DV 51;391), have a will.

> Will is a kind of causality belonging to living beings so
> far as they are rational. (G 114;446)

> The will is conceived as a power of determining oneself to
> action in accordance with the idea of certain laws. And
> such a power can be found only in rational beings. (G 95;427)

> Everything in nature works in accordance with laws. Only
> a rational being has the power to act in accordance with
> his idea of laws--that is, in accordance with principles--
> and only so has he a <u>will</u>. Since reason is required in
> order to derive actions from laws, the will is nothing but
> practical reason. (G 80;412)

> To have a will /is to have a/ faculty of determining
> /one's/ causality through the conception of a rule....
> (CrPrR 32;32)

That is, to have a will is to be the kind of being who is capable of be-

ing moved (to action) by your own idea of laws (or principles).

There is no need now to produce a catalogue of such laws and prin-

ciples--the most important kinds will be laws of cause and effect or

causal connections, principles or policies of life that one adopts, and

the normative principles of rational action (willing). A simple example

of a standard employment of 'will' should suffice to see what this

amounts to: Suppose I have the desire to be a concert pianist. I know

the empirical connection between practicing eight hours a day and my be-

coming a concert pianist (i.e., I have knowledge of a law or principle).

As a result, I begin a regular program of practicing eight hours every

day. In this case I will have acted in accordance with my idea of a

'law' (the known empirical connection): I will have performed in a man-

ner possible only for a being with a will. Only a being with a will can

pursue an end by having a conception of it as an effect possible through

a course of antecedent, causally related action. It does not follow

from its being possible for me to be moved by my idea of laws (or law-

like connections) that what I take to be a law is a law (I can be mis-

taken). Nor does it follow that I cannot be moved by other things as

well: the will is only a capacity, a power--it can perform well, or de-

viate from its pure employment. This latter feature uniquely characterizes the finite or imperfectly rational will (e.g., the human will); a purely or perfectly rational will (e.g., a Holy Will), by its nature can never be moved contrary to the dictates of reason. To have a will at all is to have the capacity to be moved—to some degree or other—by reason. Kant makes this connection explicit: to be moved by one's idea of a law, etc., is to have one's action (what one intends to do) determined by reason in its practical application—that is, by practical reason. "Since reason is required in order to derive actions from laws, the will is nothing but practical reason." None of this amounts to the claim that we are beings who can be moved <u>wholly</u> by reason. That is, what has been said so far about the will is independent of the question of the possibility of the categorical imperative, or, as that question is posed in the Second Critique: Is pure reason sufficient of itself to determine the will, or is it only as empirically conditioned that it can do so (CrPrR 15;16)? To put this another way, there is nothing in this initial characterization of what it is to have a will that would be incompatible with a Humean model of action and volition.

We need now to complicate our simple model of a volition to see more clearly the possible relations of its elements, and to highlight the features that make the actions of rational beings unique. Although we will not be in a position to appreciate the centrality of the <u>motive</u> of an action in Kant's theory until we consider its role in determining <u>the</u> maxim of an action, we should consider here a kind of typical variability in the relations of end and motive that are basic in Kant's conception of human volition. Consider again the concert-pianist example, only now in two variants. In the first, the end is becoming a concert pianist, and we will imagine the motive to be, simply, the desire to be a concert pianist. In the second case, let the end be the same, but now imagine the motive to be a desire for success and fame by age thirty. The action following from 'principle' we will assume is the same in both. The desire (motive) in each case functions as what Kant calls 'the determining ground of choice', the 'condition of the subject' in virtue of which an end is adopted, i.e. willed.[2] That is, although the end is nominally the same in both cases, the different desires the agents have call for their ends to be conceived as being of a certain kind. The force of this can best be seen in the way an agent's relation to his end (or to the pursuit of his end) is affected by changes in belief—changes, in particular, that will lead to abandonment of the end, or its replacement by another. If my drive is for success, and I discover that my musical talents are inadequate, it would be rational both for me to abandon my end of becoming a concert pianist and also to adopt another in its place. (This example moves into strangeness through the implausibility of a success motive completely detached from other interests and desires; the point of the example, which is largely structural, should be unaffected by this.) If, on the other hand, both my desire and my end are to become a concert pianist, and the requisite skill is found lacking, I would be wise to abandon my end, but there is no obvious sense in which the original desire would conjure a replacement—it would simply be frustrated. That is, the character of the end in the success story is instrumental, and therefore it could be replaced by another of that kind, so long as, following a familiar way of speaking, I did not come to desire the end for its own sake. The very conception of one's end—of what <u>kind</u> of end it is, and the way in which one is concerned with it—is shaped by the motive: the subjective ground of choice.

It will be of great importance that we remain attentive to the complexity of the relations between end and motive. This is especially so given that adopting (or willing) an end is not just a matter of hoping for some state of affairs to come about, but is the shaping of a resolve to act for the goal. In so far as one's conception of the goal is shaped by the motive prompting one to adopt the goal as an end of action, how one is to act is determined by the relation of end to motive.

An important aspect of this relation—and one which Kant frequently uses to distinguish animal and human activity—is the <u>way</u> we adopt ends, given that we have various motives. "That which can be determined only by <u>inclination</u> (sensuous impulse, <u>stimulus</u>) would be animal choice. Human choice is such that, while it can be <u>affected</u> by impulses, it cannot be <u>determined</u> by them." (DV 10;213). Animals, strictly speaking, do not adopt ends. "The power to set an end—any end whatsoever—is the characteristic of humanity (as distinguished from animality)" (DV 51; 391). "An <u>end</u> is an object of the power of choice (of a rational being), through the thought of which choice is determined to an action to produce this object" (DV 38;380). Animal choice, for Kant, is not mediated by the idea of an object, and is not free to pursue or refrain from pursuit—it is 'determined' (moved) by the presence or absence of a suitable (strongest) impulse. Rational choice, and so human choice, can be <u>with</u> <u>respect</u> <u>to</u> impulse or inclination—that is, in so far as we are rational we <u>adopt</u> our ends, we do not simply <u>have</u> them. (This is

ultimately the ground of our responsibility.) "Since no one can have an
end without himself making the object of choice into an end, it follows
that the adoption of any end of action whatsoever is an act of freedom
on the agent's part, not an operation of nature" (DV 43;384). Our desires may prompt us to seek an end (and we are not free with respect to
the desires we have), but as rational beings we do not automatically
have an end—we are not automatically moved to act—as the result of
having a (strongest) desire. "The will is not determined directly by
desire. Something becomes an incentive for the will only when the individual incorporates it into his maxim" (Religion, 19). We are not moved
to act necessarily by our strongest desire. We can determine what desire (if any) to satisfy. We can deliberate about our desires—e.g.,
about how we would most like them to be satisfied. This is what is
meant by saying that the will of a rational being is free from direct
determination by desire. (The contrast is being subject to the force of
impulse, reflex or instinct.) There is an example Anscombe borrows from
Plato that illustrates this nicely.[3] A slavemaster refrains from beating a slave who has deserved punishment lest he should do so from anger,
saying, "I should beat you if I were not angry." While one cannot
choose the motives or desires one will have, one can choose 'whether to
act from a motive': We can (at least sometimes) choose whether or not
we will allow ourselves to be moved to action by a particular motive.

The willing of rational beings is characterized by Kant in terms of
its maxim—the subjective principle by which an agent determines himself
to act.[4] For human volition, a maxim is "a practical rule determined by
reason in accordance with the conditions of the subject (often his

ignorance or again his inclinations): it is thus a principle on which the subject <u>acts</u>" (G 88n;421n). That action or volition can be 'determined by reason' at all distinguishes the human will from the subrational animal will; that it is 'in accordance with the conditions of the subject' distinguishes it from the divine or holy will, which is not subjected to the conditions of sensibility. The concept of a divine will is the concept of a will whose determining ground of action (motive) is of necessity unopposed by and independent of need or inclination—a will determined <u>directly</u> by pure practical reason. The human will, by contrast, is subjected to complex and conflicting motivation: it is moved both by reason <u>and</u> the conditions of ordinary sensibility. Human willing is naturally and necessarily with respect to ends and from motives that suit ourselves as rational <u>and</u> sensible subjects. We inevitably strive for the kind of happiness and contentment suitable to our very specific situations. The principles (maxims) according to which we characteristically act are determined by our wants, etc., or our conception of what will make us happy. They are <u>subjective</u> principles: principles on which a subject acts. The central task of the <u>Groundwork</u> might be given as describing the conditions in which an agent's subjective maxims are also <u>objective</u>: valid for every rational being, regardless of inclination or an agent's particular subjective constitution. It is because our maxims may not be objective—because our actions are not always rational—that Kant says we are subject to <u>imperatives</u>: principles which direct the will to conform to principles valid for all rational beings. For the perfectly rational or divine will, whatever the nature or conditions of the subject, volition is in accordance with principles valid for every rational being. All of its subjective principles would also be objective. Such a will is said not to be subject to imperatives.

To understand the import of this and what the point of introducing imperatives might be, we need a fuller account of what an imperative is. But before we look to a definition of imperatives, if the idea behind imperatives is based on the fact that the human will is not wholly or necessarily rational, it will be of use to pause with some examples in order to see the pre-theoretical source of this characterization of human willing. (Our purpose here, it should be recalled, is both to explain and to motivate the basic concepts of Kant's moral theory.) When I know it is both in my best interest and in my power to refrain from smoking, and I do not, it may well be said that I am subject to complex and conflicting motivation—indeed, whether I smoke or not, the choice is hard and issues from some resolution of competing desires. If it is true that it is in my best interest not to smoke, and that if one is rational one ought to do what (one knows?) is in one's best interest, and it is within my power to do so, then if I smoke, I am not acting rationally. (This form of practical irrationality is regulated by pragmatic imperatives: imperatives concerned with the promotion of happiness.) If I have chronic back trouble and want sound medical advice, but go to the doctor of passing fashion, I am again not acting rationally, although not necessarily in the same way as in the first example. (Examples such as this will be the subject of technical imperatives: imperatives governing the choice of means to ends.) A more controversial example, but c e obviously central to Kant's account of rational volition, is the failure to do what is morally right (e.g. I betray a trust for the sake of my personal advantage). In this case as well, Kant would say I am not acting rationally. (Such cases are, of course, governed by categorical imperatives.) I will say no more at this time about the 'moral' case—and, in particular, what Kant could mean by identifying a morally wrong action with a failure of rationality—since it is the object of this first chapter merely to set the stage for attempting that account. These examples are simply meant to show the kinds of willing one might think required regulation by rational norms. Given this background we are ready for the formal introduction of imperatives.

What is important at this juncture is to be clear about the sort of thing an imperative is, and in what sense we are subject to it as a constraint on action and willing.

Let us consider what Kant says:

> If reason infallibly determines the will, then in a being of this kind the actions which are recognized to be objectively necessary are also subjectively necessary—that is to say, the will is then a power to choose only that which reason independently of inclination recognizes to be practically necessary, that is, to be good. But if reason solely by itself is not sufficient to determine the will; if the will is exposed also to subjective conditions (certain impulsions) which do not always harmonize with the objective ones; if, in a word, the will is not in itself completely in accord with reason (as actually happens in the case of men); then actions which are recognized to be objectively necessary are subjectively contingent, and the determination of such a will in accordance with objective laws is necessitation.... The conception of an objective principle so far as this principle is necessitating for a will is called a command (of reason), and the formula of this command is called an Imperative. All imperatives are expressed by an 'ought' (Sollen). (G 80–81;412–13)

/Imperatives/ say that something would be good to do or to leave undone; only they say it to a will which does not always do a thing because it has been informed that this is a good thing to do.... Imperatives are...formulae for expressing the relation of objective laws of willing to the subjective imperfection of the will of this or that rational being—for example, of the human will. (G 81;413-14)

This extended quotation from the Groundwork presents the central features of the notion of an imperative with, for Kant, surprising clarity. Apart from the questions whether there are any imperatives, and if there are, which, if any, of those proposed by Kant, the question we will find hardest is how imperatives are to be applied. A less difficult task, although not for that of less importance, is determining what sort of thing imperatives are intended to be. I will try in what follows to show that imperatives (in general) can usefully be viewed as rather familiar normative principles of action, and furthermore, to show to what extent Kant's general account of imperatives is really uncontroversial.

If it is possible to imagine a creature capable of action (or at least of volition) whose activity, whose willing, is completely and naturally in accord with reason, that creature is not subject to imperatives. Beings who are subject to imperatives are those rational beings whose wills are 'exposed' to some influence in addition to their reason, which in some sense is able to contend with reason for controlling influence in the determination of the will. That is, in order to be subject to an imperative it must be possible for a being to act (or will) in a way that is not in accordance with rational principles—with reason. The obvious presupposition of this account is that there are "objective laws of willing"—principles of reason that apply to the practical

activity of all rational beings.[5] That there are some norms or principles of rationality that apply to action is a reasonable and non-
controversial assumption. An obvious candidate is the means-end principle of prudential action: if a goal is to be pursued, one ought—it
is rational—to act in such a way that one's action will be a means to
the attainment of the desired end. Also, few would dispute the requirement that a person's different ends each be pursued in a manner most
compatible with the pursuit of other ends of equal or greater importance—and that this requirement was an expression of what would be
rational for a being with various and potentially conflicting ends. And
so on. In so far as it is natural to express these requirements by an
'ought', and if it is correct to call a person more or less rational to
the degree that the means he selects in pursuit of his ends are likely
to lead to his goals, and to the extent that he does not undermine long-
term projects in pursuit of fleeting whims—then this far there is little
reason to dispute Kant's account of imperatives, as they embody such
norms of rationality. The part of the account that is controversial is
the claim that there could be a principle of reason adequate to determine the will to action in complete independence of the desires, etc.,
of the individual. But this is just the issue of whether there are
categorical imperatives and it has no bearing on the general characterization of imperatives as principles of practical reason.

Technically, an imperative is a formula expressing the relation of
principles of practical reason ('objective' principles) to a will which
"does not necessarily follow these principles in virtue of its own
nature" (G 80;413). Imperatives require ('command') the will to follow

principles of rational willing, even if the will of the individual is subjected to strong temptation to do otherwise. That is, as a rational being, one is under constraint to do what reason dictates (one 'ought' to do it) whatever else one may in the moment want. This is what Kant means when he says, "actions which are recognized to be objectively necessary are subjectively contingent, and the determining of such a will in accordance with objective laws is necessitation" (G 80;412). If a rational being necessarily conforms to a principle, it is inappropriate to say he ought to do so (or, to transpose this: it makes no sense to tell someone you know will keep his promise that he ought to do so; unless, perhaps, you want to insult him). The 'ought' is appropriate only when a practical principle does not merely describe how a particular rational being already and inevitably wills. Kant holds that the imperative form is always appropriate for us as rational beings in that while we are able (have the capacity) to follow principles of reason (i.e. we have a will), it is always possible that we will not (the human will forms subjective principles of action which are not objective, and we may act on them even knowing that they are not):

> An imperative...tells me which of my possible actions
> would be good; and it formulates a practical rule for a
> will that does not perform an action straight away because
> the action is good—whether because the subject does not
> always know that it is good or because, even if he did
> know this, he might still act on maxims /subjective prin-
> ciples/ contrary to the objective principles of practical
> reason. (G 82;414)

The notion of a 'will necessitated to act in conformity with an ob-jective law' means simply that when an action is required by appropriate rational principles, if the will (the agent) would act rationally, it is necessary that it choose those actions dictated by the principles, regardless of other inclinations, etc. which vie for dominance (of the will). In more ordinary terms: in so far as you would act rationally, you are constrained by the dictates of principles of rationality. Once again, the general account, as glossed, turns out to be straightforward, and again, the controversy is over what Kant claims the principles of rationality are: that there is a _categorical_ imperative. When Kant says an imperative is merely the formula of a '_command_', the question of the supposed _authority_ of this command _is_ a substantial one. But it is important to realize that this question applies to hypothetical as well as categorical imperatives. We are familiar with a version of this question in discussions of moral skepticism. Although it is not fashionable, in honesty one should also be prepared to question the nature and ground of our attentiveness to the voice of prudential imperatives.

The theory of imperatives performs two related tasks: the different types of imperative, considered as objective principles of willing, are intended to provide an exhaustive description of practical rationality—of what principles of action a rational being would conform to in so far as he is rational. And it is because of this that the principles (embodied in imperatives) also serve as criteria for assessing the rationality of conduct. How these standards are to be employed is the concern of later chapters. Our question _now_ is quite general: if you want to assess the rationality of conduct, what aspects of conduct are the proper objects of such assessment? Answering this question will lead to an appreciation of the significance of Kant's introduction of the idea of a 'maxim' of an action.

There is a special reason for pursuing this issue in the context of trying to come to an understanding and an appreciation of Kant's moral theory. It will allow us to see why the primary object of moral evaluation for Kant is willing (and in what sense it is), and also that the reason why Kant's theory is not a theory of consequences is to be found in the internal logic of the theory, and need not come from any extra-theoretical concern for moral purity, etc., at the expense of producing good in this world. Our immediate question concerns the aspects of conduct appropriate for consideration in the employment of norms of practical rationality. This is to ask for a concept of action suited to rational assessment of conduct. I would like to consider first what one might say in answer to this question apart from the requirements of Kantian theory.

Ordinarily, it should be clear, in the determination of the rationality of conduct, action is not construed as mere behavior—that is, as just an event in the 'external world', called 'behavior' to indicate its causal origin in a person (or other animate being). Mere behavior as an event is not standardly judged to be rational or irrational. Even the phrase 'irrational behavior' is a description of action that customarily includes reference to purpose (or purposelessness), and so already exceeds the notion of behavior-as-event I am using here. There is a standard use of 'rational' for events, as when the weather or the economy is said to be behaving irrationally. But what that most often means is that a system is not behaving predictably—not following established 'patterns of behavior'. We say 'the economy is behaving irrationally' when either it is not behaving as it has before, or it is not conforming to the rules that constitute our understanding of the economy. But the attribution of irrationality is at bottom only an attribution of **apparent** irrationality—that is, as relative to our understanding. The economy appears irrational because there are factors operating we do not perceive, or perhaps we see them but do not appreciate their importance, or our theories are not yet sophistcated enough to deal with certain sorts of local perturbations, etc. The standing (or standard) presupposition is that the events themselves are orderly, and in that sense rational; we call them irrational to indicate how they appear to us, and that in our given state of understanding we are able neither to predict nor to explain their behavior.

It is possible to look at human behavior this way too—as a sequence of events. Much of modern social science relies on just this sense of rationality in studies of 'human behavior patterns', etc. The very same presupposition reigns here: people never _really_ behave irrationally, it only appears that they do. Their behavior is not irrational in the sense that a fully adequate explanation, including all the causally operative factors in the situation, would (if such a full explanation were possible) reveal order and predictability of behavior: that is, rationality.[6]

Outside of this scientific (or quasi-scientific) context, however, we do not normally look at human action as mere behavior. We usually explain a person's actions in terms of intentions, wants and interests, and we sharply distinguish those explanations from ones we would give, for example, of the workings of someone's leg. (Along with this comes a different and often critical use of 'rationality', and the possibility of discovering real irrationality in an individual's actions.) There are, to be sure, occasions when it seems appropriate to look for causal explanations of actions: when someone performs a task known to be far beyond his capacities, or when unexpected failures occur, one wants an explanation, and typically one is seeking out a special or 'external' cause. It is reasonable in these circumstances to treat an action as an event, and therefore to abandon the customary use of wants, interests, etc. as explanatory reasons. But it is reasonable because these cases are—and because of the way they are—unusual. In addition, there are times when we want to be able to calculate the antecedent conditions necessary for a person's success in certain performances, and to be able to predict with reasonable certainty the conditions in which he will fail. When such knowledge of powers and capacities is needed, scienfific or causal explanation is appropriate. But when we simply want to understand what a person is doing when he acts, normally we offer explanations in terms of what that person wants to do and his reasons for wanting to do it.

Our estimation of the rationality of action relies to a great extent on what we understand an agent wanted to do (what end he had); we often change our assessment when we discover his end was different from what we initially took it to be. Our judgments of irrationality are not necessarily or in principle provisional; deeper understanding of the laws of human behavior may enable us to explain why the person acted as he did, but the explanation may well be of why someone acted irrationally. If Jones ruins his health by working at two jobs to accumulate enough money to buy a house, but steadily loses his extra earnings

through casual gambling, we may judge his actions to be irrational, and
not withdraw this judgment upon learning that in fact he fears owning a
house will be a threat to his freedom, and as a result succumbs to the
temptation to gamble he has otherwise been able to resist. The appropriateness of our judgment will depend upon whether he recognizes (although perhaps without being able to admit) that he does not really want
the house. If he is not aware of his fears, we may well hesitate in
judgment, as we would if he was unable to refrain from gambling. When
we are driven to look for causal explanations, we increasingly view the
agent's behavior as the product of internal and antecedent conditions,
governed by natural laws, and, to varying degrees, outside his control.
We want to know why he is unable to do what he wants and is trying to
do.

Kant's use of imperatives to assess the rationality of conduct conforms in all important respects to this sketch of the ordinary normative
use of 'rational' (and its presuppositions) as applied to action. (This
is so in detail, as we shall see, in the employment of hypothetical imperatives.) All imperatives presuppose a conception of action as something other than mere behavior or observed event, since imperatives are
defined as formulae expressing principles of practical rationality—
objective laws of willing. For Kant, the will is the locus of practial
rationality; it is only because we have a will that it is proper to call
our conduct rational or not. Thus, in assessing the rationality of
conduct, action must be conceived as connected to and issuing from volition. To treat action as 'mere behavior' would be to regard it as like
involuntary movement: it is activity of the person, in a sense, but it

is not of the will, and therefore neither rational nor irrational. Action which is to be judged or evaluated according to the norms of practical rationality (imperatives) must therefore not be detached from the agent whose action it is, but always viewed as action that is willed.

The 'action as willed' is a compound consisting of the proposed action and the volition which determines it. All the elements of volition—end, motive, principle—are therefore central to the conception of action as subject to normative assessment by imperatives. In so far as action is of the will it is to some degree a product of practical reason; thus the rationality of the action will be measured by the conformity of the volition to the appropriate objective principle of willing. The event that succeeds the volition is therefore not the primary object of evaluation.[7]

There can be no obvious, general theoretical answer to the question of what aspects of conduct will be of concern in a moral theory, as different moral theories are concerned with or emphasize different aspects. Moreover, it might even be said that the manner of concern was in itself indicative of the more central features of a moral theory: what sort of thing it considers an action to be (mere event, intentional, as willed, etc.), the relation in judgment between action and agent (or agent's intention), what aspects of conduct it selects for what sorts of evaluative consideration, and so on. In addition, a theory's resolution of such problems illuminates among other things its idea of freedom, its sense of the importance of responsibility and moral worth, its interest (or lack of interest) in a rich conception of human character—that is, in short, as a theory judges action, so it will value those features of human beings most closely associated with what is evaluated in action.

A non-Kantian example should help to show how this works out. Consider an extreme form of act-utilitarianism. Because the focus of evaluation is on the <u>consequences</u> of acts[8] the ultimate concern with human agents is (1) as producers of consequences, leading to an emphasis on the inculcation of techniques to manipulate the environment to planned effect—a kind of technology of human agency—and (2) human beings are viewed as the relevant loci of consequences, which yields a major concern for those aspects of humans which are measurable, and an obvious interest in the malleability of desires (in particular with respect to available technology). Human freedom, if an issue at all, is peripheral; responsibility—the assignment of praise and blame—is largely conceived of instrumentally,[9] as is human character, which tends to be regarded almost entirely as a causal nexus. Although all of this is unargued assertion (the argument would require too great a digression), the characteristics I point to are familiar to anyone who has ever been troubled by utilitarianism as a moral theory (because of, e.g., its lack of concern with human dignity, its difficulties in providing an adequate theory of rights, etc.). I would think there should be little difficulty in discerning the connection of these characteristics with utilitarianism's choice of the aspects of conduct which are to be the primary objects of evaluation.

Although we have not yet talked about the theory of imperatives as part of a moral theory, it should already be clear how the general treatment of conduct I have outlined as Kantian has serious moral implications. Since the moral evaluation of an action is made using an imperative, evaluation will not be made with respect to the effects of the act as a causal intervention in the world of certain bodily movements. The intended consequences (the proposed end of the action) will weigh more than the real consequences. The focus on the agent in Kant, the theoretical requirement that a person's actions not be regarded as detached from his intentions and the very nature of his willing, the concern with why an agent does what he does—how an act comes from an agent as its author, provides much of the motivation for the focus on problems of virtue and character in Kant's ethics. But the apparently peripheral role of action as event-in-the-world with causal consequences, does not amount to a lack of regard for the consequences of our actions. Action is the striving to produce consequences, and central portions of the theory are concerned with this effort: the doctrine of the Highest Good, the idea of a Kingdom of Ends, the moral arguments for republican government, the moral role of a conception of history in social and political thinking, etc. It is simply that moral evaluation is not primarily concerned with success, but rather with what effect in the world your action would produce—the proposed end of your action. Action is not judged good to the degree that its consequences are good. This view arises in Kant's ethics from the way he acknowledges that human beings have intrinsically limited physical capacities. And as we may be physically unable to produce the effects we will, so the world does not adequately mirror our efforts, and is not the final word in the assessment of our projects (see G 57;106, CrPrR 45). The theory would in a sense be consequentialist, if our physical capacities were always sufficient to produce the effects we willed and if we had perfectly good wills. But then, as Kant would be the first to point out, it would not be a moral theory.

Notes

1. There is no single passage in Kant's ethical writings which gives just this account, and there are a number where he does appear to use terms differently. E.g., at G 95;427, it appears that 'motive' is being restricted to one class of. determining ground—the objective; but this passage is extremely obscure, and it is possible even here to read 'motive' as I do given that what it is contrasted with is 'the subjective ground of desire' and not with the ground of a volition; more likely, the passage is simply confused (or confusing—because, as Beck often notes, it is not until his later works that Kant stabilizes his terminology). As we shall see, this set of volitional elements does fit the interesting passages, and furthermore, facilitates understanding of otherwise obscure portions of text. This is so, I believe because they conform in a rather direct way to ordinary usage. I see this as no coincidence, and as confirming of their accuracy to Kant's intentions.

2. Keeping 'end' and 'motive' neatly sorted is extremely difficult, in fact, as well as in Kant's account of rational volition. The line, for example, between desire (motive) and the end can appear extremely artificial, and perhaps it is. Why, for example, insist that in the above example the desire is for success but the end is to become a concert pianist, rather than saying that the desire for success issues in the end of becoming a success (to which being a concert pianist is assessed the best means)? Both are initially plausible and easily account for the relevant features of choice and volition. I think the division made in the above example is preferable because the 'end' there is more closely related to the action—to what is being done. While it makes some sense (sometimes) to talk of the end I am pursuing as success, it seems strained as the end of eight hours a day practicing. More will be said in justification of this in the section on maxims: Kant's device for setting the elements of a volition in formal relations.

3. G.E.M. Anscombe, Intention, p. 22.

4. See chapter two for a full discussion of maxims. The concept of a maxim is introduced here simply as the name of the principle on which an agent determines himself to action and to introduce the distinction between subjective and objective principles which is at the foundation of the theory of imperatives.

5. More precisely, principles of reason that apply to all rational beings with a will. It is possible to conceive of a being whose rational capacity was wholly theoretical—its conclusions about what would be good to do could have no effect on activity. This is a case of a being whose reason was not practical; such a being could not be said to have a will.

6. There is another use of 'rational'—as what is in some sense normal— that I am leaving out here because it is closely related to a normative use of 'rational' that Kant employs in his arguments for the duties of

beneficence and non-neglect of talents, and so will be taken up when those arguments are discussed. Judgments using 'rational' this way have the form: 'anyone who prefers y to x is irrational' or 'it is irrational to spend $500 on a camera you'll only rarely use', etc. Since such judgments generally presuppose that rationality is an <u>option</u> for an agent, they are not importantly different from the <u>kind</u> of assessment found in Kant, and so do not need separate treatment in this section.

7. Nothing said so far is specifically concerned with <u>ethical</u> evaluation or with anything peculiar to the categorical imperative. The argument, as it develops in the first part of chapter II of the Groundwork, is quite general, and is about the nature of rational willing, the different kinds of objective principles, etc. Even after the categorical imperative is introduced in its primary formulation (G 88;421) it still must be <u>shown</u> that the categorical imperative <u>is</u> a moral principle. We shall see in chapter five how this task is performed by the four famous examples.

8. I am ignoring here all the known difficulties in distinguishing <u>an</u> <u>act</u> from its consequences, as well as other technical matters. I am interested only in the bare bones of the theory—their influence will be felt, I believe, no matter how the details are tidied up.

9. See, for example, J.J.C. Smart, "Extreme and Restricted Utilitarianism", and H. Sidgwick, <u>Methods</u> <u>of</u> <u>Ethics</u>, Bk IV, Chapter 3.

Chapter Two: __Maxims__

The 'maxim' of an action is Kant's formal device for presenting an 'action as willed' for purposes of normative judgment. We will consider here why such a device is needed, what, exactly, it is, and also look at a number of the difficulties with the concept familiar to most readers of Kant and his many critics.

Actions are represented by their 'maxims' in two major and related contexts in the __Groundwork__. The categorical imperative is used to determine whether an action is obligatory, prohibited or permissible (DV 20;221) by running a certain sort of test on the **maxim** of the action.[1] And it is a fundamental dogma of the __Groundwork__ that the moral worth of an action depends on its maxim--"An action done from duty has its moral worth, not in the purpose to be attained by it, but in the maxim in accordance with which it is decided upon" (G 67-8;399). Given the importance of the notion of a 'maxim', one would expect it to have been the subject of considerable critical study. With the exception of a recent book by Onora Nell and some interesting brief remarks by Beck this has not been the case.[2] The absence of a good account of maxims is, I hope to show, the source of a great deal of confusion and obscuring controversy, particularly as the maxim is employed in the application of the categorical imperative.

Maxims are variously referred to in the literature as statements of the nature or purpose of actions, descriptions of actions, policies an agent follows of which his particular actions are instances, plans, projects, very general principles of conduct, rules of action that are part of someone's policy of living, etc.[3] All of these are to some extent correct, each pointing to an important aspect of the notion as it is used by Kant. But they are each inadequate as an account of what a maxim is—for example, how on such accounts does one determine what the maxim of an action is? is it possible for very different looking actions of one person to have the same maxim? if the maxim is or includes a description of an action, what is the appropriate level of generality? etc. This is just one set of questions that an adequate account of maxims should answer. In addition an adequate account of maxims should provide an understanding of what a maxim is that works: one that allows the categorical imperative to be employed as a moral criterion. It is, of course, possible that the categorical imperative, particularly in its universal law formulations, where the maxim of an action is a central feature, is itself inadequate and cannot give the results Kant intended. Even if this is the case, it should not be so because the moral theory is burdened with intrinsically problematic accounts of maxims if there is a more interesting and precise analysis. I would like to offer what I take to be such an analysis, with the proviso that it cannot decisively be established that this is what Kant had in mind (or that it is not what he had in mind, either). This should not be a disturbing state of affairs if it can be shown that (a) the account rests on good evidence, (b) it enables one to use the notion of a maxim fruitfully and in a fashion consistent with Kant's procedures, (c) it illuminates Kant's general account of rational action and volition, and (d) there is no other, better, account that does the job as well.

As is often the case, Kant does not offer clear or detailed

definitions of his technical terms. Still, we should have what he does

say available:

> A _maxim_ is the subjective principle of a volition: an ob-
> jective principle (that is, one which would also serve
> subjectively as a practical principle for all rational be-
> ings if reason had full control over the faculty of desire)
> is a practical _law_. (G 69n;400n)

> A _maxim_ is a subjective principle of action and must be
> distinguished from an _objective_ _principle_—namely, a
> practical law. The former contains a practical rule de-
> termined by reason in accordance with the conditions of
> the subject (often his ignorance or again his inclina-
> tions): it is thus a principle on which the subject _acts_.
> (G 88n;421n)

> The rule that the agent himself makes his principle on
> subjective grounds is called his _maxim_. (DV 24;224)

> A _maxim_ is the _subjective_ principle of action, the
> principle which the subject himself makes his rule (how
> he chooses to act). (Wie es namlich handeln will.)
> (DV 25;225)

> Practical principles are propositions which contain a
> general determination of the will, having under it several
> rules. They are subjective, or maxims, when the condition
> is regarded (angesehen) by the subject as valid only for
> his own will. They are objective, or practical laws, when
> the condition is recognized (erkennt) as objective, i.e.,
> as valid for the will of every rational being. (CrPrR
> 17;19)

Such texts are the ones generally used in defining 'maxim'. It is hard

to see how any definition elicited from this material could be 'ade-

quate'; for example, on the basis of these texts, how could you deter-

mine the relation between particular actions and maxims so that you

would know what it was for a maxim to be _the_ maxim of an action? It

might make better sense to pay at least as much attention to Kant's many

examples of maxims, but this procedure is equally limited, as we shall see, by Kant's apparent lack of consistency in what he says in different cases the maxim of the action is. I say 'apparent' because it is possible that the way in which Kant presents particular maxims varies with the part of his general program that is under consideration. If this were the case, then perhaps all the different kinds of maxims we find could each be taken as an aspect of a more general account that needs to be pieced together. The course I will follow here, however, looks less at the defining passages and instances than at the role the maxim is called on to play. I want to determine, in part, what a maxim is by looking to see what in the theory of imperatives requires what Kant calls a maxim. The uncertainties attendant on the other two procedures reinforce the conviction that the best way to find out what a maxim is, is to find out what it is supposed to do.

Imperatives, I have argued, are criteria for judging the rationality of conduct (in a manner yet unspecified), and the object of judgment is an action as it is willed. So the question is, what is it to ask whether a particular action as willed is rational? It will be helpful to look first at a simple ordinary case, since however strange Kant's method of analysis appears, one finds the reading of basic examples conforms closely to ordinary or natural judgment. Suppose I have a headache, and there is aspirin at hand. I decide to take two. Is this rational? How do you tell? In such a case there are certain facts I consider, on the basis of which I make a decision (will to act, or not to act, in a particular way). But why should the fact that I have a headache lead me to decide to take two aspirin? It's a silly question, of course; everyone knows if you want to get rid of a headache you should take two aspirin! But even that presupposes <u>another</u> fact in the situation: that I <u>want</u> to get rid of my headache. (If all of this is painfully obvious, that is not a good reason to discount the importance of the example. Complexity and subtlety are not in themselves virtues. If we are looking for an account of action-as-willed that makes it amenable to rational assessment, it ought to be perspicuous in the simplest of cases.) Now we have the following facts—I have a headache I want to get rid of, I have aspirin, and we want to know in this boring detail how consideration of <u>those</u> facts leads me to decide to take the aspirin. What's been left out is my knowledge of the causal connection between taking aspirin and relief of headaches. Given my want, the employment of this causal principle leads me to act. It is because aspirin relieves headaches, and that I want relief from mine, that I decide to take aspirin. It <u>is</u> a rational decision. It is <u>rational</u> because it conforms to the canonical form of practical rationality concerning wants: I want y to be the case, x is a means to y, I decide to do x. But the decision in this case is rational <u>only</u> because I <u>want</u> relief and <u>know</u> that this aspirin is a means to it. That is, if for some reason I wanted to suffer through my headache, or if in the intensity of the pain I just grabbed the nearest bottle of pills (which happened to be aspirin, though I didn't know it), then my action, what I willed to do in taking those pills, would not have been rational. In the case of ignorance we can see most clearly the way in which the actual consequences of an action do not weigh in the assessment of its rationality. It is certainly <u>better</u> that the pills I swallowed blindly were aspirin and not something harmful,—but what I did does not become rational for that. In summary, what we have been examining here are the three components of volition—want, end, principle. The action—deciding to take the pills (taking the pills) is judged as it was willed.

In this case I could be said to have acted (willed) according to two rules or principles: the rule of taking aspirin when I have a headache (that I want to be rid of) and the rule of willing the means necessary to reaching my ends. This second rule, which will be examined in chapter three, is the principle of prudential rationality—the Hypothetical Imperative. The first of the rules is the one of interest now, as it makes sense to call it the rule of my action. Kant calls it my maxim—the subjective principle on which I acted. That is, when I decide to act, my decision is in some sense based on a rule or principle to act in this way when the relevant facts stand as they do. (This, for Kant, is a necessary condition for something's being an action: an action is willed—it is determined according to the subject's idea of a rule (G 80;412).) The rationality of an action is seen in the match between the principle I in fact acted on (my maxim) and the canon of rationality for such kind of actions (the hypothetical imperative in this case). An action is rational, we might say, if it is the right kind of thing to do in a given set of circumstances. To judge the rationality of an action, then, you need to know what kind of thing is being done in response to what circumstances. The maxim of an action serves this purpose. It represents the action as it is willed, giving the circumstances (relevant facts about the agent and the world) and the rule of action the agent deems appropriate for these circumstances. For example, 'I should take two aspirin if I want relief from a headache'

would be the maxim of my action in our example. My action is rational
if the maxim of my action is: if it is a fact that taking two aspirins
will, in general, relieve headaches. The technique of analysis according to hypothetical imperatives is not important here; what is important
is the claim that in both Kant's theory and in matters of ordinary judgment, the rationality of conduct is considered through looking at a
rule, a principle on which the agent can be said to have acted. The respect in which an agent can be said to have acted on a rule will be explained shortly; before we turn to that, however, it will be useful to
look at yet another kind of examination of action, related to the assessment of rationality, which also _calls_ _for_ the kind of presentation of an
action provided by a maxim. It is to be hoped that by looking at situations which call for the use of a maxim, we will both understand why
Kant employed it _and_ get a clear sense of what sort of thing _the_ maxim
of an action must be.

Suppose someone asks me why I stayed home from work yesterday, and
I answer, truthfully, 'I had a temperature of 102'. What makes this
answer satisfactory is the implicit employment of a practical principle
which does not need to be noted explicitly, because the connection between high temperature and staying home from work is conventional. It
is nevertheless true that a high temperature is an explanatory reason
for staying home from work because everyone recognizes the reasonableness of acting that way: according to a rule (a maxim) which states
that if my temperature is high I should stay home from work. But suppose I had responded, again truthfully, 'I stayed home from work because
the begonias bloomed'. I am here offering a reason for what I did that

will not function as an explantory reason unless something like a principle is offered to show the connection between the fact of the begonias blooming and what I did. If I return with, 'The begonias just bloomed, and that always makes me ill', my action will be understood and thought reasonable. If, however, I respond to further inquiry by saying that it is dangerous to teach classes when the begonias are blooming, I am offering a reason, but it will not generally be thought to be a good one. I offer a reason when I show what it was about these particular facts that led me to act as I did—I reveal the structure of my decision by showing the principle—if the begonias are blooming I should not teach classes—my maxim, according to which I made my decision to stay home from work.

The maxim presents the action that I will to do in a form that makes the structure of my willing explicit. The maxim shows how particular features of the situation are reasons for acting by presenting them in a rule or principle that dictates doing what I did in just these sorts of circumstances, and, explicitly or implicitly, for what purpose. To ask whether the reason the agent gives for his action is a good reason is to ask of a particular action (or volition) whether it is rational—that is, is the principle according to which the action is willed a rational principle. In Kant's language, we are asking whether a subjective principle of action (a maxim) is also objective. (We will see in the next chapter; what 'objective' signifies for the different types of imperatives.)

If judgment of ordinary cases follows the lines I have sketched, the introduction of the idea of a maxim of an action should seem to be a

natural step in setting out procedures for the rational assessment of
conduct. We need now to look at the general structure of maxims, to
consider what elements of a volition enter the maxim in what form. The
maxims used in the examples were all loosely sketched and incompletely
formed in order to keep the discussion as close as possible to our ordinary sense of things. One can, however, give a more rigorous account
of what a maxim is that conforms to the data of the examples, is consistent with Kant's usage, and, most importantly, provides the material
for answering standard criticisms of the parts of Kant's moral theory
that employ maxims in a theoretically significant way.

All maxims contain a description of the action that is willed, a
clause specifying the circumstances in which such an action is to be
willed (including relevant motivational features of the agent), and the
result (end) expected from the successful execution of the action.[4] Let
me now give a few examples of maxims: To close the door when I want to
write to free myself from distractions,—To read Consumer Reports, if I
want to buy a new car, in order to get the best value,—To set fire to
the house, if I am short of money and will not be caught, in order to
collect the insurance,—To go to the grocery store, if I am hungry, to
get something to eat,—To save a portion of my salary, if I owe money,
in order to pay my debts. It is not always necessary to include both
the motive and the end in formulating the maxim of an action; our understanding of ordinary wants and purposes permits us to use one to suggest
the other, and it is often desirable to avoid redundancy to keep the
maxim as close as possible to what someone might easily say was the
maxim of his action. Often this will be the case when the motive is

simply the desire for the end—e.g., To go to the grocery, if I want
vanilla ice cream, in order to get vanilla ice cream. Although this
maxim is formally correct and complete, there would be no loss of information and a considerable diminution of awkwardness if instead one gave
as the maxim: To go to the grocery store if I want vanilla ice-cream.
Or, even more radically, one might offer as the maxim of an action: To
take my car to a competent mechanic if it breaks down. Here neither the
end (in order to get it repaired) nor the motive (my desire to have my
car working again) are stated, but again, it is clear in the maxim as
stated what they are. There is nothing surprising here—it is part of
conventional knowledge that grocery stores have ice-cream, and competent
mechanics are where you would like to bring your car when it breaks down
to get it fixed because you want it to work again. But if those who
were examining this conduct did not know what mechanics did or what
sorts of things one finds in grocery stores, then the full maxims would
have to be given. The fact that the maxims of ordinary actions can be
formulated incompletely without apparent loss of comprehensibility is
perhaps one of the reasons that different commentators have thought
maxims to be such a variety of things—the more familiar the case you
consider, the less you need to include in a rule which the agent could
be said to have acted on.[5] This is especially so, I think, in the case
of those who see the maxim only as a very general rule or policy of
life, and not, as I have been suggesting, as the maxim of an action. I
believe there are such general maxims, and that they relate in important
ways to what sorts of things will motivate an agent to act. But I do
not now want to discuss the different kinds and levels of maxims there

might be, or what roles they might play. What needs to be emphasized
is that every action has a maxim which in principle includes all three
elements, whether or not the motive or the end is presented in the maxim
explicitly.

The importance of this requirement can be seen by looking at some
cases. Consider first a pair of related examples.[6] The action appears
to be the same in both—bidding at an auction for a very expensive
painting. And the end is also the same—acquiring the painting. It is
only when the motives are included that we see that the maxims of the
actions are quite different <u>and</u> that the two <u>actions</u> are not really the
same either. In one case, the motive is the prestige the bidder believes he will have if he succeeds in acquiring this expensive painting.
The maxim of that action might be: To bid high for a painting in order
to acquire it if owning it will bring me great prestige. In our other
case, the motive is the strong desire of the bidder to own the painting.
The maxim of this action might be: To bid high for a painting, if I
really want to own it (in order to acquire it). In cases such as
these, we know <u>what</u> the agent wills to do only when we include the
motive which prompts the action. If the first patron is brought to believe that no prestige will accrue to him from buying the expensive
painting, he will no longer bid for it. This follows from the structure of his willing (if he is rational). We may imagine that the
second bidder could be indifferent to this information, but not to
other sorts, according to the structure of <u>his</u> willing. To know the
maxim of an action is to know the <u>kind</u> of action being done, and to
know that, in these cases, you need to know the motive—what it is

about the state of affairs to be brought about by the action that
interests the agent.

In other examples, the impact of including all the elements of
willing and seeing how they relate to each other is even greater. Let
me borrow the example of the grocers from the **Groundwork**. One grocer is
a prudent businessman and is scrupulous in giving his customers the
correct change so they will continue to frequent his store. A second
grocer is also scrupulous in giving his customers the correct change,
but he is primarily concerned to treat people honestly. The actual,
observed activity of the two grocers is the same—giving the correct
change, and it appears they both could be said to be following a general
policy of 'giving the correct change'. It is only when we look at the
motives with which they act that we see they are really doing very
different things. They are not, in fact, following the same policy; it
would be false to say they were acting according to the same principle.
As Kant remarked somewhat tartly—one acts on the principle that
honesty is the best policy, the other on the principle that honesty is
the only policy.[7] It is important to realize that in formulating the
maxims of these two actions, the inclusion of different motives goes
along with the acknowledgement that the ends of their actions are also
different: in the first case the end is to keep the customers happy,
in the second the end is treating people honestly. The two maxims of
these same actions are (1) To give the correct change to keep my customers happy if I want my business to prosper, (2) To give the correct
change in order to treat people honestly.[8]

These examples have hopefully made it obvious that the motive can

be necessary for the specification of the maxim of an action. Since
maxims are the basis for the assessment of the rationality of conduct,
which is often a question of the relation of an action to a proposed
end, and since in many cases the end of an action cannot be determined
without knowing the motive, maxims could not perform their function unless there was provision for including the motive. It is important to
emphasize this point as it is often denied (or ignored) in the literature. As we shall soon see, inclusion of the motive, in addition to
keeping the maxim in line with ordinary intuitions about describing
actions, also provides the means for blocking a fundamental criticism
of Kant's method—the possibility of tailoring maxims to 'beat' the
test of the categorical imperative.

The _strongest_ argument _for_ the inclusion of the motive in the maxim
of an action is that it makes much better sense of Kant's general
account of conduct and its norms than an account which ignores the motive. By including the motive, we can use Kant's technical apparatus
as a formal representation of what we would say about particular cases,
and, in addition, formulating the maxim of an action can sharpen our
perception by compelling us to elicit the components of a volition—to
see an action _as_ it is willed. All of this, however, depends on the
assumption that Kant's _general_ account of action and volition is intuitively plausible and therefore can be reconstructed along natural lines
with considerable independence from textual argument. In case the presumption is rebutted (or found presumptuous), it will be worthwhile
offering some textual support for the inclusion of the motive.

Two passages bear directly on this question. Kant says of a maxim that it is a "practical rule determined by reason in accordance with the conditions of the subject (often his ignorance or again his inclinations)" (G 88n;421n) and also that it is "the rule the agent himself makes his principle on subjective grounds" (DV 24;224). The context of the first passage is one of Kant's efforts to mark the difference between subjective and objective principles of action—between maxims and objective laws. The parenthetical phrase, as I understand it, indicates those conditions of the subject which when incorporated into the maxim of his action may determine that the maxim will be subjective and not also objective. That is, it is often true that the subject acts according to false beliefs (ignorance)—e.g., about causal relations, and then the maxim of his proposed action will not be rational (objective)[9]—e.g., his proposed action will not in fact be a means to his end. It is also often true, according to Kant, that the rule of action is determined according to inclination (need: see G 81n;413n), and therefore fails to be objective because the ground of the action in the agent—what determines the agent to action—is something peculiar to the acting subject. But what determines the agent to action is his motive for acting. When the motive is based on inclination, the full passage suggests, the maxim is not objective (not "valid for every rational being"). Two aspects of a maxim, then, determine whether or not it is objective—the subject's knowledge and his motive. It therefore seems reasonable to suppose that the conditions of the subject, in accordance with which the rule of action is determined, are included in the maxim—"the principle on which the subject acts."

The account in the Groundwork of moral worth also supports the conclusion that the motive of an action is to be included in the maxim. Here the connections are straightforward. "An action done from duty has its moral worth. not in the purpose to be attained by it, but in the maxim in accordance with which it is decided upon" (G 67-8;399). Those who, for example, preserve their lives out of 'an immediate inclination to do so', "protect their lives in conformity with duty, but not from the motive of duty" (G 65;397-8). In such cases, Kant says, the maxims of their actions have no moral content. The maxim of an action has moral content when the action is done from the motive of duty. If this sort of analysis is to be possible, the motive must be included in the maxim of the action.[10]

It must be said that in all strictness the texts do not directly support my claim that the motive is to be explicitly part of the maxim. It is consistent with all the relevant passages that the motive be omitted, although it would still have to be used in the specification of the nature of the action, the determination of moral worth, etc. It is the subjective ground of the agent's rule of action. I do not think there is a decisive argument either way. Since the motive is part of the circumstances which lead the agent to decide to act in the way he does, the inclusion of the motive makes the maxim a more complete representation of an action as it is willed. This seems to me good enough reason to include it.

It will be useful, at this point, to turn directly to some possible problems with the account of maxims. In doing this I hope to provide both a more substantial foundation for some of what I have already set out, as well as answers to some of the more obvious objections to my account and to the uses to which maxims are to be put in Kant's moral theory.

Describing a maxim as the rule according to which the agent acts may suggest that the maxim is some kind of practical policy commitment of the agent which directs him to act in such-and-such a way in such-and-such circumstances. There are two different propositions suggested here: that maxims are temporally prior to the actions whose subjective principle they are, and, that maxims are general policy commitments the agent adopts and according to which he directs his conduct. Neither of these is true: they are both unwarranted generalizations from a set of cases where they do apply. Some maxims are temporally prior; some maxims express general life policies. It is important to see just how these limited claims cannot be legitimately generalized to all maxims. We will first look at the claim of temporal priority as it can be answered independently of any decision on the general policy question. Moreover, a denial of the temporal claim will undermine some of the support for viewing maxims as very general principles of conduct.

Our question is this: In order for my action to be correctly described as determined in accordance with a subjective principle (maxim), is it necessary that the maxim be adopted prior to my setting myself to act according to such a principle? The answer, I believe, must be no, because, to state it directly, deciding to act in a certain way can itself be subscribing to a principle of action. This is not to say it must be a permanent subscription—order and consistency among one's practical principles is a different matter altogether. An example may help make this point clear. Suppose I decide to lend money to a friend who is having some hard times. The maxim of that action (supposing there is nothing odd or hidden about my motives) might be—To lend money to a friend if he/she needs financial help. The question is—must I have adopted that maxim prior to making the decision to lend money to my friend Robert? The only reason one might be inclined to think so is if we imagine my answering the question 'why did you lend money to Robert?' with something like—'I believe I ought to help friends when they are in difficulty.' We might well see this as saying that it was because I had this belief that I decided to help Robert. But it is not necessary to view the answer in this way. Quite possibly, I had no such prior commitment—if only because there has to be a first time. Surely it is often the case that in the course of deciding to do something you find that you are committing yourself to a principle and not just discovering that you already have one, nor is there need to feel that you must decide the issue in principle before you can rationally determine what to do in the particular case. You may have a principle that governs such cases, and you may decide to act according to it. But you may also simply decide to act—to adopt an end and determine yourself to do what is necessary to reach it. And as you have a conception of the nature of your end, you decide on specific means of action. But this just is acting according to a maxim. It may turn out that having made this decision to lend money to Robert I have adopted a general maxim to help friends (perhaps I have discovered for the first time that I can, or have now come to believe my help is welcome)—the reasons I had for helping Robert I find apply more generally and I am attentive to that fact. But I may not regard my decision that way. Although the maxim of my action is general in form—the reasons I had for helping Robert apply equally well to other friends—I am free to disregard their claim. I _can_ acknowledge them as reasons only once.

One other example should make this clear. Imagine someone attending a political demonstration, confronted for the first time by police trying to break it up using rather violent coercive means. Convinced that the actions of the police are unwarranted and unjust, our activist decides that it is right that he resist being moved by the police, whatever the cost. Having never been in nor imagined he would be in such a situation, he has no prior general policy (maxim) according to which he could act in this case. (We should resist as implausible the idea that he might act on a maxim to fight injustice wherever it occurs.) What one imagines is that in examining his situation he recognizes the actions of the police to be unjust, and becomes convinced that such acts of injustice ought to be resisted. Although he may never again have the courage or the commitment to act on the maxim of resisting the police when they act unjustly, it is still true that he has committed himself (_on_ this occasion but not just _for_ this occasion) to act on a principle of resisting injustice. It is the maxim of his action, and may well remain his abiding political view, even if he cannot ever bring himself to act that way again.

It is, of course, often true that we decide what to do as we have more or less clear general policies. If I am deciding between two components for a new bicycle, my general policy of choosing the best when I am buying something I expect to use for a long time will inform my decision, and work against spasms of pecuniary guilt. Also, when I am undecided, it can be because two general policies apply to a case with incompatible results. And when I decide to do something tomorrow, I will act then according to a maxim I adopt now. But there is no reason to conclude from such instances that it is always the case that action is decided upon according to a maxim adopted at some earlier time, especially when we have examples where it is clear that the priority of the maxim to the action is logical, not temporal.

I do not think it is an accident that the examples which most persuasively suggest a temporal succession from maxim to action involve what I have been calling general policy maxims. The view of maxims as general principles of conduct ('To increase my property by every safe means', 'To avenge all wrongs done against me'), like the view that maxims are temporally prior to actions, obscures the nature of the relation between the particular willed action and its maxim, and thereby masks the subtlety and power of Kant's analysis of practical activity. It is therefore appropriate at this juncture to consider the prevalent critical view of maxims as expressions of general plans and policies. When we see what is wrong with it (as well as what of it is right) we will be in a position to begin looking at the tasks which the maxim was designed to and is able to perform—in particular, the use of the maxim to present an action for purposes of evaluation by imperatives. The concept of a maxim has been faulted for being too losely attached to actions: it is thought that agents can always construct or 'tailor' the maxims of their actions in such a way as to avoid running afoul of the imperatives. If this section of the account of maxims is persuasive, it will become plain that the 'tailoring' criticism itself is based on a misunderstanding of what the maxim of an action is.

The analysis of maxims I have offered so far suggests that although maxims are general in form, the maxim of an action is specific to the action and occasion. So let us first consider why one might be inclined to view maxims as very general principles or policies of life. R.P. Wolff in The Autonomy of Reason gives an instructive list of "policies which a man might adopt and act on...: to maximize profits in economic transactions, to drink a quart of water a day, to revenge all insults (Beck's example), to commit suicide when continued life threatens more evil than satisfaction (Kant's example), and never to send a boy to do a man's job."[11] He is quick to point out that not "every act is preceded by an interior monologue in which the proposed act is brought under a policy" but that "every act implies a policy under which it can be subsumed."[12] While there is no reason to disagree with this cautionary note, it is puzzling that having recognized that actions imply policies, Wolff offers the list of maxims that he does. Let us look at his analysis of an example: "If I drink a glass of water to slake my thirst, it must be that I have a policy of drinking water to slake my thirst."[13] This seems to me an excessively casual depiction of the action. The mere fact that I am thirsty and drink water to slake my thirst by itself says very little about the policy I am following (or which is implied by my action) other than that my objective in acting is to slake my thirst. Surely it is possible that my policy is to drink whatever is at hand to slake my thirst, and since in this instance it is water, that is what I drink. Or, again, perhaps I drink water because it is my policy to drink water when I am thirsty <u>and</u> there is no beer around. In neither of these cases would it be correct to say that 'I have a policy to drink water to slake my thirst' even though it is true that I am thirsty and have decided to drink a glass of water. (Although this may seem like extended quibbling over an example Wolff probably meant as a quick illustration, I think the example and the list of maxims which precede it are so perfectly characteristic of the way maxims are generally considered that there is much to be gained in going on about it this way.) I <u>might</u> have a policy of drinking water to slake my thirst, but more about the action needs to be presented before it can be said that I do. If my act of drinking water is determined by a reason (or what I take to be one, if my bit of behavior is properly called an action), then it is true that the same reason will hold for relevantly similar cases. But it does <u>not</u> follow straightforwardly that the reason for drinking water in these circumstances is simply that water is what I believe it is good to drink in these circumstances.

Something is wrong with the way Wolff is looking at maxims such that on the one hand he lists as examples of maxims ones that are extremely general, and on the other he gives an extremely specific maxim of an action without providing the background to justify it. I think the source of his inconsistency is a natural enough error. When thinking of maxims as policies 'which a man might adopt and act on', it is likely one will picture someone setting out goals and projects for himself the way one might prepare for a program of diet or exercise. The form of thought is: this is my goal, I will set myself to do the sorts

of things that will enable me to reach it. It is looking at maxims as
such prior policy commitments that suggests maxims that are so general
in scope. For example, if I adopt the maxim 'to maximize profits in
economic transactions' I will be setting myself a task which will be
realized in different actions in many different sets of circumstances.
Each of the actions will be determined by this general policy maxim as
the reason for that action. So much I think is a fair representation
of certain kinds of action. What does not follow from this, however,
is that the general maxim or policy which in some sense determines the
action is itself the maxim of the action. We shall see in a moment
that it makes better sense of such examples to see the general maxim
instead as part of the structure of motives for an action, and the maxim
of the action be constructed from specific elements of the willed action
itself. It is perfectly understandable that a general policy maxim be
mistaken for the maxim of an action since maxims do represent actions
as actions of a certain kind, and, for example, lying about the relia-
bility of my car is an instance of an attempt to 'maximize profit in an
economic transaction' when I am trying to sell it. But, as we know,
actions can be described in any number of ways and at many different
levels of generality. We still must see why the description provided
by the general maxim is not usually correct, but first, let us consider
the other error I charged to Wolff—of overspecifying the maxim given
incomplete information—to see if we can elicit a common difficulty in
the way maxims are being thought about.

It may seem odd to criticize Wolff for being too specific in
setting out a maxim, but the issue is not specificity per se, or not

just that the maxim he offers is specific. The problem, as I described
it, is the lack of warrant in the example as he sketches it for the
particular maxim he selects. Again, it is quite understandable, I
think, why Wolff naturally moved to an action-specific maxim rather
than the general type in this example. The point of the example was to
show that even when an action did not follow from a general policy
directive already adopted by the agent, the action nevertheless had a
maxim, and one which when constructed stood in the same logical relation to the action as the policy maxim does to actions Wolff imagines
issuing from it. The theoretical point, that anything that is properly
called an action has a maxim, is correct and important. The construction of the maxim, however, is not equally sound. In this case, since
the maxim or policy is to be "rationally reconstructed" from the act,
he takes the action (drinking water to slake my thirst) as his starting
point. He then concludes that this action is to be seen as an instance
of the implied policy of drinking water to slake my thirst (or, in the
form we have been using to state maxims,—To drink water if I want to
slake my thirst). The move is very natural, but as the variants of the
maxim showed, it is not necessarily correct: everything may <u>look</u> the
same and it still not be the case that such a policy is implied by my
action. What Wolff seems to realize intuitively here is that if the
maxim is to have its foundation in a particular act, then the maxim
must contain the elements (generalized) of that action. This, I take
it, is why he included the purpose of the act in the thirst-slaking example. But note, when his attention is not on acts but on maxims independent of particular actions, he formulates a similar policy (maxim)—

To drink a quart of water every day—without feeling the same intuitive pressure to include the purpose to be served by such activity. (It is of some interest that the suicide example Wolff borrows from Kant is the only one on his list of maxims that includes motive and end.)

There is nothing impossible in someone's having as the maxim of his action—To drink water to slake my thirst. It is simply unlikely. Let me flesh out the example a bit to show why. Suppose you are playing a lot of tennis or some other thirst-inducing sport, and at the side of the court there is a cooler which contains a variety of things to drink. You get thirsty and you go over and drink some water to slake your thirst; later, you become thirsty again and this time drink orange soda, and so on, through the afternoon. There need not be any reason to presume your different choices each had a different maxim—first a water-drinking maxim, then an orange soda drinking maxim, etc. Nor, as has already been shown, is there necessarily one general thirst-slaking maxim adopted at some prior time which keeps directing you to the cooler whenever you are thirsty. In a case like this, what you may want in each trip to the cooler is 'something to drink', a fact of your volition which might well be shown in your indifference to what you pulled out of the cooler. If, on the other hand, you showed a distinct preference for one sort of drink, the maxim of your action might reflect that preference. (Other examples of this sort will be discussed, and a principle for determining their 'correct' maxims suggested, shortly.)

Wolff's remarks on maxims miss the mark because he is rather inclined to see them as a cumbersome Kantian device for talking about what are really reasons for acting. As we have seen, there is certainly some point to looking at maxims this way, but noting that maxims are related to reasons for action does not make it obvious what the maxim of a given action is—nor, for that matter, should it be obvious how you determine what an agent's reason for action is. At the risk of making this tedious, let me give one more example. Suppose, on solicitation, I give money to the Cancer Society. What is the maxim of my action? If we follow Wolff's procedure, it must be that I have a policy (maxim) of giving money to the Cancer Society when asked. But isn't it quite possible that in so far as I have any policy regarding such matters, it is to give money to reputable charities when a donation is requested? The force of this emerges when we realize that if my policy were really to give money to the Cancer Society, if that is the maxim implied by my action, then either I would not have given money if it had been the Heart Fund asking, or there would have had to be a Heart Fund policy too. As with the last case, it is possible that things **are** this way with me, but, again, in all likelihood they are not. There is no a priori way to settle this matter. What the maxim of my action is depends on my conception of what I am doing. If I give to the Cancer Society **as** a reputable charity then my maxim will be different than if I give because I want to support cancer research. It is the motive, or what it is about the act that moves me to do it, that determines the content of my maxim.

If we combine both of Wolff's intuitions about maxims—that there are general policy maxims which in some sense govern a number of actions, and that actions have or imply maxims—we will come closer to the truth. In the next section I will try to show that for Kant, there may be a number of maxims of different levels of generality governing a particular willed action. The problem will be to see how they govern together. In addition, it is to be hoped that this way of considering the relations of maxims to actions will yield an answer to the question of the maxim of an action—at least for purposes of evaluation by imperatives.

Briefly, what I want to establish is that there generally is an action-specific maxim that is the maxim of an action, and that this must be so if an action is to be evaluated in terms of its maxim. Otherwise, if the maxims of actions were very general principles of conduct, and maxims were the objects evaluated, then the evaluation would almost always be indeterminate. For example, take one of Kant's general maxims: To increase my property by every safe means. While it is possible that actions performed according to this maxim would fail the test of the categorical imperative, it is hardly necessary that this be the case. I might well act on this maxim and never do anything morally wrong—whether I do is obviously contingent on the circumstances in which I find myself (as well as other, possibly incompatible maxims I might hold). But to say that it is even possible for a general maxim to lead to morally wrong acts (and therefore, presumably to judge the general maxim as morally faulty), it must be possible to judge the action right or wrong independently of the general maxim. That is, holding the maxim in this example might lead me to break a promise in order to acquire another man's property which I held on deposit (see CrPrR 27;28),[14] and if so it would have led me to perform a morally wrong action. But if it led me to make a shrewd and perfectly fair business deal, that action would not be wrong in itself, and certainly not wrong for having its source in a maxim which might, in other circumstances, have sent me in other directions. So, if the rightness and wrongness of actions are to be judged according to their maxims, in fairness to Kant, we must assume that the general policy maxim is not appropriate (or, only rarely so) as the maxim of an action.

But even if we agree that for purposes of evaluation the maxim is to be action-specific, we must still find room for the general maxim in the structure of volition. The general maxim, I suggest, serves as a motivational feature in specific willings—what Kant calls general determining grounds of the will. The key to this interpretation is a passage in Religion Within the Limits of Reason Alone where Kant is discussing the problem of the source of evil in human nature and, in particular, how evil is to be shown compatible with freedom. Our interest in this text is not centered on its main question; what is important in it for our discussion is the structure of volition that Kant sets out:

> ...the source of evil cannot lie in an object determining the will through inclination, nor yet in natural impulse; it can lie only in a rule made by the will for the use of its freedom, that is, in a maxim.... When we say, then, Man is by nature good, or, Man is by nature evil, this means only that there is in him an ultimate ground (inscrutable to us) of the adoption of good maxims or of evil maxims.... (Religion 17)

> That the ultimate subjective ground of the adoption of moral maxims is inscrutable is indeed already evident from this, that since this adoption is free, its ground (why, for example, I have chosen an evil and not a good maxim) must not be sought in any natural impulse, but always again in a maxim. Now since the maxim also must have its ground, and since apart from maxims no determining ground of free choice can or ought to be adduced, we

are referred back endlessly in the series of subjective
determining grounds, without ever being able to reach the
ultimate ground. (Religion 16n-17n)

There is no problem, I believe, in employing this passage from the more
sophisticated and later text to problems encountered in working through
the Groundwork, as this passage is readily seen as an explanation of
the phenomenon noted in the Groundwork (75;407) of the ultimate inscru-
tability of human motivation. What I want to emphasize now is Kant's
suggestion that the subjective determining ground of a maxim can itself
be a maxim.[15] That is, we may have the following as a possible structure of volition. An action follows from the adoption of an end. The
proposed action, the hoped for end, and the motive for acting (in the
generalized form of a reason) are expressed in the maxim of the action.
If the adoption of the end is itself an action, then there will be another maxim governing that act of adoption, and so on. Consider a typical chain: a man decides to leave his job as an engineer in order to
become a carpenter, a trade he has come to consider more meaningful
than his present work. His end, in leaving his job, is to create time
for carpentry training; his motive is his desire for more meaningful
work coupled with his belief that he will find it through the work that
he would do as a carpenter. In Kant's language the subjective ground
of his end, and thus the subjective ground of the maxim of his action,
is his desire for meaningful or fulfilling work. Now let us divide the
case—first imagine this person as someone who simply came to feel that
his work was dull and inhuman, and as a result sought a way to work
that would not be so painful. If we ask, what is the ground of this
feeling, there seems to be no answer, and none that we would want.

People can just come to feel that their work is no longer supportable, and decide to seek a change. The motive is then the end of the chain: the ultimate subjective ground of the action. Now imagine a similar person having made a similar decision from the same motive. But when we ask this person for the ground of his motive, <u>why</u> he decided to seek more satisfying work, we get an answer—say, the discovery that doing work that gives no pleasure makes one irritable and less able to be a good parent. The motive of the original maxim, then, is not the ultimate subjective ground; the ground is a commitment to being a certain sort of parent (which itself <u>may</u> be grounded in moral principles, or love of children, etc.). The initial maxim contains the subjective ground of the action in the motive; the subjective ground of the initial maxim is found to be, in this case, a deeper and more general motive, which prompted the adoption of 'seeking more meaningful work' as an end. We might then construct a sequence of maxims, each more general than the one preceding it, and each the ground of the one narrower in scope that comes before it. From our case—(1) To quit my present job, in order to begin training as a carpenter (if I want more satisfying work and believe carpentry will provide it); (2) To seek more satisfying work, if I want to be a better parent to my children; (3) To do what is necessary to become a better parent, if I want to fulfill my obligations. (Of course, this chain could stop at (2), or if, in another case, the ground of (2) involved winning the respect of my neighbors, we might well go on to a fourth maxim, etc.) In this chain we can see how such a person could be said to have acted in accordance with a general policy (maxim), say, of always fulfilling obligations, and how it is nonetheless true that the more general maxim is not, properly speaking, the maxim of the action. The more general maxims express the deeper determining grounds in the agent of his action—his more ultimate and even ulterior motives. They appear in the motive clause of the next more specific maxim in the chain. The more general maxim is the ground for a particular determination of the will. Or, in plainer language, the more general maxims provide the elements of an explanation of why the agent adopted the end he did—they indicate the nature of his interest in the end for the sake of which he is acting. (This feature will assume greater importance when we try to resolve, in the next section, the problem of tailored maxims.)

At this juncture, it will help to look at an example from Kant that might appear to present strong evidence against this account:

> I have...made it my maxim to increase my property by every
> safe means. Now I have in my possession a deposit, the
> owner of which has died without leaving any record of it.
> Naturally this case falls under my maxim. Now I want to
> know whether this maxim can hold as a universal practical
> law. I apply it, therefore, to the present case and ask
> if it could take the form of a law, and consequently
> whether I could, by the maxim, make the law that every
> man is allowed to deny that a deposit has been made when
> no one can prove the contrary. I immediately realize
> that taking such a principle as a law would annihilate
> itself, because its result would be that no one would
> make a deposit.[16] (CrPrR 27;28)

In this passage, Kant appears to use a general maxim as the maxim of an action; that apparent use is what needs to be explained. First of all, it is important to have a clear view of what the passage is intended to establish. It is not so much an example of the employment of the categorical imperative as it is part of an argument to show that inclination (avarice) cannot be the ultimate determining ground of a will subject to the moral law, because a will with a maxim of avarice (or, in general, a maxim of inclination) as its determining ground may be led to act in ways that are incompatible with the categorical impera- tive. "If I say that my will is subject to a practical law, I cannot put forward my inclination (in this case, avarice) as fit to be a de- termining ground of a universal practical law" (CrPrR 27;28). Kant's task is to show that the maxim 'to increase my property by every safe means' is not "fit to be a determining ground of a universal practical law," and that task is accomplished through the deposit example.

What we have in the deposit example is a particular determination of the will which consists in my goal (end) of acquiring another per- son's property (deposited with me), by the means of breaking my promise to him by concealing his last wishes. Is the maxim of this willed ac- tion 'to increase my property by every safe means' (maxim A)? It is surely true that it is because I have that maxim as my general policy that I am prepared to act to acquire this property. But that is not to say that the general maxim is the maxim of my action. So, the question is, why does Kant think it is, or does he? What we would like to see offered as the maxim of the action is something like 'to deny that a deposit has been made when no one can prove the contrary (in order to increase my property safely' (maxim B). This, however, is what is sub- jected to the test of the categorical imperative. Kant says he wants to determine whether the maxim 'to increase my property by every safe means' could hold as a practical law, and so applies it to the deposit case, and asks "whether I could, by the maxim (to increase my proper- ty...), make the law that every man is allowed to deny that a deposit has been made when no one can prove the contrary." If the second _Critique_ is to be taken as consistent with the most central claims of the _Groundwork_, then we must conclude from this passage that maxim B and not maxim A is the maxim of the action. It is because maxim B does not pass the test that maxim A is not appropriate as the determining ground of a will subject to practical law.

What has really been shown so far is that Kant's purposes with this maxim and example can be met if the example is construed on the model of actions and maxims I have suggested is correct. What still needs to be accounted for is the way Kant presents the example—and in particular, why Kant speaks of applying the maxim (maxim A) to the 'present case' and then asks "whether I could, by the maxim, make the law that every man is allowed to deny that a deposit has been made..." (again, the maxim in question is maxim A). We have already seen that the maxim in this example tested by the categorical imperative is maxim B, suggesting, obviously enough, that there are two maxims at work in Kant's example, and the interpretive problem is setting out their relationship to each other. When maxim A is 'applied to the present case' we get maxim B. The significance of this simple relation can be readily seen if it is fleshed out. The 'present case' is the act of denying a deposit (if there is no chance of being found out). Now the act in itself is neither clearly right or wrong. The rightness or wrongness of a particular act depends on the maxim according to which it is performed—using 'act' here as a behavioral description detached from the content of volition.[17] For example, if my denial of a deposit falls under or is according to a maxim of increasing my property by all safe

means, then the categorical imperative should rule it impermissible.
If, on the other hand, the maxim that suggests this action is a maxim
of beneficence, then it is <u>at least</u> not clear how the categorical imperative would rule. To show that an act of a certain kind is always
wrong, you would have to show that <u>all</u> maxims involving acts of that
kind (e.g. promise-breaking) were not capable of passing the test of
the categorical imperative. The point, I think we can conclude, of
Kant's <u>applying</u> maxim A to the deposit case was to provide the proper
form for determining the appropriate action-specific maxim: that is,
that <u>this</u> denial of a deposit is an instance of promise breaking for my
own safe profit. Maxim A determines the form of maxim B; it tells you
that the agent is acting in these circumstances out of a motive of
avarice. In this case, you could not formulate the maxim to be tested
by the categorical imperative <u>unless</u> you knew both the point of and the
motive for the action; only then do you know what <u>kind</u> of action it is—
and that tells you the form of <u>the</u> maxim of the action.

In <u>Religion Within the Limits of Reason Alone</u> (20-26) the analysis
of volition in terms of a hierarchy of maxims is used to resolve the
paradox of evil. Briefly, the will is described as performing two
sorts of acts: the will is said freely to adopt a disposition (<u>Gesinn-</u>
<u>ung</u>)—a very general maxim which influences and directs the adoption of
<u>all</u> other more particular maxims. The disposition is "the ultimate
subjective ground of the adoption of maxims" (<u>Religion</u> 20)—and thus
itself a maxim. The dispositional act of the will is its free decision
to subordinate either its sensible nature to its moral nature, or vice
versa. This free (noumenal) act of adopting a most general maxim

determines for the agent (through his own choice) whether the specific acts of his will are to stem from respect for the moral law or whether they are to stem from his merely subjective interests. It is the having of a disposition -- which for Kant is the result of an act of freedom -- that is the ground in this late work of moral responsibility. It is not possible here to give more than this spare sketch; it is simply offered as support for the view that maxims are conceived by Kant to operate hierarchically -- that he provides a place for more general maxims, although not necessarily as the maxims of actual or proposed actions.

Our conclusion so far is that neither Kant nor good sense would have us select very general maxims as maxims of actions we were interested in testing with imperatives. For the sake of completeness, however, it must be acknowledged that it is possible for a person to act in such a way that it is proper to assign highly general maxims to his actions. But it must at the same time be realized that this situation is rare, and in many ways distressing. We can imagine someone, for example, who always acted on the maxim 'to do whatever I most strongly desire to do'. The example is extreme, but it will make the nature of these cases perspicuous. Let us further suppose, then, that at this moment I most strongly desire to go to the movies. Since I have, as my settled policy, decided to do whatever it is I most desire to do, I set off for the nearest movie. To say of my act of going to the movies that its maxim is 'to do whatever I most strongly desire to do', however, is really to say that the only thing about what I am doing that concerns me is that it be the thing I most desire to do. That is, what we are imagining is someone who does not want to go to the movies, as we ordinarily might, but who goes to the movies without caring particularly _that_ he is going to the movies. We are trying to imagine someone who does not care what he desires to do, but is only concerned that what he does be what he most strongly desires to do. _Any_ act would be as good as this one, if it was, in the moment, what he most desired to do. A less extreme example may make this point sharper. Let us take up one of Wolff's general maxims—to maximize profits in economic transactions. Recall, now, we are not trying to imagine someone with this policy or commitment as the source of motivation for what he does (i.e. he is not someone who merely chooses between otherwise comparable alternatives the one from which he will make the most profit—nor someone who attempts, in whatever he does, to look for profitable angles); our subject is to be one whose _specific_ actions are governed by the profit-maximization maxim. Imagine doing the family shopping according to such a maxim, or selling a car, or playing the stockmarket, or buying a present, or playing in an orchestra. The maxim of an action tells you what it is about an action that is of interest to the agent. If we are to believe that the maxim of these actions is in each case to make the greatest profit, then it is the profitability of each action that is the governing reason why it is being done. The only cases where this does not look suspicious (selling a car and playing the market) are those where either the activity itself or the conventional way of going about it has making a profit as its governing end and motive. If the maxims of a person's actions are general as in the above examples, then such a person is not concerned with what he is actually doing, but strictly with what _kind_ of action it is. A striking parallel example

of this is Kant's moral fanatic "who admits nothing morally indifferent
and strews all his steps with duties as with man-traps; it is not indifferent, to him, whether I eat meat or fish, drink beer or wine, supposing that both agree with me" (DV 71;408). The nature of Kant's dis-
agreement with the man of 'fantastic virtue' is with his blindness to
particular cases and his tendency to generalize the moral maxim into
the wrong sort of general policy—it is important to act morally according to the right sort of maxim, but that is not equivalent to adopting
a perverse moral maxim as the maxim of all one's actions. Part of what
it is to be a moral person is to know when to raise moral questions and
when it is appropriate to ask what is the morally correct thing to do
before going on with one's affairs.

The normal structure of volition is represented in a hierarchical
array of increasingly general maxims. The maxim of a willed <u>action</u> is
the last and most specific of the chain. But that still leaves unre-
solved the question of how to specify the appropriate action-specific
maxim in a given case—a problem we touched on briefly in the Cancer
Society case. The difficulty of providing an answer to this is found
again, and in the same form, in the problem of the tailored maxim. The
essence of the issue in both is the old refrain that every action is
susceptible to a wide variety of possible descriptions—with respect to
kind, descriptive detail, level of generality, etc. Since the maxim of
an action contains a description of the action, unless there is some
means of selecting a 'correct' description of an action, then we will
be unable to determine <u>the</u> maxim of an action, and it will seem possible
for an agent to tailor his maxims with adequate precision so that the

test of the categorical imperative for the permissibility of the action
will not be able to work. As the tailoring problem is more amenable to
direct solution, we will work on it first. If we can block the suggestion that maxims can be tailored by showing that there are not many
possible correct maxims of an action, we will have found a working criterion for selecting the maxim of an action.

Let us take the tailoring criticism as it is made by two commentators, one hostile to Kant's project, the other rather sympathetic:

> The doctrine of the categorical imperative provides me
> with a test for rejecting proposed maxims; it does not
> tell me whence I am to derive the maxims which first pro-
> vide the need for the test.... (T)he Kantian test of a
> true moral precept is that it is one I can consistently
> universalize. In fact, however, with sufficient ingenu-
> ity almost every precept can be consistently universal-
> ized. For all that I need to do is to characterize the
> proposed action in such a way that the maxim will permit
> me to do what I want while prohibiting others from doing
> what would nullify the maxim if universalized.... /The
> description of the action is/ devised so that it will
> apply to my present circumstances but to very few
> others....[18]

> (The 'universal law' formulations of the categorical im-
> perative) tell us to act only on maxims which we can will
> to become universal laws.... To apply the test, we must
> first specify a principle as the principle of an actual
> or proposed action. How are we to do this?... Notori-
> ously, the same act can be described in a variety of
> ways. For example, the same act might be characterized
> simply as 'a lie', or as 'answering an hysterical woman
> in the only way that can prevent her suicide'.... The
> results of Kant's test depend upon which description we
> decide to call 'the maxim'.[19]

I have quoted extensively so that the tone and feel of this rather
standard criticism might be evident. It turns on two supposed facts:
that it is in some sense up to the agent to say what the maxim of his
action is, and that there are many possible 'correct' descriptions of a

single action, all of which are available to the agent as the description he will decide to include in his maxim. Let us ignore now the details of how the categorical imperative is supposed to work as a test, and focus simply on the fact that it rules on the permissibility (etc.) of actions by performing some sort of test on the maxim of the action. Since the test (see G 88-9;420-21, CrPrR 72;70) does ask for a judgment to be passed on the maxim imagined as if a universal law, apparently similar actions with different maxims will have their maxims 'universalized' to very different effect. This very loose characterization of Kant's moral test will be detailed enough for us to see the oddness of the tailoring criticism and the way to defuse it.

First of all, it is worth marking the oddness of supposing an agent is free to characterize his action any way he wants, as if satisfying the requirements of the categorical imperative were ultimately a matter of the agent's descriptive ingenuity. Consider the case of a used car salesman who omits telling his customer that the car he is about to purchase had been in a serious accident. Now are we to suppose that the salesman has a choice between describing his action as 'deceiving a customer in order to make a sale' or 'not telling the customer something that would cause him anxiety'? Ordinarily, it will be perfectly clear that the salesman is not aiming to maintain the psychic ease of his customer, but is holding back information which if known would jeopardize the sale. Of course it is possible that there exists a used car salesman who would omit the information because it in fact had no bearing on the quality of the car and would, if known, produce such a state of anxiety in the customer as to prevent his seeing that the car had been successfully repaired, etc. In either case, however, the salesman is likely to know what he is doing, and although our first salesman might say, if pressed, that all he was doing was trying to prevent unnecessary worry, saying that's what he was doing does not make it true. The possibility of the morally neutral description of his action derives from the fact that the customer's not suffering anxiety about his new car is a consequence of his not being told about the accident. But you cannot take just any consequence of your act—even if foreseen—as the (purported) end of your action. It is not open to you to describe what you did in terms of your action's unintended consequences, or to describe your act as directed to an end which is in fact only a means to another end (making a sale no matter how) you won't acknowledge. Concerning this sort of case, one might want to say, simply, that there is no imaginable good reason why a moral theory should be required to have a way of preventing someone from lying about what he is doing. If your action has consequences x, y, and z, and you acted so as to produce y, it is simply false to say after the fact that you were merely trying to achieve z. In a similar vein, it is wrong to take credit for unintended good consequences, if they are not what you were trying for in acting. If they were foreseen as side-effects, and then became part of the reason why you acted, they are to your credit, even if you would have acted the same way in ignorance of their being a consequence of your act. But this begins to get us far afield.

Let us turn to a case where it is less likely that what we have is someone intentionally misrepresenting his action. Suppose, if I do x, I will increase my income considerably, and Jones will lose his business. We will assume that doing x is legal. What we want to know is whether this is an act of becoming rich by legal means or an act of ruining Jones by legal means. Both are, from the outside, possible descriptions of the action, but are they both equally available to me as descriptions of my action, and if they are not, how do we tell which is correct? We can tell which it is by the following sort of counter-factual question: if I could become rich by doing x, but Jones would not be ruined as a result, would I still do x. If I would, then there is good reason to believe that becoming rich or increasing my income is my end, and therefore (in this oversimple schematic way) the ground for the correct description of my action. I have a motive for doing x be-cause I want to increase my income and I believe that doing x will lead to that as a consequence. If, on the other hand, I could increase my wealth by doing x and Jones would not be ruined, and I was no longer moved to do x, then the end I am seeking would not be (or not complete-ly) getting rich. I am at least partly motivated by a desire to ruin Jones. In this latter case it would be incorrect and misleading to ex-clude 'ruining Jones' from descriptions of what it is I am doing since it is a necessary part of what I would like to bring about through my action.

To determine the correct description of what an agent is doing, we need to know the nature of the circumstances which motivate his acting in such a way. The circumstances include the supposed consequences of an action, some subset of which is the desired end of the action. Since even the foreseen consequences may be numerous and of very differ-ent types, there must be a way of insuring which of the consequences is actually the end—thus securing the correct description. It is the motive—what, in the results of an action, one wants—that picks out the end and thus the correct description. An end is adopted because an agent has an interest in it; it is an agent's motive that gives the nature of the agent's interest in the action, and thus his end. It will also reveal whether he is interested in the end for its own sake or only as a means to something else. Thus of two possible descriptions of an action, the correct description is the one that includes those features of the action and its expected consequences which are the conditions of the agent's being motivated to do that act. Descriptions of the action which do not refer to the agent's motivating interest in the action are not permitted. An agent wills an action for a particular reason. Therefore, he cannot decide to describe his action in such a way that if there was no more to the action and its consequences than was contained in the description, he would not in fact have had what he would view as adequate reason to do it.

The argument against the more familiar form of 'tailoring' will be essentially the same, but it will be worth the repetition to regenerate it to allay once and for all this tiresom criticism. We have just shown that an agent is not free to just _say_ what _kind_ of action he did or intends to do. We must now address the question of his freedom to include details in the maxim of his action which have an effect on the ruling of the categorical imperative. This sort of problem is endemic to _any_ moral principle or criterion that requires the generalization of an action with an eye to consequences: the description under which the action is generalized will have an effect on the result.

The following is a standard instance of a tailoring-criticism example: George is in severe financial difficulties from which he can extricate himself only if he borrows money from Arthur, on the promise that he will pay it back, although George knows he will not be able to do that. He plans to make the deceitful promise at lunch on Thursday when he will meet Arthur, who, incidentally, has red hair and is 28 years old. The action is, minimally, 'making a deceitful promise to resolve money problems'; the question is, may George, in approaching the categorical imperative, bring as the maxim of his action, 'To make a deceitful promise, if I am in financial difficulties, in order to borrow money, only if the promisee is r-d-haired, 28 years old, and the promise is made on Thursday'. We will suppose, strictly for purposes of this discussion, that such a 'tailored' maxim will pass the test of the categorical imperative, whereas the less detailed maxim 'To make a deceitful promise, if I am in financial difficulty, in order to borrow money' would be rejected.

Again, we should be aware of the moral oddness of such a question. As a _real_ question, it imagines someone _aware_ that under different descriptions his action will be judged differently, and therefore wanting the description that will cause the ruling to go in his favor. It is surely a misunderstanding of what a moral principle is to see it on the analogy of tax laws with their inevitable loopholes. And it is surely an open question whether a moral principle should be required to block such 'misunderstanding'. Still, if it is a mistake to regard moral principles from the point of view of slipping through their formal strictures, it is nonetheless of use to say why, from a theoretical point of view, you cannot tailor the maxim of your action. That is, it is of importance to understand why the difference between deceitful promises for personal gain and deceitful promises to red-headed 28 year olds for personal gain is not a moral difference. What we will see is how the theory of maxims can be used to explain this moral fact and also how it can be employed in blocking the tailoring of a maxim.

The tailored maxim is, again, 'Whenever I am in financial difficulties, I will make a deceitful promise, in order to borrow money, if the promisee is red-haired, 28 years old and it is a Thursday'—and it is proposed as a possible 'correct' maxim of the act of deceiving a red-haired 28 year old (Arthur) next Thursday, in order that George may extricate himself from his financial embarrassments. The procedure for blocking this variety of tailoring will be to construct a set of counterfactual questions to test the relevance of the various features in the descriptive portion of the maxim—that is, those parts of the maxim which exhibit departures from a wholly general characterization, e.g., deceiving for personal gain, etc. For example, we will want to know how George would answer, 'If Arthur did not have red hair, would you still make the deceitful promise?' and 'If the occasion for making the promise turned up on Tuesday instead of Thursday, would you still make the deceitful promise?' If the answers to these questions were affirmative, then we would have excellent grounds for declaring 'red-headedness' and 'being on a Thursday' irrelevant to a description of what it is the agent (George) wills to do. If, however, we asked 'If you did not need money (or could get it some easier way), would you still make the deceitful promise?' and received a negative answer, then we

should conclude that this feature is properly part of the description
of the action as willed, and that the correct maxim of the action is
'Whenever I am short of money, I will borrow money and promise to pay
it back, though I know this will never be done (if there is no easier,
etc., way to get the money)'.

The justification for this fairly mechanical procedure is to be
found in the way the motive for an action relates to its description.
In the set of circumstances I have described, what is motivating George
to act is his need for money and his belief that through a deceitful
promise he will be successful in securing a loan. The other circumstances—that Arthur has red hair, etc.—do not figure in the aspects
of the proposed action that motivate George to act, as he would act the
same way if they were either absent or different. It is not impossible
to imagine a case where Arthur's having red hair would be part of the
circumstances that gave someone a motive for acting: suppose George
had an irrational grudge against all red-haired people (having been in-
jured by a red-haired bully as a child), and took every opportunity to
cause them injury. But in such a case we would do well to rethink the
structure of the maxim, as it is no longer clear what kind of action is
being contemplated.[20] This, obviously, is not the normal example, or
in any case, not the sort of example at which the tailoring criticism
is directed. If the force of that criticism is that given the large
number and variety of possible descriptions of an action, the maxim of
an action is not a fully determinate notion, that criticism should now
be defused. There is a criterion available for selecting the correct
maxim of an action, and that is the agent's motive in acting as he does.

A maxim which includes only those aspects of the action (and its expected consequences) which functioned as reasons for a person acting
the way he did is the maxim of that action.

When what I want to do is cheat in order to get into medical
school, that, from the perspective of maxims, is what I am doing. I am
not, e.g., cheating in pencil, on Wednesday, wearing a blue sweater—
even though all of what I describe is the case. When the nature of my
concern with the particular circumstances in which I find myself is
merely how to manipulate them so I can successfully reach my goal unde-
tected, then neither those particulars, nor the unintended or indifferent consequences of my action, are legitimate parts of the description
of my action as willed. What belongs to the description of my action
are the consequences I anticipate and for the sake of which I am moved
to act—what I want in acting—as well as those features of the action
which are essential to what I am trying to do. The elements of the
'privileged' description for the maxim are selected according to the
agent's motive in acting. (Thus the enormous theoretical importance in
Kant's theory of identifying the subjective ground of an action.) Although I use a pencil in my cheating, if I am indifferent to that fact,
or use it simply as the most efficient means, 'using a pencil' is not
to be part of the description of my action that goes into the maxim.
So long as either any other implement would do, or I would be just as
happy with something else equally or more efficient, then I am ultimately indifferent to using a pencil, and using it is not an essential
part of what I want or what action I believe will get me what I want.
Similarly, among the many expected consequences of an action, the one

that is the end, and thus to be included in the maxim, is the consequence you want—that is, because you want that, you are moved to act.
It is the motive that picks out the correct description of the action's
end for inclusion in the maxim.

The motive, the determining ground in the subject of the action,
is thus to be used to select a privileged description of an action for
inclusion in the maxim. Any description or elements of description
which are unrelated to that ground are to be eliminated from the proposed maxim. We have now resolved both the questions that initiated
this section. We have a procedure for determining the maxim of an action. And, we can see that it is not possible to tailor the maxim—an
action (as willed) has a maxim. If an agent is free regarding what he
wills, having willed, he is not free to say what he wants about how he
has willed. In so far as he is rational, he wills the realization of a
state of affairs, according to a principle. The willing is determinate,
and so, therefore, is its maxim.

The source of the tailoring criticism is to be found in the general tendency among critics and commentators to overlook what I have been
arguing is the central fact about Kant's view of action: action is
never to be thought of merely as an event, but always as of an agent—
as something willed. It is when you see acts as events detached from
agents that it is easy to imagine a variety of equally 'correct' descriptions of a single action. There may be occasions when it is appropriate to regard actions as events (perhaps when one is looking into
the general consequences of an action), but it is not appropriate in
the context of imperatives and maxims. The maxim of an action provides

a description of an action that follows from the very nature of the action as willed by a particular individual agent. It is therefore uniquely suited to be the point of assessment of our actions by imperatives.

The striking exception to our diagnosis of the source of misconceptions about maxims is to be found in Onora Nell's Acting on Principle. Nell sees the maxim in the context of the problem of relevant descriptions: a problem endemic to moral theories which employ a universalizability principle.[21] It is not that she offers the maxim as a general solution to the problem of relevant description, but rather that she sees Kant as unique among the universalizability theorists in that he has a solution to the problem: the maxim. Nell correctly sees the maxim of action as part of Kant's account of volition; she sees that the maxim need not be conscious or antecedent to the action; she proposes as a general form for maxims, "To do——if....in order to——"; she argues that an agent cannot include specific detail in his maxim unless he intends his act to be contingent on those specific restrictions;[22] and yet she does not think there is a maxim of an action. Rather, she contends, there is a maxim for each intended component of our action:

> We may break down acts into components and phases to each of which a relatively specific maxim corresponds, or compound acts into sequences to each of which a compound or abstract maxim corresponds. It is one of the merits of Kant's solution of the problem of relevant descriptions that it does not preclude us from assessing morally either small but intended components of our actions such as firing a gun or large intended sequences of actions such as "committing murder" or "betraying the cause."[23]

What we need to see is why Nell might have been drawn to this characterization of maxims and to what extent it is plausible.

The oddness in the account is that each intended part or component
of an action is treated as a separate volition, with its own maxim,
whereas Kant conceives of the willed or intended action as emanating
from the adoption of an end. The motivation for the account, then,
does not come from the theory of volition, but, we must suppose, from
the desire to have all intentional aspects of an action available for
assessment. The question is, in order to do this is it necessary to
deny that an action has a maxim and to assert instead that an action is
to be represented by a set of maxims?

Nell does not discuss in any detail her reasons for the intentional-
aspect account of maxims. We can best see what she has in mind by looking at examples she thinks an account of maxims like the one proposed
in this essay cannot adequately manage. In a section at the end of the
book discussing theories of action which offer a privileged description
of a voluntary action, Nell gives the following example: "an employer
fires an employee who has a dependent family, with the intention of
providing summer employment for the son of a business associate."[24]
Since this example occurs within a short discussion of Anscombe's Intention we may suppose it is to be looked at as analogous to Anscombe's
rather famous example (discussed by Nell on the previous page) of an
agent poisoning-the-inhabitants-by-pumping-at-the-well. That is, according to Anscombe, the relevant intentional description of the action
is formulated according to the end: poisoning the inhabitants. This
is the intention with which the agent acts, and is therefore the

intentional act description which is relevant for moral assessment.[25]
On this model, Nell assumes, we would describe the act of firing the
employee with respect to the end for which we act: to provide summer
employment for the son of an associate, and omit from the description
the act which is morally problematic: the firing of a trusted employee,
because it was a 'means' rather than an 'end' description in a series
of intentional act descriptions. We need not digress to consider what
Anscombe's reply might be, for the criticism applies to the account of
maxims in this chapter as well. That is, if our account makes the appropriate discriminations in the examples which concern Nell, we will
have shown that there is not adequate motivation for her account, for
it does not arise naturally out of the Kantian portrayal of the nature
of volition.

The first thing to note is that the examples are _not_ analogous.
In the water-pumping example there is _one_ action which falls under a
number of intentional act descriptions which are sorted as means or
end. In the firing-hiring case there are plainly _two_ distinct actions,
one of which is a means of enabling the performance of the other. The
successful firing will not bring about the desired end without _a hiring_.
On our account, this example would be represented by _two_ maxims: 'To
fire _x_ in order to make a place for _y_' _and_ 'To hire _y_ in order to
please his father'. The Anscombe example, on the other hand, being a
single action, would be represented by a single maxim. Thus we have
available to us just the distinction Nell wants for the moral assessment of actions. There is no reason and no need to treat the firing-
hiring example as a single action with two aspects or components. What

the agent does is fire x with the intention of making room for y. That
is, he fires x. Later he will act to hire y. Each is an action; each
has a maxim. As our account is more natural than Nell's, and since it
requires no sacrifice of moral sensitivity, it is clearly preferable.

There is one kind of case that should be mentioned as it seems to
call for the kind of account Nell offers: a number of maxims for an
action. Suppose that in a single action I will promote a number of independent ends: e.g., in selling my land I will a) increase my fortune, b) make my mother happy, and c) ruin my tenant. Each of these is
an end for which I act in selling my land and each would provide sufficient motivation for the action. Earlier (p.64) we discussed a similar case which differs from this in that one of the ends was a necessary part of what I would bring about through my action. That is, if
the action would not ruin my tenant, my increase of fortune and my
mother's pleasure—both of which I want—would not be sufficient to
move me to act. Then, we said, ruining my tenant had to be included in
the maxim of my action, whatever other ends I also had in acting. In
the case at hand, however, we cannot argue this way for the inclusion
of all the ends in the maxim since each end is a sufficient independent
motive for action. How then do we specify the maxim of the action? If
we include all the ends in a single maxim we misrepresent the structure
of this volition. If we select one of the ends (say, making a profit)
we may omit a morally relevant aspect of the action (ruining my tenant).
The solution is to represent the action-as-willed with three maxims,
each governed by one of the independent ends. This is not to concede
the point to Nell, however, since the reason for doing this is not that

the action has morally relevant intentional aspects or components, but because this strategy in this case best represents the agent's volition. The agent has three ends and would act for each of them. As a matter of contingent good fortune the agent can promote them all in a single action. It is because the action is a means to each of three ends that it is appropriate to represent the agent's volition in three maxims.

Apart from cases of this sort—where there is good reason to stipulate the use of more than one maxim to represent an action-as-willed—the claim that there is a maxim of action, specified according to the motive with which an agent acts, is still closest to Kant's general account of volition and most plausible in its own right. Even in the multiple end case, we should note, it is not that the action may be represented by any maxim you like: it is to be represented by one maxim for each independent end, and the specification of each of these maxims must satisfy the requirements on description we have set out. Thus in allowing for the possibility of more than one maxim to represent an action we do not depart in any essential way from our account of maxims. Other cases may suggest further modifications, but as we have seen in this instance, a virtue of our account is its flexibility in meeting complexities of volition. An account of maxims ought to be flexible in its representation of willed actions since, we should remember, it is an essential part of Kant's theory of volition.

Before concluding this chapter, a number of issues should be discussed, if only briefly, for the sake of completeness. From the account of tailoring we have presented, it should by now be clear that the problem of tailoring maxims to meet the requirements of normative principles is not restricted to the categorical imperative. There is little interest in the tailoring of prudential maxims, but there is, in principle, no difference. It is equally necessary to establish the maxim of an action in the evaluation of actions as they fall under hypothetical imperatives. As we shall see in the next chapter, this is the basis for determining whether failed actions are mistakes or the results of irrational willing.

Also, although we have rejected the idea of tailoring a maxim, there may be cases where it is legitimate to include in the maxim the sort of detail excluded by the general argument against tailoring. These will be cases where the specific circumstances do make a difference to what the agent wills to do. The most important set of such cases will involve an agent's choice to violate a moral prohibition, say, against deceit or theft, because of the very special and morally significant circumstances in which he finds himself. There is serious question whether Kant would go along with this suggestion—"The alleged right to lie" suggests he would not. But even if he would not, it may offer us a way of making the moral theory more flexible without our having to depart from its central insights. How such cases might be treated within the framework of the categorical imperative will be considered in chapter six. For now, the point to be attentive to is that it is not the amount of circumstantial detail in a maxim that causes problems—it is the relation of that detail to the agent's volition.

Another sort of example we have not considered might be called that of the 'underdetermined maxim'. What I have in mind is a maxim such as 'To eat truffles, if (or whenever) I am hungry'. This presentation of an action suggests that for purposes of analysis, and indeed, for ordinary comprehension, the proposed action is incompletely described. One feels that either the action is being described too specifically, or some condition of the volition has been omitted. Eating truffles does not flow from the expressed volition and its implied end (the appeasement of hunger). Now it is possible that the description in the maxim is not incomplete: there might be a creature whose hunger was satisfied only by truffles, or, it might be a description of an irrational volition. If it is the expression of a rational volition of a human being, it is, as it stands, incomplete. This suggests that what will count as completeness of description may often turn on conventional assumptions about means-ends relations and the nature of the individual whose willings are being examined.

Finally, we must acknowledge as a real problem the possibility that the agent's motive may be inaccessible to an observer as well as to the agent himself. That is, if the correct description of an action for inclusion in a maxim is selected by reference to the motive according to which the agent does or would act, then if we cannot determine what the motive is, we will be unable to formulate the maxim of an action. We may be misled by apparent motives—e.g., it may look to others and seem to the agent that he wants to go to medical school in order to be of service to his community, when in fact he is motivated by a need for professional respectability or financial security, but cannot admit the nature of his motivation, even to himself. Often, as time goes on, the original motive emerges in attitudes toward the profession or choices of medical specialty, but it need not. Also, actions can be overdetermined with respect to motive, or numbers of motives can be working, and it is not clear which is the 'real' motive. Thus, given the frequent opacity of motives, it may often not be possible to determine the correct description of an action. Where the motive is inaccessible, then, no certain maxim can be elicited. This is a problem, but it is not a problem that results from some inadequacy in Kant's theory or my interpretation of it. It is a real problem, and one which Kant acknowledges in talking about the difficulty in telling whether someone is acting from the motive of duty (e.g., G 75;407). That is, rather than posing a problem for Kant's theory, it seems to me confirming of the theory (or of the theory as I have interpreted it) that it is sensitive to the opacity of motives, and limited in its applicability by what we do not know about ourselves and others. (Of course, whether or not we can elicit the correct maxim, an agent's action has a maxim.) The problem of actually specifying a maxim reflects obvious and basic facts about human motivation. It is not that you can never tell what someone's motive (or 'real' motive) might be, often it is plain what it is. When it is not, then at least one can usually tell what someone's motives were not. Whether this is enough we shall find out when we see how maxims are used in the application of imperatives.

Notes

1. One of the things I hope to show is that **all** imperatives look to the maxim of the action to assess the rationality of conduct, and that as a result, criticisms that have been directed at the categorical imperative which turn on difficulties in specifying maxims, are not difficulties peculiar to that moral principle, but belong as well to the account of prudential action and its norm—the hypothetical imperative.

2. L.W. Beck, <u>A Commentary</u> on <u>Kant's "Critique of Practical Reason"</u>, pp. 80—81; O. Nell, <u>Acting</u> on <u>Principle</u>, especially chapter three. I do not include Nell's account in the characterization of the customary treatment of maxims that follows. Nell sees maxims as a solution to the problem of determining the relevant description of an action for use in universalizability tests. She is right, I believe, in placing the maxim in this role. What she does not provide is any motivation from within Kant's general account of rationality for the introduction of maxims. Since Nell's account of maxims is structurally similar to the one to be given here, in order to motivate that structure I have postponed consideration of her account of maxims until later in this chapter. What is missing in the Nell account is an explanation of why Kant solved the problem of relevant description with **maxims**. With such an explanation at hand we will be better able to see how to resolve familiar problems in the specification of the maxim of an action.

3. For examples of this see T.E. Hill, "The Kingdom of Ends", p. 311, R.P. Wolff, <u>The Autonomy of Reason</u>, p. 88ff., J. Harrison, "Kant's Examples of the First Formulation of the Categorical Imperative", pp. 230-233, ~~ibid~~., L.W. Beck, op. cit., pp. 80—81, 118—119.

4. In courses in which John Rawls discusses Kant's ethics I have seen him use the following schema for a maxim: To do____, if (or whenever) ——, in order to...., unless____. This seems to me correct, and I will often use this format in presenting maxims, except when doing so is unnecessarily awkward. I should say that I do not know whether Rawls would agree with my rendering of the 'if' clause of the maxim to include the agent's motive. Nell employs the same schema for representing maxims (see <u>Acting</u> on <u>Principle</u>, pp. 34-38). She includes the motive in the 'in order to' or end clause since she views ends and motives as reciprocal concepts: "The connection between motives and ends is logical. If an agent desires some state of affairs, x, we may attribute to him either the motive 'desire for x'...or state that x is one of his ends" (<u>Acting</u> on <u>Principle</u>, p. 103; cf. also, p. 38). We have already looked at cases (p.5) where two apparently identical ends were distinguished by the different motives the agents had in adopting them. We will argue, as a general claim, that it is the motive that determines the agent's conception of his end and therefore his maxim. Since motive and end <u>are</u> often reciprocal, their relation can seem simpler than it is. To preserve the complexity of this relation in the specification of the maxim, we have put the motive among the circumstances of an action.

5. Beck, and those who follow his analysis of maxims, like Wolff, are the only ones who have an argument for what a maxim is. Beck (op. cit., p. 81) tells us that "the term 'maxim'...is...taken from logic, deriving from sententia maxima, the name of the first major premise in a polysyllogism." There is no reason to dispute the derivation, but it need not follow, as Beck seems to think it does, that the maxim therefore has to be a very general personal policy principle—e.g., 'To avenge a wrong is always my purpose'. If my account of the variability of the content of maxims is correct, the real authority for this kind of maxim being archetypal—that Kant uses it (CrPrR 17;19, "For example, someone can take as his maxim not to tolerate any unavenged offense...") —no longer stands without independent argument from the nature of willing and the uses to which the notion is put.

6. These examples are borrowed from S. Hampshire, Freedom of the Individual, p. 46.

7. This phrasing is from Kant's essay "Perpetual Peace".

8. I have omitted the motive clause in this maxim, but not because it is obvious what it would be. Moral maxims pose a set of special problems given the requirements of Kant's criteria for moral worth. A distinction must be made between two possible motives in this sort of case: the motive of treating people honestly, and the motive of doing what is morally right (which in this case calls for treating people honestly). It is not clear which is better suited to Kant's requirements. But it is not essential that we resolve this problem here to appreciate the gross difference between the moral and the non-moral maxims. As the complex problem of moral maxims and their appropriate motives cannot be resolved without lengthy discussion of moral psychology, it must be set aside as the subject of future investigation.

9. In such cases the maxim may not be irrational either. See chapter three for more on this.

10. It has been suggested (see J. Murphy, "Kant's Concept of a Right Action") that Kant has two kinds of maxim—one which includes the motive and which is used in determining the moral worth of the agent, and one which excludes the motive and which is used in determining the moral rightness or wrongness of actions. The intuition that prompts this view is that one wants to be able to say that the grocer who gives correct change, from however base a motive, is still performing a morally correct action. It is not clear to me that one should want to say this—although, of course, the point of the intuition is plain: such a merchant violates no one's rights—no customer is harmed or wronged by what he does. All of that provides good reason for not pressing him through the law, but it does not seem to me good reason to say that what he is doing is morally right. That what he is doing is morally right may well be an altogether contingent characteristic of his activity; it therefore gives no more reason to call his action right than there is good reason to call morally wrong an act that by excusable accident harms. This is a larger claim than I can defend here; I will

have more to say on this subject in later chapters. Quite independently of this, the suggestion that Kant has two versions of 'maxim', one of which excludes the motive, ought to be undermined by the considerations already brought forward concerning the role the motive plays in determining what sort of act a given action is.

11. R.P. Wolff, The Autonomy of Reason, p. 69.

12. Ibid.

13. Ibid.

14. For those familiar with this example in the second Critique, it should be clear that I am not presenting the example here as Kant does. I will consider the details of Kant's example a bit later in this section, and will explain there how the parts of it that appear to contradict what I say here are to be read.

15. In the case of action from the motive of duty the subjective determining ground is necessarily a maxim; in other cases, it may be a maxim, but it also may be a need or 'sensuously based' inclination. One of the ways Kant ultimately distinguishes truly from only apparently moral action is that in the moral case the chain of determining grounds includes only maxims, whereas in the non-moral case, the chain ultimately terminates in 'inclination' or 'natural impulse'.

16. I will not pay attention to aspects of this example that rely on issues of the technique of employing the categorical imperative. I assume the reader has enough basic familiarity with examples similar to this one in the Groundwork to permit my treating it at the present time as if it were one of the four examples. I discuss those examples in chapter five where the general problem of the application of Kant's moral principle is examined.

17. This is an important claim and requires substantial argument in its support. For the time being, the only available support is intuition about the cases. In chapters four to six I will return to the task of supplying the necessary foundation for what must here remain a conjecture. This seems to me a reasonable procedure, as it would be a serious flaw in Kant's theory if it could not accommodate the moral distinctions I make here. Of course, many believe Kant's moral theory fails in just this way, but as I hope to show, it is not necessary to read it so ungraciously.

18. A. MacIntyre, A Short History of Ethics, pp. 197-198.

19. T.E. Hill, "The Kingdom of Ends", p. 311.

20. The motives for such an action are probably complex, and the maxim would have to reflect that complexity. But if George would be moved to make the deceitful promise only if the victim had red hair, then that fact must be included in the maxim. Less schematic examples are more

difficult—suppose, e.g., that although George is moved to injure red-haired people, he also would make a deceitful promise if he could not find a suitable red-haired victim. Cases like this are overdetermined with respect to motive, and need special consideration. They make no material difference to the point being discussed here.

21. O. Nell, *Acting on Principle*, pp. 4-31.

22. *Ibid.*, p. 72.

23. *Ibid.*, pp. 41-42.

24. *Ibid.*, p. 140.

25. *Ibid.*, p. 139; G.E.M. Anscombe, *Intention*, pp. 45-47.

Chapter Three: The Hypothetical Imperative

It has become a matter of convention to emphasize differences between hypothetical and categorical imperatives. We are often reminded,
for example, that hypothetical imperatives tell you what you ought to do
given that you have some particular end, while categorical imperatives
tell you what you ought to do without any regard to the particular ends
you may or may not have. This, as well as other differences familiar to
students of Kant's ethics, is fundamental, but excessive or exclusive
concern with such elemental facts obscures basic and useful similarities
between the two types of imperative. I place considerable emphasis on
Kant's account of hypothetical imperatives for two principal reasons.
First, the account and analysis of prudential action is interesting in
its own right--and, in addition, it sets in relief details of the structure of Kant's employment of concepts such as will, maxim, principle,
etc. Second, as a methodological rule of thumb, I have found that it is
often useful, when considering difficulties with the categorical imperative, to examine with care the analogous problem and solution as it appears in the account of hypothetical imperatives. This is possible, as
I hope to show, because the structural similarities of the two kinds of
imperatives are as thoroughgoing as the differences are profound.

For example, the categorical imperative is said to be the principle
of morality: it describes what we are doing when we are acting morally.
Kant's conception of the categorical imperative often seems perplexing,
particularly in the claim that if there is to be a moral principle, and
if its relation to the will is to be one of necessity (obligatoriness),

then the moral principle must be a priori—it must not have its source in (contingent?) experience. (Why this is thought to be so must be left unexamined here.) If the categorical imperative were a principle of reason itself (i.e. a principle any rational being would follow in so far as he is rational), that would satisfy Kant's condition. But what a principle of practical reason might be is more than marginally elusive. We can get a handle on it, however, by looking at the hypothetical imperative as such a principle: it too governs action, necessitates the will, and is established a priori. A second aspect of the hypothetical imperative's usefulness is to be found in the formidable task of making out Kant's claim that it must be possible to derive actual duties from the Categorical Imperative[1] in the following sense: if the Categorical Imperative tells us what obligation is, we must be able to show how those things which we take to be our duties are our duties (if they are) by reference to the Categorical Imperative. The difficulties with the supposed derivation of duties (in the Groundwork, G 89-90;421-423) are infamous: what does Kant mean by 'derivation'? how are we to evaluate the use of supposedly 'forbidden' empirical data in the derivations? how is the Categorical Imperative to be used as a moral test for moral actions? is it the source of substantive moral rules?[2] etc. Here, careful examination of the proper mode of employment of hypothetical imperatives provides the key to answering these questions, as well as suggesting an argument for a structural unity in application of the principles of practical rationality.

In this chapter, then, while looking at the nature and proper method of application of hypothetical imperatives, we will be emphasizing similarities among imperatives. This, in addition, has the virtue of following the order of presentation in the Groundwork, and so will place us at the same point of argument as Kant is when we formally introduce the Categorical Imperative. The importance of this ordering in the present program will be appreciated as we become able to talk of imperatives as principles of rationality with an increasingly clear sense of what that might mean. One last thing should be mentioned—there is an obvious reason to begin with hypothetical imperatives, and that is their intimacy with ordinary intuitions concerning purposive rationality. We are able to move easily through Kant's remarks on hypothetical imperatives because there is nothing, on the surface, that is counter-intuitive. While this feature facilitates reading—and lends credence to Kant's claim that he is trying to elicit the categorical imperative from ordinary intuition—it should not lead us to overlook the detail of Kant's presentation. It is in this often ignored detail, and the interpretive interpolation necessary to fill out the account, that Kant's theory of action and the norms of practical assessment make their initial appearance in roles they will not later abandon. The argument in the Groundwork depends on our familiarity with prudential action and the prudential 'ought', and our following the way this intuition is embedded in Kant's system of practical rationality. We must first learn to recognize familiar forms of action and judgment in new formal garb if we are to be able to follow Kant's efforts to explicate our 'confused' moral intuitions.

As will be recalled from chapter one, we introduced imperatives in

general as formulae expressing the norms of practical rationality—
principles of rational willing.

> An imperative...tells me which of my possible actions
> would be good; and it formulates a practical rule for a
> will that does not perform an action straight away because
> the action is good—whether because the subject does not
> always know that it is good, or because, even if he did
> know this, he might still act on maxims contrary to ob-
> jective principles of reason. (G 82;414)

A principle is an imperative (for us) just in case it is appropriate to
express the principle to human beings in 'ought' form, and the principle
is one that any fully rational person would follow. Human beings are
subject to imperatives because they can act according to a conception of
a rule, and can thus modify their intentions according to an accepted
prescription. But they are subject to imperatives (a command, an ines-
capable 'ought') because it is possible for us to recognize that it
would be good or right to do something, and yet act contrary to what we
(in some sense) know we ought to do—either out of weakness of will, or
the sly effort to exempt oneself from an almost willfully misconstrued
principle, etc. Beings not subject to imperatives are exempt either because they are perfectly rational, and therefore necessarily act according to objective principles of willing, or because, like animals, they
are thought not to have a will, and therefore lack the capacity to act
according to a conception of a rule or principle—i.e., there is no
question of the categories of practical rationality applying to them.
The complete set of imperatives, or rather the complete set of the principles they embody, define practical rationality. In this and the next
chapter we will be examining the least and the most controversial elements of this theory—the means-end, or technical imperative, and the

categorical imperative. Pragmatic or prudential imperatives will not be
ignored, but as they do not contribute to the formal theory of rationality, and since Kant does not really provide an adequate account of them,
they will be included as they enhance the theory of hypothetical imperatives and add confirming evidence to this interpretation.

Hypothetical imperatives are concerned with what is rational for an
end-setting creature with desires (wants) that require at least some
satisfaction. There are standard sorts of examples where, given what I
desire, there will be problems about what is the rational thing to do
(will). I might desire a variety of things (wealth, fame, etc.), but
not all of them would be things it would make good sense for me to will--
adopt as ends, which I would strive in my actions to achieve. To use an
old example, if I have a desire to be a concert pianist, but my musical
abilities are nil--and there is nothing I can do about that--if I am
rational, I do not commit myself to a course of action with that end in
mind (it's a vain desire), and I would be irrational if I did, however
strong the desire for that end. Other things I desire (fame by 30) I
may know are within my power, but I am 'unwilling' to do what is necessary to achieve such a goal--it would require the sacrifice of too many
other things I desire (friendship, tranquility, etc.). Then, given what
I care about, it would be irrational for me to adopt the end of ambition.
Both of these are cases of conflict where regardless of the strength of
a given desire, we would say it is not rational to pursue the object of
that desire, or if the end were one already adopted, that rationality
dictated its abandonment, because one is either unable or unwilling to
support the necessary means. These, I think, are the interesting cases,

but to understand their relation to the theory of hypothetical imperatives, we must first work through the standard case to see, in particular, what the constraints of rationality are on the willing of an end.

In the standard case, there is something I desire (want), it is
within my power to satisfy that desire, and there are no competing desires whose satisfaction will be made impossible by acting on this one.
Here, where my desire is the source of some project (willed goal) my
rationality is measured by the appropriateness of the means I select.
That is, if I want x, I ought to do y, when y is the available means to
x (other things equal, as we assume they are in the standard case).
What makes the 'ought' appropriate, in a general sense, is that it is
true of me 'by nature' that I may want x, know y is the means to what I
want, but balk or be tempted away. This 'ought'—that 'I ought to do
y'—is appropriately addressed to me because of the goal I have set myself and the objective relation of y as means to my end. If I have
adopted an end, know the means necessary to reach it, have no competing
ends, and what needs to be done is well within my power, then if I act
some other way, without thereby changing my goal, I am, in the most ordinary sense of the word, acting irrationally. What now needs to be
shown is how the theory of hypothetical imperatives can be seen as not
only a theory that produces the same judgments as we arrive at intuitively, but explains the force and authority of those same intuitive
judgments. We should look, then, at how Kant presents the idea of a
hypothetical imperative.

> All imperatives command either hypothetically or categori-
> cally. Hypothetical imperatives declare a possible action
> to be practically necessary as a means to the attainment
> of something else that one wills (or that one may will).

A categorical imperative would be one which represented an
action as objectively necessary in itself apart from its
relation to a further end.

Every practical law presents a possible action as good and
therefore necessary for a subject whose actions are determined by reason. Hence all imperatives are formulae for
determining an action which is necessary in accordance
with the principle of a will in some sense good. If the
action would be good solely as a means to something else,
the imperative is hypothetical; if the action is represented as good in itself and therefore as necessary in
virtue of its principle, for a will which of itself accords with reason, then the imperative is categorical.
(G 82;414)

(I have left in the comparative remarks concerning categorical imperatives for the sake of completeness; they
will not be discussed until the next chapter.)

Hypothetical imperatives enter when one has adopted or plans to adopt

some end. They govern our relations to possible actions, indicating

what is good for us to do, given our ends—what we take as good for us.

Hypothetical imperatives fall into two classes along a principle of di-

vision according to the nature of the end involved. Imperatives that

govern ends rational agents can possibly have are called either 'techni-

cal' or 'problematic' (hypothetical) imperatives. They are concerned

with all sorts of possible ends and actions, indeed, with every "possible

purpose of some will; and consequently there are in fact innumerable

principles of action so far as action is thought necessary in order to

achieve some possible purpose which can be effected by it" (G 82;415).

These imperatives tell us, given an end, how it is to be attained. Kant

therefore also calls them 'imperatives of skill'. They tell us nothing

about "the rationality or goodness of the end, but only about what must

be done to attain it" (G 82-3;415). That is, if, for example, my end is

to go to Paris this weekend, a technical imperative will indicate (in a

way we have not yet determined) the appropriate means—e.g., flying PanAm

from Logan Friday night. What it will be silent about is the fact that
the pursuit of this end conflicts with other, more abiding ends of mine
(e.g., the flight will exhaust funds I was saving for something else),
as well as, perhaps, with obligations and commitments I have already incurred. It does not speak about whether this end is 'good for me' or
'good in itself' but only about the merits of possible means I could
adopt in pursuit of my Paris goal. There is a form of hypothetical imperative that deals with the relations among my ends. Kant calls it
'pragmatic' or 'prudential'; it is the "hypothetical imperative which
affirms the practical necessity of an action as a means to the further-
ance of happiness" (G 83;415). Of course, the Categorical Imperative
and the principles it subtends also govern relations among ends by
setting what Kant calls a 'limiting condition' on the willing of ends.
We will not now be concerned with the problems that arise when willed
ends conflict with moral requirements, and how the theory of imperatives
both expresses and resolves such problems. The kind of conflict at
issue for hypothetical imperatives is among ends we take to be mutually
necessary for our personal happiness as we conceive it.

The end of happiness is, however, special. It is not, according to
Kant, an end it is merely possible to have, it is an end we all necessarily have:

> There is, however, one end that can be presupposed as ac-
> tual in all rational beings (so far as they are dependent
> beings to whom imperatives apply); and thus there is one
> purpose which they not only can have, but which we can as-
> sume with certainty that they all do have by a natural
> necessity—the purpose, namely, of happiness. (G 83;415)

Although the end is necessary (which distinguishes this type of imperative from imperatives of skill), as the imperative is still (in principle

concerned with "the choice of means to one's own happiness", it is a hypothetical imperative. "(A)ction is commanded, not absolutely, but only as a means to a further purpose" (G 83;416).

Even though we will not dwell on pragmatic imperatives, something should be said about the nature of this end--happiness. We might well ask why it should be presupposed that we have this end given that 'we are dependent beings to whom imperatives apply'. What does our being subject to imperatives have to do with our necessarily having happiness as an end? And further, why is it an end we are said to have 'by a natural necessity'? Two elements are operative here. First is Kant's well-known remarks to the effect that the end of happiness is indeterminate: "the concept of happiness is so indeterminate a concept that although every man wants to attain happiness, he can never say definitely and in unison with himself what it really is that he wants and wills" because, the elements of happiness are empirical, and only an omniscient (and hence not-finite) being would 'be able to deside with complete certainty what will make him truly happy' (G 85-6;418). That is, whatever conception of happiness we have is partial and presumably without complete internal consistency. Connected with this is a second relevant feature--and that is the personal nature of happiness. In short, happiness is always someone's happiness, and there is no reason to suppose that my conception of my happiness would make you happy. What follows from all of this is that we have and adopt ends which are neither singly nor in conjunction necessarily good or rational. In part this is because of our imperfect empirical knowledge, but it is also in part a product of our taking our subjective-empirical differences as the basis

for our adoption of ends. We are beings of needs, and so demands of our
non-rational constitution are put on the will—and these are demands
that must be met. That is our nature. We are neither wholly nor domi-
nantly rational beings. Combined, this is the basis of our being subject
to imperatives: we are rational beings—we use reason in acting and
deciding—but we do not necessarily adopt ends and will according to
principles of rationality.

But why should it follow that we necessarily have happiness as an
end? Some distance toward an answer can be made by considering what
kind of notion 'happiness' is. For Kant, it is best interpreted as a
generic term by which reference can be made to all the particular ends
an agent desires, including priority, ordering and other structural
considerations. It is the sort of conception of ends Rawls calls a plan
of life. In this sense, it appears that all rational beings who act for
a variety of ends would necessarily have happiness as an end, and thus
the claim would be trivialized. But the appearance is misleading. What
we must recall is that for dependent beings (rational beings who are not
wholly rational—let us leave until later further examination of what
Kant means by 'dependent'), the set of ends and their ordering, etc.,
will be different for each. And this is what distinguishes the ends of
dependent beings (called happiness) from the ends of purely rational
beings (called the Good). That is, the ends of all purely rational
beings would be the same. They would not act to realize ends unique to
each as a subject. Human beings, however, conceive of happiness as the
attainment of certain goals set in terms of their own interests, desires,
beliefs, commitments, etc. This is not to say that human happiness is

selfish or even amoral. A conception of happiness can of course contain moral and social goals--and that as a matter of course. But if happiness refers to all the ends desired by a particular agent, then it will not be the same for all human beings. What is true (and, according to Kant, necessarily true) is that every human (dependent) being will have a conception of happiness, and this because he necessarily has a complex and interconnected set of goals. It is certainly plausible to call the desire for the satisfaction of one's general projects, plans, etc., a desire for one's happiness.[3]

It should be a striking feature of this account that it includes no mention of Kant's infamous attachment to a crude form of hedonism. Neither the notion of happiness nor the ends of which it consists were hedonistically described. It is certainly true that Kant does sometimes employ a pleasure-pain analysis of any non-moral interests an agent may have, and he must be faulted when he does that. But what I hope this brief depiction of the concept of happiness has shown is that psychological hedonism is not (at least here) a necessary element of Kant's theory. It is impossible to know how deeply committed Kant was to psychological hedonism as a theory of human nature. However, the issue can be reduced to one of 'merely' historical interest--in the narrowest sense--if we can make good sense of his theory of action and ends without it. One might propose a parallel account of the 'motive of self-love', according to which self-love is not to be seen as a separate motive with its own peculiar object (e.g., 'happiness' or pleasure seeking and pain avoidance), but rather, again, as a generic term, standing for all the particular motives an agent has that point to desired ends.

Only in this latter sense will it be correct to say that the object of
self-love is happiness--when happiness itself is not regarded as a separate end.

The most important difference between technical and pragmatic imperatives is in the nature of their ends; the ends of technical imperatives are determinate and given; the ends of pragmatic imperatives are
indeterminate and at best supposed. That is, technical imperatives
regulate willing after the adoption of an end. They are indifferent to
the nature of the end except as it poses technical problems. The problem of ends for pragmatic imperatives, however, turns rather on the
'fit' of an end within a program, and in addition, on the internal coher-
ence and possibility of the program itself. But since our concept of
happiness is indeterminate, "we cannot act on determinate principles in
order to be happy, but only on empirical counsels, for example, of diet,
frugality, politeness, reserve, and so on--things which experience shows
contribute most to well-being on the average" (G 86;418). However, as
Kant points out, if we assume that we could have a determinate notion of
happiness and that the means to attain it could be found out, then pragmatic imperatives would be formally the same as technical imperatives--
both commanding that he who wills the end also will the necessary means.
There would still be a difference with respect to the end--for an imperative of skill "the end is merely possible" (i.e. it is an end that some
rational beings can adopt), but the end of the imperatives of prudence
is given (i.e. every dependent rational being has it--although, not
necessarily as the end of every action, otherwise moral willing, as Kant
understands it, would be ruled out). We can, then, for most of the rest

of this discussion of hypothetical imperatives, restrict our focus to imperatives of skill as the paradigm of 'willing an action _only_ as a means to some further purpose'—which is defining for what makes an imperative hypothetical.

Although commentators have often underestimated just how penetrating Kant's analysis of action and volition actually is, it must nonetheless be acknowledged that he does not provide, and did not, I think, intend, anything like a complete theory of practical rationality. An adequate theory of practical reason must in addition to general structural norms include subsidiary principles. A good example of such a principle might be Rawls' principle of inclusiveness[4] which would provide an element of the needed supplement to a Kantian account of prudence.

What is most important in Kant's theory is the introduction of the three distinctive types of imperative or principles of practical rationality. That is, there are, it is claimed, three different forms of rational thought about action, embodied in the principles of the three types of imperative: the technical apparatus of successful means-ends manipulation, the development of a coherent and possible set of ordered ends, the realization of which constitutes an individual's conception of happiness, and a formally distinct **moral** principle. While we have not yet examined Kant's arguments for this division, and in particular his argument for the categorical imperative, it is to be noted that this is what his claim concerning practical reason amounts to in the theory of imperatives—there are _three_ principles normative for practical reasoning. The moral principle is, of course, the one Kant is concerned to present in detail. We, however, must be interested in a general way in all of them if we would appreciate where the categorical imperative fits in a theory of practical reason as well as how it differs from the more familiar principles of technical and prudential rationality.

I shall take it as by now well established that hypothetical and categorical imperatives are not to be distinguished from each other in terms of distinctive grammatical or logical form.[5] It was once thought that hypothetical imperatives in general had the form 'If you want A, then you ought to do X', while a typical categorical imperative would have the form 'You ought to do X'. The problem with this was that many moral imperatives were in hypothetical form, or as Hill puts it, "A major problem with this way of distinguishing types of imperatives is that the distinction does not coincide, as Kant intended, with the distinction between moral and nonmoral imperatives."[6] One would not want to be committed to a view that required 'If you promised to return that book today, you ought to do so' to be classed as a hypothetical imperative. And obviously, apart from Kant's tendency to talk as if the difference were merely one of form, even if there were such a uniform difference, it would not be a morally significant one. It seems equally well-established that the difference between the types of imperative is to be marked in terms of the nature of the willing: in the relation of the will to its end. Construing the difference this way also allows us to keep perspicuous the distinction between pragmatic and technical imperatives that Kant takes such pains to draw. Wolff uses a schema that sets this out clearly:[7]

> An imperative of skill says that an action is good to some possible purpose.

An imperative of prudence says that an action is good to
some actual purpose.
An imperative of morality says that an action is good to
some necessary purpose.

We will not be in a position to appreciate the significance of this por-
trait until we examine the complexities surrounding the categorical imperative.[8] What is important for our account here is that we recognize
the central structural similarity of both types of hypothetical imperative: The validity of any hypothetical imperative--the legitimacy of
its authority over an individual--depends on whether the individual has
willed a particular end. That is, if a hypothetical imperative says a
certain action would be good (rational) to do in the pursuit of some end,
if I have not adopted that end, if I have not committed myself to its
pursuit, then that hypothetical imperative has no authority over my action. Now the authority of an imperative of prudence would seem not to
fit this model, given that such imperatives govern an end which Kant
claims all human beings necessarily have (happiness). But if it is
possible for us ever to abandon the goal of happiness--either for a
short time or in a more enduring way--in response to some moral claim,
then happiness cannot be a necessary end in the way it might initially
appear. For Kant to have a moral theory at all, we must understand the
end of happiness to be one we necessarily desire (however indeterminate
our conception of it), but not an end that we necessarily and on all
occasions adopt as the end of our action. Thus for our present purposes
we will not differentiate between the two forms of hypothetical imperative, but examine the nature of the constraint imposed by both of these
principles on the willing of action 'only as a means to some further

purpose willed'. This, as we shall see, essentially identifies all hypothetical imperatives as they are 'not categorical'.

We want now to look in detail at how hypothetical imperatives govern action.[9] A hypothetical imperative says, we should recall, 'if you want y, you ought to do x'—where x is some available means to y. Our first question is, what is the force of that 'ought'? Let us begin by looking at an example of a hypothetical imperative that fits the pattern and is the sort of practical injunction one would intuitively expect a hypothetical imperative to be. We will be interested both in the way such an imperative would regulate volition and in the question of whether an imperative of this form is the norm for hypothetical imperatives (directed at specific ends). We will be working toward the full answer to these questions throughout the rest of this chapter; the conclusions that appear to be established as we go along must therefore be regarded as provisional or incomplete.

We will take as our sample hypothetical imperative, 'If you want to be physically fit you ought to run for at least 15 minutes each day'. First we should ask what is meant by calling it a hypothetical imperative, even if it seems that the answer is obvious. "A hypothetical imperative...says only that an action is good for some purpose..." (G 82; 414). Our sample does not strictly say that running at least 15 minutes each day is a good way to realize the purpose of physical fitness, but we surely understand it to imply that. So the physical fitness imperative is hypothetical because it posits a means to end relation between running and fitness. (We will assume for the present that there are no problems in establishing that the suggested means do in fact provide a

good way of realizing the stated end.) But this does not explain the
point of calling it an _imperative_. An imperative, we have said, embodies a principle or norm of practical rationality. Without now going
into the way _this_ imperative could be said to embody such a principle,
we can say that what this means is that an imperative includes an expression of what it is rational for an agent to do. That is, our sample
is an imperative not merely because of its form, but because its form
implies that if you want to be physically fit then the rational thing to
do is run for at least 15 minutes every day. It is a _hypothetical_
imperative because it says that a possible action would be good or rational to do _given_ that you have physical fitness as your end.

If running is in fact a means to physical fitness then the sample
is, in a sense, a hypothetical imperative whether or not there is any
agent who wants to become physically fit. It states a means-end connection which _would_ be the basis of action for a being with fitness as an
end who did what was the rational thing to do. This is the sense of
hypothetical imperative that is present in the following:

> Everything that is possible only through the efforts of
> some rational being can be conceived as a possible purpose
> of some will; and consequently there are in fact innumer-
> able principles of action so far as action is thought
> necessary in order to achieve some possible purpose which
> can be effected by it. All sciences have a practical part
> consisting of problems which suppose that some is possible
> for us and of imperatives which tell us how it is to be
> attained. (G 82;415)

Our sample imperative looked at this way might well be found among the
rules for good health in an exercise manual. But this does not capture
the central role of these imperatives in Kant's theory of action. What
we need to see is how and under what circumstances our imperative governs

an agent's willing.

We must recall from our earlier discussions of imperatives what the function of the 'ought' is in the formula--it indicates what it is rational to do, but to an agent who while capable of acting rationally, will not necessarily do so just because he knows that something is rational (good) for him to do. The point of this 'ought' is to tell me, an agent, that if I have adopted an end of physical fitness, then if I am rational I will begin a program of daily running. The power of an imperative to tell me what to do is dissolved if I am indifferent to the claims of rationality, but as we shall soon see, if this is my stance, it will be hard to understand what I take myself to have done in adopting something as my end. Even in such an extreme case, however, the imperative still dictates a norm of action for a rational being in my circumstances. Of course, the power of an imperative is also contingent on my having adopted and continuing to affirm the end the action it dictates would have as its effect. If I do not have that end, then the imperative says nothing to me. And if I do not want to accept the means to my end that rationality dictates, it is not necessary that I do, so long as I then abandon my end. If I feel that running every day would be insufferably boring, I can, with full rationality, refuse to run, so long as I am willing to forego the end of physical fitness--assuming there is no other means by which I could pursue it.

This last qualification (the possibility of 'other' means than the one included in the imperative) raises an important question about the appropriate formulation of a hypothetical imperative. If playing one hour of tennis every day would serve the goal as well, surely I need

not, if I do not want to, run 15 minutes, regardless of what the imperative says and without any loss of rationality. It is not at this point
in our discussion clear in what direction we will find an answer to this.
One could, for example, construe the 'ought' of our sample imperative as
having merely prima facie authority, and thereby accommodate the rationality of playing tennis with some regulatory principle such as: if two
imperatives govern action to an end equally well, but the agent prefers
the means specified in one over the other, then the 'ought' of the pre-
ferred imperative over-rides—or some such equivalent notion. But an
equally successful solution would be to include both means in a single
imperative: If you want 'A' you ought to do x or y, and then explain
the apparent problem of our sample imperative as one of incomplete formulation, etc. Or, we could avoid the problem altogether by requiring
that imperatives be formulated in a more general way—for example, we
could have the means clause be something like, 'you ought to do some
adequate regular exercise'. We will eventually need to determine a solution for constructing appropriately specified hypothetical imperatives,
but as it is not immediately necessary, having acknowledged the problem
we will postpone the answer until the reintroduction of maxims.[10] All
we need to be clear about so far is—if our sample imperative is a
possible hypothetical imperative (and most commentators would think so),
then the real circumstances of the agent can affect the stringency of
its requirement.

If I have adopted an end, I will, if I am rational, at least propose and attempt a course of action I anticipate will lead me to my
goal. If I adopt an end but do not embark on appropriate means I may

well be open to charges of irrationality. For example, if I adopt the
end of losing 2 lbs. a week and then proceed to pay no attention tð what
I eat, or allow myself to 'forget' what I had at different meals, then I
will not, in an ordinary sense, be acting rationally. If I want to diet,
but discover that my proposed rate of weight loss will weaken an already
fragile physical constitution so that I will be unable to do the work I
planned on during the period of the diet, then my not doing anything to
restrict my food intake need not be a mark of failed rationality, but
might instead indicate my determination of priorities among ends that
were circumstantially incompatible (i.e., although the ends themselves—
losing weight and doing my work—are not incompatible, the means circumstances prescribe for one undermine the realization of the other). The
point is, when other things are equal—i.e. the pursuit of my adopted
end will not interfere with other higher-order ends, the means involve
actions I know are possible for me, etc.—the 'ought' of a hypothetical
imperative marks the fact that if I then do nothing in pursuit of my
goal, I am not acting as a rational person would act in my circumstances.
We are not here concerned with why an agent might refuse to take steps
toward the goal he has resolved to pursue, but only with understanding
that, other things equal, such action is judged irrational. So far,
then, what we would say based on the command of a hypothetical imperative accords with our natural judgment.

We remarked earlier that a hypothetical imperative binds only so
long as the agent holds onto his end—if he is willing to abandon it,
the imperatival 'ought' no longer applies. We should examine this
phenomenon a bit more closely. One feature can be brought out in a

comparison with the moral 'ought', If at some earlier time I have made a promise to do something now, that promise is binding (other things equal) until I have carried through on whatever I promised to do, regardless of any change my attitude toward making that promise may have undergone in the period of time between my making it and my obligation coming due. This is not the case with a hypothetical imperative. Even though two weeks ago I adopted a physical fitness goal, if today I do nothing toward it, the charge that 'I ought to' is inappropriate if I no longer have that goal. That is, the 'ought' of a hypothetical imperative that governs either a course of action of some duration or an action to be performed in the future retains its authority over a rational agent only if the agent remains constant in his commitment to the end of the imperative--up to the time of the action. A hypothetical imperative does not prohibit an agent's changing his mind about what he wants; what it does prohibit is, as Hill puts it, "The irrational refusal to implement decisions one continues to reaffirm."[11]

A hypothetical imperative is a formula containing an expression of what is good (rational) for an imperfectly rational agent to do given the ends he has adopted, and it is presented to the agent in the form of a command (an 'ought') because an imperfectly rational agent will not always want (desire) to do what is good for him to do. A valid hypothetical imperative will in this way be like the moral 'ought' in that it will be experienced as a constraint on what an agent might like to do.[12] That is, if I want x, and although y is the means to x (and I know that), I might still prefer doing z, which, although not a means to x, would be a lot more fun. If I am responsive to the claims of rationality (expressed in the imperative 'if you want x you ought to do y'), and continue to be clear that I do want x, then I might well feel constrained to do something other than what I in the moment would most like to do. The experience of constraint by norms of prudential rationality need not be of a different order (nor even of a different magnitude) than that produced by moral principles.

We must now turn to the question of the source or ground of the authority of particular hypothetical imperatives. To put the question schematically—if y is the means to x, and x is an end I have willed, why does rationality dictate doing y? (Given, of course, that other things are equal; I will drop this qualifier to avoid excessive repetition in what follows; it should be assumed to be operative unless a case is obviously constructed to show the consequences of other things not being equal.) Up to this point we have taken the theory of hypothetical imperatives to be a formal representation of our intuitive ideas of practical rationality, and, indeed, as a result, there has seemed no need to exercise special caution in moving back and forth between the Kantian and intuitive accounts. What has been left out is the part of the Kantian program that offers a justifying explanation of our intuitions and a ground for the authority of hypothetical imperatives. This, in Kant's language, is the question, 'How are these imperatives possible?'

> This question does not ask how we can conceive the execu-
> tion of an action commanded by the imperative, but merely
> how we can conceive the necessitation of the will ex-
> pressed by the imperative in setting us a task. (G 84;
> 417)

The question is not nearly as obscure as it looks. What Kant is in essence asking is--in virtue of what could an imperative be <u>binding</u> on an agent such that in so far as he is rational he can recognize and will acknowledge its authority over what he wills? This will be clearer if we consider an analogy borrowed from Wolff.[13] He asks, in virtue of what are the commands of a military officer binding on agents? We might offer two conditions: that they be addressed to agents who are in his 'command' (say, his company) and that what is commanded be within his authority as an officer (this to cover moral and other limitations of the scope of military authority). If these conditions are satisfied, then we can explain why, if someone is a member of the officer's company, he ought to obey the officer's legitimate commands (as well as why, for example, if you are not a member, his commands do not apply to you). This, along with more on the roles of soldier and officer, is to answer the question 'how such a command is possible' because it shows 'how we can conceive the necessitation of the will (of a soldier) expressed by the (officer's) command in setting (a soldier) at task'. To answer the question for hypothetical imperatives we must find some characteristic of rational agents that will function as 'being a member of the officer's company' did for military commands. We will also find the scope of authority of hypothetical imperatives limited by moral and other principles of valuation.

The answer is to be found in understanding what is meant by 'willing an object' as an end (G 85;417). What Kant in effect argues is that in the very conception of willing an end there is present a principle of rational willing: "Who wills the end, wills (so far as reason has decisive influence on his actions) also the means which are indispensably necessary and in his power" (G 84-5;417). This is The Hypothetical Imperative; it is the principle of all particular hypothetical imperatives and the ground of their authority. Not to accept the Hypothetical Imperative as binding on one's will is, as Beck puts it, "to fail to be a rational being concerned with desires."[14] That is, to be a rational being concerned with desires is to have at least some desires you would prefer satisfied rather than not. As a rational being (with a will) you would not merely wish or hope for their satisfaction, but would perceive the need to propose a course of action to a desired end. The Hypothetical Imperative is the rational principle of acting for an end—thus the force of Beck's remark. Of course, accepting the Hypothetical Imperative does not in itself entail that we will act rationally in pursuit of our ends—and our failures of prudence will be as important in understanding the theory of hypothetical imperatives as our ability to do what we ought.

We want now to see how Kant establishes the claim that the Hypothetical Imperative is present in the very conception of willing an end, and thus derives its authority from the very nature of the will it commands. Let us look at the full text:

> Who wills the end, wills (so far as reason has decisive influence on his actions) also the means which are indispensably necessary and in his power. So far as willing is concerned, this proposition is analytic: for in my willing of an object as an effect there is already conceived the causality of myself as an acting cause—that is, the use of means; and from the concept of willing an end the imperative merely extracts the concept of actions necessary to this end.... (I)t is one and the same thing to conceive something as an effect possible in a certain way through me and to conceive myself as acting in the same way with respect to it. (G 84-5;417)

From this Kant concludes, 'If I fully will the effect, I also will the action required for it' is true and, he says, analytic. The connections are as follows: to will an end is to will an object (state of affairs, etc.) as an effect—something that will follow from some cause. But not just any cause. The Paton translation is really insufficient here: 'my willing of an object as an effect' does not capture the full point of the German "als meiner Wirkung".[15] So what we have is: to will an end is to will an object as my effect—that is, to will that an object (end) come about as an effect of some action of mine (as its cause). "The causality of myself as an acting cause" is the causality of a being who is moved to act (cause effects) in accordance with its idea of a connection between means and end. There is a conception of myself as a cause and of my ends as possible effects of my causality. ("Only a rational being has the power to act in accordance with his idea of laws...and only so has he a will.") And to be moved to act by my conception of the law connecting means to end is to 'will the means'. Thus the concept of willing an end can be said to include the willing, by the agent, of the necessary and available means. To will an end is to conceive of oneself as an agent—as a source of voluntary intentional action. It is also to appreciate the limits imposed on one's agency by the circumstances in which one would act as a cause for a desired end. "Who wills the end, wills also (necessarily, if he accords with reason) the sole means which are in his power" (G 85;418).

A perfectly rational being who willed an end would, by the necessity of its nature, will the means to that end in its power. In its willing an end, it would perceive itself as the potential cause of the

realization of its end as an effect, and knowing that effects are connected to causes according to empirical laws, it would attempt (if that
were possible) to act according to its conception of the law connecting
the desired effect with an action it might perform as its cause. An imperfectly rational being would not necessarily act that way, although as
a rational being, it ought to. The 'ought' is appropriate because an
imperfectly rational being does adopt or will ends—an act possible only
for a rational being and constitutive of its being rational. That fact
alone subjects him to rational requirements (what Kant means by the
'ought'), and therefore having willed an end he ought to will the available means. An imperfectly rational being may fail to appreciate the
constraints of rational agency—he may mistake the nature of his causality, in general, or in particular instances. He may act irrationally,
or even neurotically. There may also be a failure to coordinate the
complexes of action required by the variety of ends such an agent typically wills, and so a failure to will possible means. Much more needs
to be said about these failures—they provide the lineaments of a successful account of Kant's understanding of human agency—and we will return to them in our discussion of the use of the Hypothetical Imperative
as a test of prudential rationality. What we have established thus far
is the foundation for such a test: we have shown the ground in the will
of a rational being for a principle governing all action for ends, and
why Kant holds that even this principle is experienced by imperfectly
rational beings (and so by human beings) as a constraint, an 'ought'.
We can, following Hill, give a formula for the Hypothetical Imperative:
"If a person wills an end and certain means are necessary to that end

and are within his power, then he ought to will those means."[16] This is
what a rational person would do.

In short, the source of the authority of the Hypothetical Imperative is the nature of the rational will itself. The Hypothetical Imperative embodies a principle which describes how a wholly rational will
acts upon willing an end, and it is thus normative for imperfectly rational wills. The authority of particular (action-guiding) hypothetical
imperatives is the Hypothetical Imperative as their principle. A hypothetical imperative is valid or in force for a given rational agent if
it conforms to the principle of all hypothetical imperatives—the Hypothetical Imperative: if it contains the end the agent has adopted and
continues to affirm, if the course of action it proposes is possible for
the agent, and if the proposed actions are means to the agent's end.
The presence of these three elements constitutes conformity to the Hypothetical Imperative. 'You ought to quit smoking if you want to maintain
your health' will be a valid imperative for me if quitting smoking is a
means to the maintenance of health, if quitting smoking is a possible
action for me (i.e. I do smoke and it is possible that I could stop),
and if I want to maintain my health more than I want to continue smoking. (The case where my ends simply conflict—requiring, as it were,
equal and opposite courses of action—does not affect the validity of
the imperatives, but I will not be able to satisfy all the imperatives
currently valid for me.) The validity of a hypothetical imperative for
an agent is in its being an empirically specific instance of the principle of rational willing of ends, and its end being one the agent
affirms.

The theory of hypothetical imperatives concerns the ends an agent happens to have (ends of his choice or because of his nature) and not ends we are under obligation to adopt. The Hypothetical Imperative, on the other hand, governs more than just the contingent ends of agents (or the end of happiness); it applies whenever action is for an end. Since, according to Kant, all action is purposive, the Hypothetical Imperative is always operative. The nature of its governance depends, however, on the kind of end to be willed. In the next chapters we will see in just what sense the Hypothetical Imperative could be said to apply to moral as well as empirical, contingent ends.

It is now time to examine the fit of hypothetical imperatives into the account of human volition I have been arguing is Kant's, and, in particular, to set out the formal relations between maxims and hypothetical imperatives as one of their norms of rationality. We will be looking at how maxims are tested for their prudential adequacy, and so we will want to move with caution through this section of the argument as it will provide a possible model for the correct method of employment of the Categorical Imperative, which tests maxims for their moral adequacy. The general structure in both types of imperative is strikingly similar. In both, maxims are assessed as they conform to a particular imperative (or directly on the standard of the principle for all such imperatives), and in both, the ground of the legitimacy of particular imperatives is a general principle of practical rationality (an objective law of willing) expressed as a formal requirement on the will: the Hypothetical Imperative or the Categorical Imperative. Although, as we have seen, the operation of the Hypothetical Imperative is readily understood and close to intuition whereas the Categorical Imperative, with its strange demands on the agent's willing, is simply hard to make out, to say nothing of any close correspondence to intuition, nevertheless, the ambition of this argument is to demonstrate the formal uniformity in Kant's theory of practical reasoning. As we progress, it may seem that prudential judgment is made unnecessarily cumbersome; it may be so, but I think it will still prove illuminating in certain important ways; but above all else, we will see how the familiar feeling that the Categorical Imperative suddenly arrives (in the Groundwork) with no adequate preparation and no basis for its being understood, is ultimately only an appearance. There are great difficulties stemming from Kant's elliptical mode of presentation; our ambition here is to fill in enough gaps to produce a coherent and well-motivated account.

To return briefly to fundamentals: As we have already remarked, the neglect of maxims in Kant's discussion of hypothetical imperatives in the Groundwork should not be taken to suggest that they are in any way inessential.[17] Imperatives are norms for the assessment of the rationality of action. Since this assessment requires the inclusion of the agent's volition in the data to be evaluated, and the maxim of an action is the formal means of representation of an action-as-willed (other more general maxims or policies relate to the ground of motivation), it must be possible, and indeed it ought to be necessary, to take the maxim of an action as what is tested by hypothetical imperatives. We appreciate the rationality of our purposive undertakings by looking at the relation of the maxims of our actions to the principle of all

hypothetical imperatives (i.e., the Hypothetical Imperative—'Who wills
the end, wills (so far as reason has decisive influence on his actions)
also the means which are indispensably necessary and in his power' (G
84-5;417)).

At this point it will be useful to introduce some further terminology from the Groundwork (see G 81;413, 88n;421n, etc.). The maxim of
an action—the principle on which a person ('subject') acts—is called a
subjective principle; an objective principle is one which a rational being would act on if he were completely rational (or was acting in a completely rational way). Imperatives, therefore, express objective principles of action in a form suited to the condition of imperfectly
rational beings. A maxim will be called a 'subjective maxim' as it is
the principle on which the subject acts; an agent's subjective maxim will
be called (in addition) an 'objective maxim' if it is (or embodies) a
principle valid for all rational beings in so far as they are rational.
This last requires qualification: the validity of objective hypothetical principles (hypothetical imperatives) always depends on the empirical fact of what a given agent wills—hypothetical imperatives are
therefore, in Kant's terms, only conditionally valid (in contrast with
the purported/unconditional validity of categorical imperatives—a claim
whose import will be examined in subsequent chapters). To ask, then, if
an agent's purposive action is rational—that is, to ask if his willing
is in accordance with a hypothetical imperative (or the principle of all
such imperatives)—is to ask if his subjective maxim is also objective.
His purposive maxim will be objective if it is a principle appropriate
for any rational being who adopted the same end: it would be rational

for any agent with that end to have the same maxim of action. To determine whether a subjective maxim is also objective (in the ordinary purposive case) you look to the principle that governs such maxims--the Hypothetical Imperative.

Before displaying how this works in an example, we must return to a problem raised earlier in this discussion (pp. 100-101), as its solution is necessary before we can proceed. In the exercise example, it was noted that if the 'ought' of the imperative was to be binding, in the sense that if the agent did not do what the imperative indicated he ought to do he would not be acting rationally, and since in many cases any number of possible actions would be equally good means to a willed end, we need a method to specify the content of the relevant governing imperative such that it makes sense to say its 'ought' is binding. Put another way, what is being asked for is a way to make sense of Kant's claim that "hypothetical imperatives declare a possible action to be practically necessary as a means to the attainment of something else one wills" or "Every practical law presents a possible action as good and therefore necessary for a subject whose actions are determined by reason" (G 82;414, emphases added). In what sense is the action necessary? Suppose an imperative with the following content: If you want to spend a weekend in the mountains you ought to go to New Hampshire; and suppose the imperative is valid to the extent that it does include an end I will, going to N.H. is a means to my end, and it is a possible action for me. Given my end, however, is it necessary that I go to N.H.? That would seem to impose an absurdly stringent requirement on what I ought to will. As we shall see, the resemblance of this problem to that of the specification of the correct level of generality of the maxim of an action is not accidental, and the solution to the problem of maxims will hopefully be able to serve as our guide. It will be helpful, therefore, to pose the question yet again, in the terminology for maxims we have just introduced.

A hypothetical imperative is said to embody an objective practical principle; a maxim expresses the subjective principle on which the subject acts. Whenever someone acts on a rational principle (according to an imperative) his subjective maxim is also objective. If I acted according to the imperative of going to N.H., my subjective maxim (which, since it would conform to an imperative, is also objective) would be 'To go to N.H., if I want to spend a weekend in the mountains'. Now, if this maxim is correctly said to be objective, then it is the maxim every rational being with the same end (of spending a weekend in the mountains) would follow if he were rational. Here we have our problem again: given the information we have, it seems perfectly possible that some rational agent could, without imputation of any irrationality, plan a weekend in the Sierra Nevadas. The problem seems to be that the proposed maxim is too specific for it to be true that any rational being with my end would act on it if he were rational. So once again we have come around to the question of the maxim of an action. I suggest that the answer to this question of how a subjective maxim can also be objective will also turn on the role of the motive for an action, and the way in which the motive determines the description of what it is the agent wants.

Suppose my car breaks down and I decide to take it to Joe's Garage to be repaired. Is the maxim of my action to <u>do</u> <u>that</u>—i.e., take it to Joe's Garage? It seems prima facie plausible that it is, and that such a subjective maxim ought also to be objective, for if I want to get my car repaired, and taking it to Joe's is in fact a means to that end, then surely I am doing what the appropriate hypothetical imperative would direct me to do. The problem is, the maxim so described is not 'objective': many rational beings with cars they wanted repaired would, on this model, act on different maxims, each of which would also satisfy a governing hypothetical imperative. To escape this problem we could simply jettison the requirement as presently formulated that for my maxim to be objective (for it to conform to the appropriate imperative) <u>any</u> rational being with the same end would act on it (if he acted rationally). There does seem to be a way of doing this within the spirit of Kant's account; I will give a brief sketch of what it is and then explain why I believe it is not adequate.

For a maxim to be objective one could require, simply, that it conform formally to the Hypothetical Imperative: that the action called for <u>be</u> a means to the willed end. As for Kant's remarks about objective principles being ones all rational beings would act on if reason had full control, they could be interpreted also as referring to the Hypothetical Imperative itself. Then two agents with the same end but different proposed actions could both be acting on objective maxims if both of their subjective maxims conformed to the Hypothetical Imperative; in that sense they would both be acting on the same principle as well—as would all agents who acted rationally in pursuit of <u>any</u> <u>kind</u> <u>of</u> end. In short, the maxims of all agents who acted according to the principle of prudence would be objective in the sense that each of their maxims would be a concrete instance of the Hypothetical Imperative—a principle to which (by definition) any fully rational being (with ends) would conform.

There is much to be said for this account in terms of its clarity and straightforwardness. (Hill seems to flirt with it indecisively when he describes an objective principle as "a principle, or an application of a principle, that any fully rational person would follow.")[18] One is said to act on an objective principle (one's maxim is objective) if the principle of action is an instance of a principle constitutive of practical rationality. There is a sense in which I think this description is exactly right, My hesitation in accepting it is that as the whole story about objective maxims, it produces a truncated and not altogether plausible view of hypothetical imperatives, and it does not solve the problem of particular imperatives which enjoin, Kant says, as necessary, actions as means to an end, appearing thereby to rule out perfectly reasonable alternatives. Furthermore, and for reasons discussed in another context in chapter two, a maxim of 'going to Joe's Garage' is arguably not always (indeed, not even usually) the right formulation of my maxim when I go to Joe's Garage; for related reasons, an imperative instructing me to go to Joe's when I want my car repaired may not be the model instance of prudential instruction our initial account suggested. As I cannot rebut the above sketch directly, I will try to present as much indirect support as possible for a more complicated but, I believe, more satisfactory account. The nature of the support should make clear the relevant virtues of this way of looking at imperatives.

We will be able to bring into relief the object of my objection by working through the car-repair case to see what we would intuitively want to say about it. What we need to see is the very special nature of the circumstances which would warrant the imperative 'You ought to go to Joe's Garage, if...", where what is meant is: if getting the car repaired is your end, then taking it to Joe's is the 'possible action' that is 'practically necessary as a means to the attainment' of the end you will. The question is, given the end, what principle _would_ it be rational to act on: 'going to Joe's', simply, or some other, more general principle which indicates that going to Joe's is the right _kind_ of thing to do (e.g., to take the car to a competent mechanic)? (This of course is just another way of asking what maxim would be rational, i.e. 'objective'; I will continue in the rest talking about maxims, using 'objective maxim' in place of the imperative with which it conforms.)

An action-specific maxim is warranted if the agent intends his action to be contingent on the restrictions that specify the action (e.g. 'to _Joe's_') and not merely if he is pursuing his end by those means (since 'means' as taken are necessarily specific). For such a specific maxim to be appropriate, the following counterfactual would have to be true: that I would abandon my project of getting my car fixed if Joe's Garage had gone out of business, even if there were other competent mechanics, etc., available. If the project _is_ contingent on the specified particular means, then the maxim should reflect that specificity. For example, it might be that I do not understand what it is about Joe's such that whenever I bring my car there it gets fixed. Perhaps I think Joe is the one magically 'chosen' to fix cars. Or, it might be that I believe that Joe is the only honest garage owner in town, and I would rather not have the use of my car than pay good money to crooks. And it might be that given what ails my car, Joe is the only one who could fix it. In such cases as these, where the agent will act for his end only if means of a highly specified sort are available, an action specific maxim appears to be in order, as the agent really is acting on an extremely restricted principle. Given what the agent believes, it is 'rational' for him to do so, and in a sense his maxim will then be objective.[19] Often, as in the case of my desire to have dealings only with honest mechanics, a subsidiary desire modifies the end I am pursuing and therefore affects what it is rational for me to do by narrowing the range of possible actions and principles.

While it is true that with complex and intervening desires, oddities of circumstance and belief, etc., the maxim moves in the direction of increased specificity—as the action it would be rational to do becomes selected by increasingly narrow specifications, it is questionable whether the objective maxim (or the hypothetical imperative which embodies it as its principle) ever picks out an action. That is, we might well want to question the rationality and hence the objectivity of the maxim formulated out of the spiritual conviction of Joe's divine designation. And if a garage run by Joe's moral twin opened up across the street, we might expect a rational principle of action to allow its selection as a viable alternative means suitable to my complex end. And similarly, if I found out that someone else had been trained in the exotic mechanical procedures hitherto known only by Joe, then surely, if I am rational, the principle on which I act should direct me there on discovery of Joe's demise.

This requirement may seem to have greater plausibility if we look at it in terms of the more normal case. For example, when, wanting to have my car repaired, I bring it around to Joe's Garage, we can see that the principle on which I am acting is not 'to go to Joe's' when we see that upon discovering Joe has gone out of business, I initiate a search for another equally competent (trustworthy, cheap, convenient, whatever) mechanic. It might also be visible in the way I express my displeasure at the situation I am now in--every other mechanic I know about is no good, and I am afraid of what an incompetent mechanic will do to my car. The point should now be evident: the principle on which I was acting in going to Joe's was something like 'to take my car to a competent mechanic', and I went to Joe's because he was (or I believed he was) competent. Going to Joe's was doing something _of_ _a_ _certain_ _kind_--and in so far as I am rational, if I cannot go to Joe's and still want to get my car repaired, I will do something else _of_ _that_ _kind_. If, on discovering I cannot go to Joe's, I complain, 'there's no other competent mechanic around who doesn't charge an arm and a leg for his work'--then we can conclude that my initial end had been complex, and I had gone to Joe's because he was competent _and_ inexpensive--I went there because it was a garage of a certain kind. And so the maxim would have been, 'To go to an inexpensive competent mechanic, if I want my car fixed _and_ want to spend as little as possible to get a good job done'.

Formally, if the maxim is objective (it conforms to the Hypothetical Imperative), the action taken follows from the agent's determining what it is possible to do in his particular circumstances that will be the _kind_ of action called for by the principle of ends being acted upon.

Acting on a maxim is acting on a principle, and that in most cases requires an **exercise** **of** **judgment**. The principles that normally characterize our purposive projects set out criteria for the determination of an
appropriate action, given the ends the agent is striving to realize.
When only one action is possible as a means to our end that will generally be because the circumstances in which we have to act are limited
(or our understanding of them is). If Joe's is the <u>only</u> garage that
meets my criteria of economy and efficiency, going there is the action I
must (necessarily) perform if I would now act for my end. It would not
in such a situation make sense to say that I was acting on a principle
of 'going to Joe's', although, given the principle on which I <u>am</u> acting,
I ought to go to Joe's. The 'necessity' of <u>this</u> <u>action</u> is circumstantially contingent. What is <u>necessary</u> is that my action be of a certain
kind--the kind specified in my maxim. (It should be remembered that it
need not be the case that we consciously employ a principle in judging
how we are to act for what we want, but that our action always <u>has</u> a
maxim--there is always a principle at least implicit in the voluntary
and intentional acts of a rational being. The principle emerges when,
for example, untoward circumstances force an agent to consider the nature
of what he wants to do so that he can adjust his actions to permit successful pursuit of his ends in unanticipated ways. Or, it is what we
try to construct in understanding what someone is trying in his actions
to accomplish, or what can be offered in response to 'Why are you doing
<u>that</u>?')

In chapter two we used an example from Wolff to explicate a characteristic misunderstanding of maxims; it should not be surprising that we

can find an analogous useful mistake in his discussion of hypothetical imperatives; conveniently, he uses the same example[20]--an agent with the maxim or policy 'To drink water when I am thirsty'. The policy is adopted as it will further a purpose the agent has; it is judged to be a rational policy/maxim if "all rational agents similarly constituted and possessed of the same purpose" would have an equally good reason to adopt it. It would not be a rational maxim for agents whose thirst "would not be slaked by drinking water" or for agents "who have not chosen the slaking of their thirst as their purpose", etc.[21] Wolff then posits "an objectively valid principle of practical reason corresponding to this policy:" "Physically normal thirsty humans who seek to slake their thirst drink water" and an imperative expressing this principle-- "Having it as your end to slake your thirst and being as you are a physically normal human being, drink water!"[22] Wolff is a perceptive reader and he does present maxims (as he understands them), objective principles and particular hypothetical imperatives in the right rela- tions. But because he does not understand what a maxim of an action is, or how you <u>determine</u> what it is, the correct formal insight is under- mined. To put it briefly, his conception of the agent's maxim leads him to offer something as an 'objectively valid principle of practical reason' which it plainly is not. While physically normal human beings can and may slake their thirst by drinking water it is not a principle of reason that they should: a normal human being who, with that end, drank milk, would not for that be acting contrary to a principle of reason. You could justify an imperative to drink water in differently specified circumstances--e.g., Having it as your end to slake your

thirst, and given that you are a normal human being, and if the only
available liquids are water and sulphuric acid, drink water! This variation is absurd, of course, but what ought to be striking is that it,
and not Wolff's example, is an instance of a valid--if odd--hypothetical
imperative. An imperative should not specify an action unless there is
only one possible action that can be taken for a given end. If what I
want is a drink-of-water, that's a different story.

The source of all this confusion, I contend, is in the original
conception of the subjective maxim of the action. Without rehearsing
the arguments of chapter two, the point can be made briefly. It is
peculiar to construct an action-specific maxim when the end of the agent
is not also specific (or the circumstances such that there is only one
possible path of action to the end). Ends are not characteristically so
narrowly conceived. To see this point graphically, suppose my end is to
read Bleak House. Now imagine the conditions that would have to obtain
to warrant 'You ought to buy the Penguin edition at Reading International'
as the governing imperative or 'To buy the Penguin edition at RI if I
want to read Bleak House' as a rational principle of action. I might
well, if I wanted to buy rather than borrow, go to RI, but that would be
what I would judge I ought to do, given my principle (maxim) and my appreciation of the circumstances determining possible choices. Again, to
avoid any possible misunderstanding, there might be certain conditions
of volition--other than the one indicated in the example--that would
call for a maxim including the Reading International specification (say
I had a policy of reading only books I purchased and of buying books
only at RI; if this was a characterization of my wants then my maxim

would be specific to include their satisfaction). The point of all this
is to bring back to mind the relation of motive, which gives the agent
his conception of his end as of a certain kind, to the maxim which describes the principle of his volition. If I am thirsty I want something
to drink, and my maxim ought to be constructed around the principle of
getting something suitable to slaking my thirst. If I want to acquire
the complete Dickens, unless there were further wants involved--to get
it quickly, or cheaply, or in first editions, etc.--one would expect a
rather general maxim, and a correspondingly general imperative (or objective principle).

It might well be asked at this juncture, why not construct the
maxim in the most general way--'If I want some end x, I will take whatever means are necessary and in my power to obtain x.' Again, such a
maxim would generally not be the maxim of my action. It could be the
maxim of an action, but the circumstances that would generate it would
be when, for example, I adopt an end I do not now know how to realize,
but still I commit myself to that end--to finding the means and acting
accordingly if I am able. In most cases, when I act, or propose an action, I do so as I perceive that action to be of a kind suitable to my
understanding of my end as an effect of possible causes (possible actions).

To return to our original question--when is a subjective maxim also
objective, or, how are we to specify the appropriate content for a valid
hypothetical imperative--I believe enough has now been said to provide a
convincing case for not having either action-specific or wholly general
objective practical principles (hypothetical imperatives) as a matter of

course. And, it should now be possible to say with Wolff, that when an
agent has a rational (objective) maxim, "all rational agents similarly
constituted and possessed of the same purpose" would have good reason to
act on the same maxim. Since once again the nature of the agent's motive
is the decisive element in determining the content of practical principles, and so their level of generality, we can expect that agents who
really do have the same end (i.e. they conceive of it in the same way),
and who are similarly constituted, will, if they are acting rationally,
act on the same principle (subjective maxim). To return to our original
exercise example, if I understand my goal of physical fitness to require
that I raise my pulse rate to 120 for at least five minutes of exercise
each day, then that way of understanding my goal dictates the principle
on which I should act. My maxim would not specify either tennis or running (a subsidiary maxim might, but it would be with a different end),
although, given my maxim, each could be shown to provide the appropriate
exercise for my goal. The problem arose because of the natural assumption that since running was a good exercise if one wanted a regular fitness program, then it made sense to think that the maxim of someone running regularly would include 'running' in its principle governing what
to do, given the end. And, since running was indeed a means to the end,
an imperative enjoining it was in order. The mistake was in thinking
about the volition as centrally directed to running (the act) rather
than to physical fitness (the motivated end). It should now be obvious
that the story establishing the validity of 'If you want to be physically fit you ought to run 15 minutes each day' would be considerably
more complicated than merely showing the agent has the end, and running

is a means to it.

With this part of the problem of subjective and objective maxims out of the way, our next task is to see how hypothetical imperatives act as norms for subjective maxims, and to examine the kinds of judgments concerning an agent's rationality they yield. A hypothetical imperative is a formula expressing an objective practical principle in a manner suited to the condition of an imperfectly rational will. Accordingly, the principle can be used in two intimately related ways: to direct the agent's action (appearing in the form of an imperative), and as a standard of rationality for maxims of action (i.e. for judging whether subjective maxims are also objective). As we should now expect, in order to perform these tasks, the objective principle itself must reflect the agent's motive, for if it is to posit the means a rational being would take in pursuit of an end, it must do so in light of the nature of an agent's interest in his end.[23] This does not, of course, mean that imperatives are valid only if they reflect what an agent wants to do. Whether anyone actually acts on a principle is irrelevant to whether it is an objective principle. But an objective principle will bear on an agent's purposive volition only if it is constructed from the same motivational elements as the agent's subjective maxim. We should now turn to some examples to see how this part of the theory works.

Let us return to Joe's Garage, where you take your car when it breaks down. If asked why you're taking it there you are likely to offer such reasons as 'he's a superb mechanic', 'he has done the same job on a friend's car', 'he has a great sense of humor', etc. Your

(subjective) maxim indicates the kind of reason you are acting on. If
your maxim is <u>objective</u> it indicates reasons you ought to act on—the
kind of reasons for action that will be <u>good</u> reasons, given your end.
That the garage has a qualified mechanic is a good reason for taking
your car there. That you like the color and shape of its sign is not.
If getting a car repaired is the end, then, other things not entering to
modify your end, the means it would be rational to adopt is 'taking the
car to a competent mechanic' (we assume the agent knows what 'mechanic'
means). The functional relation between end and means is the basis for
a hypothetical imperative to govern this case. The objective principle
or imperative does not tell you to go to Joe's; it does not even tell
you to go to a garage. It can only indicate what kind of thing you will
need to know so that you will be able to judge what to do to get your
car repaired: knowledge about cars sufficient to tell you that it might
be repaired, what mechanics can do and where they are to be found (e.g.,
in auto garages), ways of telling if a mechanic is capable, etc. The
principle founded on just this end does not determine other features of
the situation—e.g. whether the mechanic you choose should be one who
can get the job done faster or for less money than some other mechanic,
although such choices may well be governed by other imperatives connected
to quite different ends. The imperative merely determines what <u>sort</u> of
thing you must know or do if you want your car fixed and will do what
has to be done to get it fixed. Given this imperative alone, if Joe is
not the cheapest or the fastest, it is not irrational for you not to
care (he may be a friend, or you may appreciate the way he works). What
would be irrational would be for you to want your car fixed and not care

whether the mechanic you chose was competent. The irrationality of not caring about such matters (required by the particular hypothetical imperative) comes from (is derived from) the 'principle' of all such hypothetical imperatives: "Who wills the end, wills (so far as reason has decisive influence on his actions) also the means which are indispensably necessary and in his power." And it is through the particular imperative's conformity to the principle that it determines what kinds of things will be appropriate to do by providing a criterion for which reasons are good reasons in acting to produce a desired end.

Actions governed by such imperatives can go wrong in a number of characteristic ways. For example, the facts can be wrong (the car is damaged beyond repair, the mechanic works only on foreign sports cars, etc.), and if they are, the desired end will not be attained. A mistake (in fact or judgment) has been made that was in principle corrigible. In cases where the agent could not be expected to have known better, if he was acting on a maxim which conformed to the governing hypothetical imperative, the objectivity of the maxim is unaffected, and the untoward outcome does not give grounds for attributing irrationality to the agent. If, on the other hand, I set out for Joe's Garage (acting on a rational maxim of going to a competent mechanic), but on the way I am attracted by Pete's Auto Palace, which is shiny and modern and gives its customers free glasses with each repair job, then the maxim on which I am acting is affected—indeed I would be acting on a new maxim, and one that is not rational. The new maxim would not conform to the original imperative which still governs the case, if the agent is continuing to act for the sake of the end of getting the car repaired. We might even

say (in preparation for difficulties with the categorical imperative)
that the new subjective maxim is shown inconsistent (or even that it is
self-contradictory) through violation of the principle of all such
maxims: "Who wills the end, wills also (necessarily, if he accords with
reason) the sole means which are in his power."

The 'principle' of hypothetical imperatives (the Hypothetical Imperative) thus provides a criterion for determining when a given maxim
is consistent with the requirements of rational willing--and it does
this via the objective principle or particular imperative constructed in
accord with the agent's end. This consistency does not guarantee what
the outcome of acting on an objective or rational maxim will be, it only
insures that it is a rational _form_ of action. Successful outcomes remain (properly) in the province of knowledge and judgment about the particular situation. Thus while the application of the principle requires
information about the case to determine if the means are reasonably commensurate with the end willed, its relation to the maxim is only in the
requirement that they be commensurate, whatever they are.

In summary: a particular hypothetical imperative is valid for an
individual when it prescribes the means to an end the agent is committed
to; thus the _character_ of a hypothetical imperative that is in force for
an individual is contingent upon the nature of his goal. A particular
hypothetical imperative is a formula (appropriate to certain conditions
of the will) expressing the principle of action--the maxim--that would
be acted upon by an agent whose will was determined solely by rational
considerations. It is therefore an expression of what we have been
calling an 'objective maxim'. The particular hypothetical imperative is

related to the Hypothetical Imperative as a specific instance: that is, specific to a given end. The Hypothetical Imperative is its principle, and so also the principle of all objective purposive maxims. A subjective maxim will conform to the rational requirements on purposive willing (expressed in the Hypothetical Imperative) when it conforms to the objective principle (imperative) formed according to its end any wholly rational being with that end would act on. Such a subjective maxim is also objective and a specific instance of the principle of all hypothetical imperatives. What a particular imperative requires of an agent committed to an end is that he act on the objective principle the imperative embodies. A violation of a valid imperative entails acting on a maxim which is not objective. According to Kant's theory, this is what it is not rational to do.

The level of generality for particular imperatives will vary as the end is more or less specifically conceived and as the means are known to be various or there is only one act which leads to the proposed end. For example, we might well say that if you want to get to L.A. within a day, you ought to take a plane. This is specific both because of the nature of the want (it is not _just_ to get to L.A., but also within a day), and because of known (if contingent) empirical fact—taking a plane is the only possible means to the end. If we were attempting to produce a formally precise system of presentation, we should replace 'taking a plane'—which is contingent on our present state of technology—with a generic description such as 'to utilize a mode of transportation that permits crossing the country in under 24 hours'—which would be a technically correct and sufficient description for an objective principle.

This is not a correction we need worry about as it is generally quite clear what role such things as airplanes are taking in imperatives.

In an earlier example we considered someone with a maxim of becoming a concert pianist; the appropriate objective principle would probably include the prescription 'to practice however many hours are necessary' and not 'to practice 8 hours a day' when that _is_ what is necessary. If we were more like machines, with fixed rates of change and development, the 8 hour injunction might well be in order, but then precisely because no judgment is needed to modify behavior according to changes in the agent's situation. It is precisely characteristic of such _human_ activity that what we need to do in pursuit of a long-range developmental goal often changes as we progress toward it. The principle of our action, if we are rational, should reflect that, and require that we judge what really is necessary to do for our end as we go along.

On the other side, we have cases such as Kant's example of an objective principle: "in order to divide a line into two equal parts on a sure principle I must from its ends describe two intersecting arcs" (G 85;417). This principle is action specific (although not _fully_ specified) because it is presumed that this is the sole possible means of bisecting a line (with straightedge and compass). That is, there is no place here for exercise of judgment concerning the _kind_ of action appropriate to the end. This example provides a model for the type of imperative Kant believes to be present in the practical part of all sciences which, he says, consists of "problems which suppose that some end is possible for us and of imperatives which tell us how it is to be attained" (G 82;415). For practical matters _without_ pre-established techniques, however, the degree of specificity of the imperative's charge will not be fixed but will vary with the nature of the end, its relation to known principles and procedures (including the state of empirical knowledge and technology), and the specificity of the agent's desires. Formally, an objective principle of ends contains the description of possible means such that a specific action falling under that description would realize the object of the motive that set the agent to act.

We will best be able to see the import of all this by considering the role of objective principles (hypothetical imperatives) in assessing the rationality of conduct. The fundamental characteristic of judgment by imperatives (see chapter one) is that it is _maxims_ and not actions that are assessed for their rationality. Thus although not every objective maxim will yield _successful_ action (in which the end of the volition is realized), _if_ the maxim is rational, the action cannot be called irrational, even in an extended sense. This claim may still seem surprising, especially in cases where action is untoward as the result of faulty exercise of judgment; perhaps we want to say that if an agent's judgment or his beliefs are irrational, so, therefore, is he. An example will help us explore whether we really do judge an agent irrational when his judgment is faulty. It will also give some of the reason we have so tediously stressed the question of the appropriate level of generality of the principle of a hypothetical imperative. (Another way of posing this problem is to ask how or whether the content of an objective principle itself is affected by the empirical knowledge possessed by an agent whose volition is governed by that principle.)

Suppose an agent to be acting on the now familiar subjective maxim, 'To take my car to a competent mechanic if I want it repaired'. And further, suppose that this agent determines the competence of mechanics as they charge higher fees for their services. If his judgment is faulty, if this is not the way to determine competence, then isn't it true that the agent is both acting on an <u>objective</u> maxim <u>and</u> that he is acting irrationally? Two things need to be established here to guard against this temptation: First, the presumption in favor of looking at the case this way is likely to depend on a view of maxims as principles adopted by an agent prior to his acting and on the basis of which he judges how to act. Only this picture, it seems, could explain how you might say an agent acting in the manner described was acting on a principle directing him to take his car to a <u>competent</u> mechanic. If, instead, we looked at what he was <u>doing</u>, and used that as the basis for constructing a maxim of action, it would be much more likely that the maxim of his action would be 'To take my car to an expensive mechanic if I want it repaired'. Then, if we are inclined to think this was not an appropriate means to the willed end, we would judge the volition (and so the agent) irrational, but now because the <u>maxim</u> is not objective. (It should not be forgotten that the agent's judgment partially determines the content of his subjective maxim as well as guiding him to a specific action as a means.) If this agent <u>said</u> he was acting on a 'competent mechanic' maxim, we might well wonder whether he knew what the word 'competent' means.[24] As usual, we can concoct a story such that an apparently counter-intuitive result stands. Here, for example, we might imagine that the agent had been brought up systematically deceived about the meaning of 'competent', and so actually did act on the maxim as originally formulated, only now to be understood within the framework of his idiosyncratic meaning. But such stories, while possible, mainly demonstrate their own unlikelihood and thus the force of the theory's accommodation of ordinary intuition. Beyond that, they remind us that a rational agent not only acts according to a rule, but according to _his_ _conception_ of a rule. It is because of this that practical reason is impotent without knowledge of the world.

We should be cautious about hasty conclusions here since the entire question of the rationality of belief is large and more complex than the questions the apparatus of imperatives is competent to manage. What I want to establish are certain minimal claims, leaving the larger issue aside. We need to accommodate cases where given what the agent believes to be true, his actions are rational as they are based on his beliefs— at least sometimes—even when those beliefs are false. For example, if I want to learn a foreign language and believe this is most effectively done by playing a special set of records in the room where I sleep, then even if it is false that this is a way to learn a language, it need not be irrational for me to act in this way, especially if, as might ordinarily be the case, the maxim of my action was something like, 'If I want to learn Chinese, I will employ the best language-learning technique I can find'. Again the basis for assessing action on this maxim as _rational_ depends on the _conception_ I have of the means clause—i.e., if it is demonstrated to me that _other_ means are more effective or the record technique completely ineffective, then, if my maxim is objective, I will determine to act differently, but still _on_ _the_ _same_ _maxim_.

If I am rational, if my volition is rational, then I have committed myself to finding the best language-learning technique, and to the records
<u>only</u> as I believe that is what they are. If on receipt of decisive in-
formation discrediting the records, I <u>persist</u> in using them as my sole
means of acquiring fluency in Chinese, that is at least good <u>evidence</u>
that the maxim I was acting on was not a 'best learning-technique' maxim.
The alternatives of judgment here are either that I have some independent motive for playing these records while I sleep, so preserving my
claim to rationality (and requiring the discovery of a different maxim
as the one I am acting on), or, I am being irrational.

A mistaken empirical belief is not <u>itself</u> grounds for attributing
irrationality. It is a good rule of thumb to presume that if an agent
believes <u>x</u> is the means to <u>y</u> and acts on that belief, then there is no
<u>necessity</u> to judge the agent irrational if in fact <u>x</u> is not the means to
<u>y</u>. It will depend on the agent's <u>maxim</u>--his conception of the <u>kind</u> of
act he believes it is good to perform, given his end. We may even take
it as a condition of practical rationality that an agent who adopts a
certain end and proposes to undertake a certain kind of action in pursuit of that end, <u>believes</u> that the end in question is possible of attainment <u>as a consequence</u> of the action he proposes to take. He must
believe <u>both</u> that the end ha adopts <u>is</u> possible to attain <u>and</u> that it is
possible <u>through</u> the means he determines appropriate. Both beliefs may
be mistaken. Nonetheless, they can form the "ground for the actual employment of means to certain actions"; Kant calls them "pragmatic beliefs" (CrPuR A823-4;B851-2).[25]

Again, caution is necessary so as not to misunderstand the import of this; it will be helpful in this connection to consider a likely objection to the above account. One might wonder, if the criterion for a subjective maxim also being objective is that it be a maxim any rational being with that same end would act on, in so far as he was rational, then isn't it strange to be saying that a fully rational being would act on a maxim which is based on a mistaken empirical belief? Now this points out the way we must be cautious. There are two very common types of case where the requirement on objective maxims is easily met. If the problem is that the agent is wrong in believing his action is a means to his end, it does not follow that his _maxim_ contains any such error. (Imagine someone who, finding himself lost, decides it would be best to ask directions from the first local resident he encounters. If the directions he gets and acts on are wrong, his action, while based on a mistaken belief, is still according to a rational maxim: it was the sort of thing it is reasonable to do in such circumstances.) Or, if an agent believes the end he adopts is possible when in fact it is not, the maxim of his action will be founded on a mistaken belief, but again, it need not for that be irrational (not-objective). Any agent, with _that_ end, would also have made the same mistake. (We must not confuse practical rationality with omniscience; a being with perfect practical rationality may yet err in his judgments about the world.) If the agent had that end (while assuming it possible), he would act on the appropriate mistake-induced maxim. That rational agents who did not have this end (or who knew it was impossible) would not have the maxim says nothing about the maxim a rational agent _would_ have _if_ he adopted the end on the (mistaken) assumption that it was possible. There is a third

type of case that is somewhat harder to know how to resolve. It is
where the maxim itself contains a faulty means-end connection, although
one believed to be effective by the agent. One might think here of fad
health regimens where putative authority convinces people that if only
they refrain from eating x or just increase their intake of y they will
find the health and spiritual ease they seek. It is hard to find pure
cases of this sort--i.e., not contaminated by an agent's independent
interest in the fad, or some other more subtle psychological determinant.
Obvious candidates for this class are the objective principles in the
'practical part of all sciences' which possess an aura of authority sufficient to induce agents to act on them, though they may well be incorrect. Here it is clear that we have cases where a maxim does not in
fact agree with the principle of all hypothetical imperatives, and yet
it seems inappropriate to judge the agent irrational for acting on such
a maxim. I do not at this time know how to manage this sort of case in
detail, but the direction of the solution may well be in the development
of criteria for evaluating information about the conditions of the subject—including the state of his empirical beliefs—which bear on the
agent's acting on an empirically faulty maxim. That is, some way of defining 'objective maxim' would have to be found which would include all
relevant empirical circumstances of the agent; then we could say a subjective maxim is objective if it is a maxim appropriate for any rational
being with the same end who is similarly constituted and with the same
beliefs about causal connections--relevant to the adopted end. The
theoretical justification for such a move is in the fact that an agent's
empirical beliefs determine how he conceives of his end as an effect of

action, and thus partially determine what maxim he acts on. Although some empirical errors will be evidence of irrational maxims (volitions), sometimes surely, given what an agent believes, he does not act irrationally when he acts on his belief. This last is really the position we have been trying to make credible within Kant's system. In the end, we may want to express a qualified caution and say of these cases where there is empirical error at the level of the maxim that the maxim is _not_ objective (to retain the strictest sense) but also that it is _not irrational_ either. This way would diminish the need to make the theory of imperatives depend on a theory of 'justified false belief', while retaining and highlighting the insight that practical (ir)rationality has to do with volition, and not with the state of an agent's knowledge. There is no independent or easy way of telling at this juncture which of the solutions is preferable. What we can see is necessary for any solution is that it preserve the attribution of (ir)rationality for volitions.

The archetypal cases of irrationality occur when the agent _knows_ what he ought to do (given his end), but cannot or will not act accordingly. "What the Hypothetical Imperative condemns is...the irrationality of continuing to profess, work toward, and hope for certain ends even though one is unwilling to take some essential means to realize them."[26] If it is true that some action is essential to the pursuit of one's end, and one balks at carrying through with these necessary means, _and_ one also refuses to withdraw from the commitment one has made to pursue this end, then one is acting irrationally. The case is straightforward enough; the question is how to describe this kind of irrational volition in terms of the agent's maxim and its relation to the Hypothetical Imperative.[27] There is one mistake we must not make: it does not follow from an agent's knowing what principle it would be rational for him to act on, that this principle _is_ his maxim. His maxim, it must be kept in mind, is _of his action_. That he knows what maxim he ought to have is evidence on which we base the conclusion that the maxim he is acting on is not rational (and not merely untoward). The irrationality follows from not doing what one at the same time acknowledges it would be rational to do. To put this another way, a maxim is irrational when the means clause is not believed by the agent to be the means to the realization of his end. If I know that x is the means to y and I also know that z is not, but I nevertheless do z wanting y, then the maxim of my action is, schematically, 'to do z if I want y', although, as I know, the maxim I ought to have (the maxim I would have if I were acting rationally) is 'To do x...'. Central to a Kantian conception of this phenomenon is the fact that the dictates of reason are not _external_ to the agent's will; it is _his_ reason that indicates what ought to be done, and the experience of being unable or somehow unwilling to act as one believes one ought is of a kind of self-alienation. These are clear cases where it is correct to say that an agent's subjective maxim is not objective, and that because it does not conform to the Hypothetical Imperative--the maxim is not one a wholly rational being would act on, with the same end, etc.[28]

If an agent does not believe that what he intends to do is a means to his end, then _if_ he is rational he will either abandon his end (and with it his proposed action _conceived as a means_--he may perform the act for some other reason), or, he will try to find a way of acting he does believe will lead him to his end. A note on this: if an agent does not know whether it is possible to realize his end, then while he might rationally act on a maxim of finding out whether his desire is for a possible end, I think he would not, if he were acting rationally, just adopt the end and act on a 'whatever means turn out to be necessary' maxim. Such a maxim is not normally the maxim of an action. It would have to be an extraordinary commitment to an extraordinary end that gave sanction to any means.

An agent acts irrationally when he does not believe his intended action is a means to his end. The irrationality is located in the maxim--the expression of his volition. What he wills does not coincide with what his reason indicates he ought to will. By contrast, in the case of mistaken belief about means or the possibility of an end, the agent is not at odds with his reason, since what reason (aided by judgment) dictates is dependent on the agent's empirical beliefs. (Reason divorced from the agent's understanding of the world is practically useless.) This is not true, however, of all cases of mistaken belief. There is, for example, a kind of irrational volition which involves the agent maintaining a faulty belief in 'the face of the facts'. E.g., either he acts on a maxim with plainly irrational means (If I want my car repaired I will begin a course of meditation and continue it as long as necessary), or, having successfully employed a certain kind of means to a recurrent end I now, having that end again, deny the efficacy of those proven means and commit myself to some other, implausible course of action--e.g., having suffered many times from back trouble and always finding relief through extended periods of rest, this time, suffering back pain, I determine that what is needed for relief is a series of strenuous exercises I have heard about from a friend. These are extremely difficult cases as the root of the trouble is often a hidden motive which prevents the agent from acting rationally with respect to the motive he has taken up as his end of action. The reason why I exercise when I ought to be resting my back may be that I have developed some acute anxiety about passivity which is triggered by the back injury and dominates my willing. It dominates my willing, however, without necessarily occurring in my volition as an end I have adopted. The dominance (or effect) of such factors on volition may well prevent the agent from acting on a maxim at all--even though he might well think his action had a maxim and even be able to produce one for consideration. There is room here, I believe, for extensive contribution from the theory of the unconscious to unravel the thread of the effects of different levels of motivation on volition and action. While we can hardly pursue that here, what we can see is the way a hidden motive can result in an agent's not acting rationally, since it affects his behavior by bypassing the volitional act itself: it does not inform the agent's conception of what he is doing. Discovering the operation of such a motive, an agent can recover rationality by accommodating his future volition to it; by adopting it as an end, by taking it as a limit to what other ends he can adopt, by overcoming its effects on his behavior, etc. All of this is connected, I believe, to Kant's view that it is a necessary truth about imperfectly rational beings that the ultimate springs of their action are hidden, and, to modify his famous remark, it is possible that there has never been a case of a human act that was perfectly (and transparently) rational.

There is, we should add for the sake of completeness, an important set of cases where one motive can control the expression of action based on a different motive within the norms of practical rationality. These are cases in which more than one end the agent has adopted can be acted on in a given situation, and either a choice has to be made between them or the nature of one end is such that what it requires can be accomodated as a condition on the maxim of acting for the other. As Beck describes it, "Material maxims themselves stand in a hierarchy. My desire for money may be expressed in one maxim; my desire to live slothfully in another; and one of these can control the expression of actions done under the aegis of the other."[29] This picture of volition under these circumstances seems correct, and it points out a possibility that we have not before considered—that an agent might, in one action, act on more than one maxim. That is, if, given my desires for money and to live slothfully, I find a job which both pays well and requires only an hour's easy work a day, in taking that job, I am certainly acting for two ends, and it may well make sense to say I am acting on two different maxims—I would not act this way unless I wanted to make a lot of money and do as little work as possible. This would be obvious if we suppose that the easy job I decide to take is also very boring, or dangerous, and I would not have taken it if it had not been both easy and well-paying.

If there are two maxims operative, the content of one is affected by the end of the other. If, for independent reasons, one wants to say every action has, by definition, only one maxim, then you would want to construct a maxim with a composite end such that it reflected (in so far as the agent is rational) the agent's priorities concerning those ends, or the conditions each end places on the fulfillment of the other. I see no a priori reason for insisting on a single maxim in such cases: an agent's motives in acting a particular way may be varied, and it is possible to realize more than one end in the same act. This is not to concede that because an action can be described in different ways there is a maxim possible for each description; more than one maxim is sanctioned just because there is more than one end, and the same arduous justification in terms of motivational source would have to be performed for each of the maxims offered as one of the maxims of the complex action.

It should be clear from the little said so far on this subject of an agent's ends controlling each other's expression in action, that we have moved away from the rationality of technical imperatives into that of prudential or pragmatic imperatives. If we were concerned in this essay with the (re)construction of a Kantian theory of practical reason, we would now begin to look at examples, and at what little Kant has to say about pragmatic imperatives; we would need to set out his views on the nature of happiness, and his theory of the Highest Good. Even then I doubt we would find sufficient consistent material to work out a satisfactory formal theory, but that is not the reason for not pursuing that project in this context. What we needed to know was not Kant's complete theory of practical reasoning; we needed, rather, to see in detail what an imperative is, what its source of authority is claimed to be, and how it is employed in assessing the rationality of conduct. If we take Kant at his word (G 86;418-19), the difficulty with pragmatic imperatives is in constructing a determinate conception of happiness and not in the formal structure or authority of such imperatives, then our lengthy examination of technical hypothetical imperatives (and the principle of all hypothetical imperatives, the Hypothetical Imperative) should give us the answers we may hope will facilitate understanding the Categorical Imperative as an imperative.

In preparation for the transition to the moral imperative it will be useful to highlight some features of the analysis of hypothetical imperatives that may not have been perspicuous as we went along, and which will be especially useful in getting a handle on the Categorical Imperative. Particular hypothetical imperatives (of the form 'you ought to x', where x is some action) are derived from and receive their authority from facts about the agent's end and his circumstances of possible action entered as specific values in the formula of the principle of reason for all willings of ends—the Hypothetical Imperative. The Hypothetical Imperative functions, to paraphrase Kant's claim about the Categorical Imperative, like a formula in mathematics, enabling the mathematician to 'determine what is to be done in solving a problem without letting him go astray' (CrPrR, 8n). While the principle itself is completely formal and in no way empirical, it cannot be employed without the introduction of empirical information about the agent's ends, etc. We might say that to derive a hypothetical imperative, you first take the governing formula, 'If you will the end, you ought (if you are rational) to will the means that are indispensable and in your power'; then you enter the agent's proposed end and fill in the means

clause according to known empirical connections, limited by the resources (including knowledge) in the power of the agent. The resulting
imperative is binding on a rational agent with that end in those circumstances.

An analogous procedure is used in assessments of an agent's practical rationality. The agent's maxim is _what_ is assessed by the imperative, and it is assessed as it conforms to an objective principle which
has the same end as the agent's maxim, and which is derived from the
Hypothetical Imperative as its principle. That is, for a maxim to be
objective--for a volition to be rational--it must satisfy a certain form
dictated by the imperative governing this type of volition. In this
feature, hypothetical and categorical imperatives are virtually identi-
cal--although, of course, the forms they require an agent's maxims to
match are radically different: The Hypothetical Imperative requiring
the satisfaction of a means-end relation, the Categorical Imperative
that the maxim qualify for the willing of universal law. Each type of
imperative is also characterized by the nature of its relation to an
agent's end: the Technical Imperative takes the ends an agent happens
to have, whatever they are; the Pragmatic Imperative requires that an
agent's ends by adjusted to one another so as to promote their maximal
orderly satisfaction--called Happiness; the Categorical Imperative being
either indifferent to the ends an agent happens to have or generating
ends it requires the agent to adopt (ends an agent has a duty to adopt).
The task of the next chapter is, in part, to exploit the similarities
between categorical and hypothetical imperatives in order to appreciate
Kant's claims about the significance of their differences.

Notes

1. A terminological note: I will call the "supreme principle of morality" the Categorical Imperative (capitalized), and particular moral imperatives, categorical imperatives. A similar form will be used for the Hypothetical Imperative and the various prudential oughts derived from it.

2. "Moral principles are not grounded on the peculiarities of human nature, but must be established a priori by themselves, and yet that from such principles it must be possible to derive practical rules for human nature as well, just as it is for every kind of rational nature" (G 78;410n).

3. It is not clear to me what Kant would say about a dependent rational being who was constitutionally unable to conceive of more than one end at a time—and, in particular, whether such a being could reasonably be said to have happiness as his purpose. I suspect the example is moot, as I doubt it would make good sense to call such a being rational; it would certainly not be a moral agent.

4. See J. Rawls, A Theory of Justice, § 63 ff.

5. See, e.g., L.W. Beck, "Apodictic Imperatives", pp. 7, 17 ff.

6. T.E. Hill, "The Hypothetical Imperative", p. 441.

7. R.P. Wolff, The Autonomy of Reason, p. 132.

8. It may seem surprising and in need of some immediate explanation that the categorical imperative is here expressed in terms of a relation to an end—even a necessary end—when everyone 'knows' Kant requires that a categorical imperative represent an action as necessary (good) apart from any relation to ends. I will say at this point only that it will be the concern of the next chapters to demonstrate the implausibility of this textbook view of Kant.

9. It should be noted at the outset that in the preliminary account of hypothetical imperatives and the kind of constraint they are thought to place on one's actions and volitions, the notion of the maxim of an action will not be employed. Given the emphasis already put on maxims, this may seem surprising. The reason for proceeding in this odd fashion is two-fold. First, I would like to keep the account as close to intuition as possible, at least for the first stages. Second, the general theory of action that I am eliciting will, I believe, gain support from our seeing how once again maxims are called for as a natural component of both the intuitive and the Kantian account. We have already established that in the ordinary assessment of the rationality of a willed action the maxim of the action plays a central role. We want now to see how it will enter in the employment of hypothetical imperatives. Therefore, we first need to see how hypothetical imperatives are to be

employed. In addition, and somewhat incidentally, Kant himself does not use maxims in his discussion of hypothetical imperatives in the Groundwork. I do not think there is any interesting reason why he did not; in general, his discussion of hypothetical imperatives is intended as an intuitive approach to the idea of a categorical imperative, so he does not give them the kind of attention, e.g. as a formal test of the rationality of purposive volition, that would have required the introduction of maxims. There is, however, no reason to believe one should not use maxims in working with hypothetical imperatives, and, indeed, early in the discussion of imperatives Kant talks of someone who, even if he knew an action was good "might still act on maxims contrary to the objective principles of reason" (G 82;414, emphasis added). I take this as conclusive evidence that Kant is certainly prepared to consider maxims with all imperatives; there is no possible question along this line in the more careful presentation in the second Critique. But surely this is enough on a very minor point.

10. See pp. 112 ff.

11. T.E. Hill, "The Hypothetical Imperative", p. 434. Kant remarks of hypothetical imperatives in general: "we can always escape from the precept if we abandon the purpose" (G 87;420).

12. A hypothetical imperative of the form 'If you want x you ought to do y' is valid just in case the agent has x as his end, etc.

13. R.P. Wolff, The Autonomy of Reason, p. 129.

14. L.W. Beck, A Commentary on Kant's "Critique of Practical Reason", p. 87.

15. This is one of the few passages where the Beck translation of the Groundwork is markedly superior. He gives "This proposition, in what concerns the will, in analytical; for, in willing an object as my effect, my causality as an acting cause, i.e. the use of means, is already thought..." (Beck, 34).

16. T.E. Hill, "The Hypothetical Imperative", p. 429.

17. See note 9.

18. See T.E. Hill, "The Hypothetical Imperative", pp. 439, 440.

19. These qualifications are necessary as, of course, there is a perfectly clear sense in which an agent going to Joe's because of his magical gifts is not acting rationally. How we are to deal with such cases is a problem that must be postponed for a bit. The point at issue, however, is clear: if we take the circumstances of action to include the agent's empirical beliefs, then any rational agent with this end and in the same circumstances would act on that maxim. What rubs here is the use of 'rational', and that will simply have to stand until we are ready to look into the question of the relation of the status of an agent's

beliefs to the rationality of his willings. But we can hardly do that before we are clear as to what <u>sort</u> of thing a rational or objective maxim is.

20. R.P. Wolff, <u>The Autonomy of Reason</u>, p. 128.

21. <u>Ibid</u>.

22. <u>Ibid</u>., pp. 128-129.

23. It should be emphasized that this is not a claim about <u>all</u> imperatives. The object of attention here is limited to how particular hypothetical imperatives or objective principles govern purposive maxims. None of what is set out in this discussion is to be taken to apply without separate development to other forms of imperative.

24. We should not be misled by the possibility that price is used as a rough indicator of quality; this would be consistent with the agent's acting on a competent-mechanic maxim. It is not the situation being described.

25. For more on the notion of "pragmatic belief" see Allen Wood, <u>Kant's Moral Religion</u>, p. 20 ff.

26. T.E. Hill, "The Hypothetical Imperative", p. 435.

27. The omission of maxims from the account of practical rationality according to hypothetical imperatives is, I believe, the major flaw in Hill's otherwise perceptive and helpful article, "The Hypothetical Imperative". He has the right idea of what the Imperative requires of a rational agent, but he does not see the relation of it to the structure of rational volition--which is displayed in the agent's maxims. As a result, he tends to make errors which attention to maxims would prevent-- e.g., his supposition (see 431-2,433) that hypothetical imperatives characteristically require of an agent the performance of a particular action, when in fact, as we discovered from attending to maxims, they rarely, if ever, command <u>an</u> action.

28. A full discussion of this kind of case would obviously require an account of 'weakness of will'. What is given here does no more than present the relevant phenomenon in the form a Kantian account of weakness of will would use.

29. L.W. Beck, <u>A Commentary on Kant's "Critique of Practical Reason"</u>, pp. 118-119.

Chapter Four: The Categorical Imperative (The Formula of Universal Law)

The present chapter continues the order of argument of the Groundwork we have been more or less closely following throughout this essay.
It has the task of introducing and explicating Kant's central moral
notion of a categorical imperative, along with its primary formula (the
Formula of Universal Law) in the light of and with the help of the basic
concepts introduced in earlier sections of the Groundwork--concepts
which have been the concern of the first three chapters of this study:
the maxim of an action, imperatives, the Hypothetical Imperative, etc.
We will examine the claim that categorical imperatives are objective
principles or laws of willing, and we will be concerned to explain the
point of the sharp contrast Kant draws between hypothetical and categorical imperatives, while at the same time making it clear that and how
categorical imperatives are imperatives: that is, norms of willing. We
will then attempt to show how Kant generates the first and most famous
formulation of what he says is the only possible categorical imperative
from the 'analysis of the mere concept of a categorical imperative'. It
will be the task of chapter five to show that this supposed objective
principle (or law) is in fact a moral principle, and that it can be used
to assess actions as morally right or wrong or permissible.

The argument we have been tracing in the Groundwork begins (at G
80;412) with the introduction of the concept of the will—the defining
feature of a rational agent. It proceeds through a characterization of
the relation between reason and the will, distinguishing perfect from

imperfect rational volition, and then using this distinction, it gives a definition of the basic term 'imperative'. Kant next provides a classification of the different types of imperative—hypothetical imperatives (technical and pragmatic) and categorical imperatives—after which he asks the necessary transcendental question: How are such imperatives possible? (G 84;417) In essence, the 'possibility question' asks—what in the nature of a rational being gives an imperative authority over the will of that being? As we know, Kant claims the answer is relatively straightforward for hypothetical imperatives, and that the formula of the Hypothetical Imperative emerges as part of the same analysis of the concept of a rational will which demonstrates the possibility of hypothetical imperatives ('Who wills the end...wills the means...'). Turning to categorical imperatives, Kant argues that the question of their possibility has no easy answer for, first, there is no (possible) empirical evidence that anyone has ever acted on a categorical imperative (G 86; 419), and second, it is not possible to derive the concept of a categorical imperative from the 'concept of the will of a rational being' (G 87n;420n). (We will return to and examine the bases of these claims later; the present purpose is simply to recall the argument in broad outline.) Although unable to answer the transcendental question at this moment in the Groundwork, Kant nevertheless contends that it is possible to elicit the formula of the Categorical Imperative (the Formula of Universal Law)[1] from the concept of a categorical imperative in general (G 88;420-21). This moment in the Groundwork has often seemed strained or contrived. As I believe Kant is not indulging in a sleight of hand when he produces the formula, and that trying to reconstruct how he could see

the formula emerging from the careful consideration of what is contained
in the concept of a categorical imperative gives a precise sense of what
a categorical imperative is, the obvious next step is to look back in
the text for the elements Kant takes to constitute the concept of a categorical imperative.

Let us, then, look at Kant's characterization of categorical imperatives:

> All imperatives command either hypothetically or categori-
> cally.... A categorical imperative would be one which
> represented an action as objectively necessary in itself
> apart from its relation to a further end. (G 82;414)

> Every practical law represents a possible action as good
> and as necessary for a subject whose actions are deter-
> mined (determinable?) by reason.... If the action is rep-
> resented as good in itself and therefore as necessary, in
> virtue of its principle, for a will which of itself accords
> with reason, then the imperative is categorical. (G 82;414)

> (Beck: If the action is thought of as good in itself, and
> hence as necessary in a will which of itself conforms to
> reason as the principle of this will, the imperative is
> categorical.)

> A categorical imperative...declares an action to be objec-
> tively necessary in itself without reference to some pur-
> pose—that is, even without any further end.... (G 82;415)

> (T)here is an imperative which, without being based on,
> and conditioned by, any further purpose to be attained by
> a certain line of conduct, enjoins this conduct immediately.
> ly. This imperative is categorical. It is concerned, not
> with the matter of the action and its presumed results,
> but with its form and with the principle from which it
> follows; and what is essentially good in the action con-
> sists in the mental disposition, let the consequences be
> what they may. This imperative may be called the impera-
> tive of morality. (G 83-4;416)

> Willing in accordance with /the/ three kinds of principle
> is...sharply distinguished by a dissimilarity in the neces-
> sitation of the will. /The principles are therefore named/

rules of skill...counsels of prudence...commands (laws) of
morality. For only law carries with it the concept of the
unconditioned, and yet objective and so universally valid,
necessity; and commands are laws which must be obeyed--
that is, must be followed even against inclination....
/A/ categorical imperative is limited by no condition /in
contrast with a hypothetical imperative which is valid
only under a subjective and contingent condition/ and can
quite precisely be called a command, as being absolutely,
although practically, necessary. (G 84;416-17)

(T)he categorical imperative alone purports to be a practical law, while all the rest may be called principles of
the will but not laws; for an action necessary merely in
order to achieve an aribtrary purpose can be considered as
in itself contingent, and we can always escape from the
precept if we abandon the purpose; whereas an unconditioned
command does not leave it open to the will to do the opposite at its discretion and therefore alone carries with it
that necessity which we demand from a law. (G 87;420)

Two related aspects of categorical imperatives emerge in a striking

manner from this extended compilation of texts. The first is that it

declares an action "objectively necessary in itself apart from its rela-

tion to any further end", "good in itself and therefore as necessary",

"objectively necessary in itself without reference to some purpose--that

is, even without any further end", etc. These are the sort of passage

that generate the all too familiar picture of the Categorical Imperative

as a principle indifferent to ends--a merely formal principle, a prin-

ciple concerned not with the matter (end) but only with the form of a

volition. An even minimally attentive inspection of these passages at

least precludes using them as the basis for such a contention. All Kant

says, in drawing a contrast between categorical and hypothetical impera-

tives, is that categorical imperatives declare an action necessary with-

out reference to any further end. This yields a second aspect through

contrast with hypothetical imperatives, that is, a hypothetical imperative

is said to enjoin a line of conduct only 'mediately': as it is in fact
a means to a prior willed end. The necessity of the action is mediated
by or conditioned by its being a means, and therefore by there being an
end (some 'further end') to which it is a means. Or, to put the familiar
claim plainly, a hypothetical imperative of the form 'You ought to do x'
is only valid for an agent if x is an indispensable means to some y and
y is an end the agent has adopted. Thus it is, as Kant says, with hypothetical but not with categorical imperatives 'we can always escape from
the precept if we abandon the purpose!'. The difference Kant is pointing
to is a difference in the grounds of an imperative's validity. A categorical imperative is valid regardless of the ends an agent happens to
adopt or abandon: its validity for an agent is not contingent on the
line of action it enjoins being a means to some end of the agent. It is
in this sense that Kant talks about a categorical enjoining conduct
'immediately'—not-mediately. For example, if we suppose a categorical
imperative requiring of me that I give truthful testimony, in order to
know whether I ought to give truthful testimony,

> it is not necessary for me to search for an end which I
> might propose to achieve with my declaration, since it
> matters not at all what sort of end this is; indeed, the
> man who finds it needful, when his avowal is lawfully de-
> manded, to look about him for some kind of /ulterior/ end,
> is, by this very fact, already contemptible. (Religion, 4)

This is not to say that an action enjoined by a categorical imperative
has no end, but simply that its necessity is independent of any further
end it might serve as a means.[2] In Kant's language, the enjoined action
is good in itself and not merely good for something else.

All of this, it should be remembered, is intended by Kant merely as

a formal characterization of a <u>kind</u> of imperative—a categorical imperative—which, at the point in the argument where it is introduced, may or
<u>may</u> <u>not</u> be a valid objective principle. After the preliminary descrip-
tion of this type of imperative, Kant says, "This imperative <u>may</u> <u>be</u>
<u>called</u> the imperative of morality" (G 84;416). He does not show that it
is, in any recognizable sense, a moral principle, nor does he provide
argument to support the existence of any such imperative. Although
categorical imperatives are described with an eye to the features Kant
believes a moral principle will have to have, such a description is not
tantamount to the claim that there is or that this is a moral principle—
i.e., that it is valid for all rational beings and is not reducible to
either form of hypothetical imperative, and that it <u>is</u> the principle
which supports valid moral 'oughts'.

The essential features of categorical imperatives are, then, that
they enjoin a line of action 'immediately'—without the relation to an
agent's ends that is necessary for the validity of a hypothetical imperative—and that, because of this, it is not possible to 'escape from
the precept by abandoning the purpose'. This last suggests another
characteristic of categorical imperatives: that they alone purport to
be practical <u>laws</u>: the nature of their necessitation of the will dis-
regards just those differences among rational agents that are respon-
sible for the restricted scope of application of hypothetical imperatives. If a hypothetical imperative is valid for a rational agent only
so long as he sustains his commitment to the end contained in the imperative (the end for whose realization the imperative is a directive),
a categorical imperative is to be valid for an agent without regard to

his commitment or lack of commitment to ends, his desires, or the courses of action he, in the ordinary ways, has an interest in pursuing. Thus to the degree that different rational agents are distinguished from each other by their desires and interests, these are differences that determine the applicability of hypothetical imperatives but make no difference where categorical imperatives are concerned. It is this feature of categorical imperatives that suggests they are properly to be looked at (if they exist) as pure principles of practical reason (or principles of pure practical reason)—they do not depend for their validity on contingent empirical features of agents, but merely on the fact of the agent's rationality—that the agent has a will.

This has all been set out without much elaboration since, while it is necessary that we have a clear picture of what a categorical imperative is before us, none of what has been said so far about categorical imperatives is particularly new or startling. What follows is true of categorical imperatives in general: They are objective principles of willing. This is so because they are defined (G 82;414) as formulae which direct the will to an action which is (in some sense) good—that is, they direct the will to the action a wholly rational being would perform if similarly situated. Also, categorical imperatives are imperatives because they necessitate a will—they require an action of a will "that does not perform an action straight away because the action is good" (G 82;414). Categorical imperatives differ from hypothetical imperatives in that they do not depend for their validity on ends an agent happens to have willed, and thus the actions they enjoin cannot be escaped by the foregoing of an end. Therefore, if imperatives embody

principles of practical rationality, and if there are categorical imperatives, then there are rational principles which provide norms of action
or volition that do not depend on what a given agent wills.[3] We will
not be considering whether Kant succeeded in making out the claim that
there are categorical imperatives--that they are possible. Our concern
is to show that the concept of a categorical imperative is coherent, and
that it stands in some fundamental relation to what we know as moral
principles and can recognize as moral judgment. The first task is now
completed; we have a coherent description of a non-hypothetical type of
imperative.

Our approach to the second task will be through the passage where
Kant introduces the Formula of Universal Law as the formula of the one
Categorical Imperative. The idea of there being a single Categorical
Imperative will be relatively easy to make plausible. What will be more
difficult to reconstruct in a way that convinces is Kant's argument that
the Formula of Universal Law is the Categorical Imperative. When we
have done that we will be in a position--both conceptually and in the
order of the text--to address the question of its status as a moral
principle.

Let us now look at Kant's argument to the Formula of Universal Law:

> (W)e wish first to enquire whether perhaps the mere con-
> cept of a categorical imperative may not also provide us
> with the formula containing the only proposition that can
> be a categorical imperative.... When I conceive a hypo-
> thetical imperative in general, I do not know beforehand
> what it will contain--until its condition is given. But
> if I conceive a categorical imperative, I know at once
> what it contains. For besides the law this imperative
> contains only the necessity that our maxim should conform
> to this law, while the law, as we have seen, contains no
> conditions to limit it, there remains nothing over to

> which the maxim has to conform except the universality of
> law as such; and it is this conformity alone that the im-
> perative properly asserts to be necessary.
>
> There is therefore only a single categorical imperative
> and it is this: Act only on that maxim through which you
> can at the same time will that it should become a univer-
> sal law. (G 88;420-21)

Even at the risk of tedium, it is nonetheless worthwhile to work through

this passage practically sentence by sentence to reduce to a minimum the

aspects appearing either ad hoc or unintelligible, and to raise the

level of our clairty about this most basic concept. Although in a way

we already know the answer to the obvious question arising from the

first sentence, we will take it up in turn to get a sense of the whole.

Why, we might ask, does Kant open with the supposition that when we in-

spect our concept of a categorical imperative we will get a formula con-

taining the "only proposition that can be a categorical imperative"?

Does he think there can be but one categorical imperative? Would that

mean 'You ought not to make a deceitful promise' is not, according to

Kant, a categorical imperative? We must understand him to be again re-

ferring to the relation of a general formula to its particular in-

stances—the particular embodiments (e.g., no deceitful promises) are

instances of categorical imperatives only if they are instances: if

they conform to the formula containing the only proposition that can be

a categorical imperative. We can see the quite ordinary claim Kant is

asserting in a trivial example: Suppose one said there is a formula

containing the only proposition which can be the Pythagorean Theorem.

The assertion that there is only one such proposition does not deny that

there can be many instances of possible triangles whose dimensions sat-

isfy the conditions of the formula $c^2 = a^2 + b^2$. The use of such a

formula to explain Kant's intentions is not as far-fetched as it might
at first seem. We should recall his remark in the second Critique when
he defends himself against critics who belittle the importance of his
work because "there is no new principle of morality in it but only a new
formula" by comparing what he has done to the achievements of mathematics:

> Those who know what a formula means to a mathematician, in
> determining what is to be done in solving a problem with-
> out letting him go astray, will not regard a formula which
> will do this for all duties as something insignificant and
> unnecessary. (CrPrR 8)

In any case, on the fair presumption that categorical imperatives
would bear a gross formal resemblance to hypothetical imperatives, we
should have expected to encounter a principle of all categorical imperatives as there was a principle of all hypothetical imperatives--the
Hypothetical Imperative. So there really should be no surprise when we
find Kant introducing the Formula of Universal Law as the formula of the
unique principle from which, he claims, all 'imperatives of duty' can be
derived.[4] When he says, "there is...only a single categorical imperative", I believe this is meant in the same sense as one might say 'there
is only a single hypothetical imperative'--that is, all such imperatives
derive their authority from their being instantiations of the one governing imperative. We will see how this works when we try to unravel the
arguments of the examples. So far, then, the structure of the two types
of imperative is parallel; as with hypothetical imperatives, although
there are many categorical imperatives, there is only one Categorical
Imperative.

In the next stage of the argument Kant contrasts the two types of imperative in a way that opens onto the Formula of Universal Law. When, he says, we conceive a hypothetical imperative in general (überhaupt) we do not know what it will 'contain' until its condition is given, whereas, with a categorical imperative (überhaupt), what it contains is said to be known 'at once'. We might suppose that Kant means by a hypothetische Imperativ überhaupt simply an abstract particular hypothetical imperative (an 'ought' with respect to an agent's ends); when you 'conceive' it, then, what you would have is an empty formal representation, e.g., If you will x, you ought to will y. To know what such an imperative-schema contains, you would have to know what the x, the willed end, was. (As well, of course, as knowing facts about the means possible for the given agent, etc., although even this is contingent on knowing the end.) The agent's end would then be the condition which must be given to know what a hypothetical imperative in general (Beck: as such) contains. With a categorical imperative, by contrast, as soon as we conceive it we are supposed to know what it contains. We should then be able to see the difference according to a parallel expansion. We will suppose that Kant is talking about some particular categorical imperative, abstractly, as it were—an 'ought' that makes no reference to the agent's ends. Now do we know what it contains? If we suppose that a particular imperative of this form could be 'If you make a promise, you ought to keep it', or even just the command 'Keep your promises!', you could hardly know such content by conceiving of a categorical imperative in general. It looks as though you no more know what a categorical imperative contains in this sense than you do for a hypothetical imperative—in both cases something needs to be given before we can determine any specific content.

But perhaps our conception of what an imperative 'contains' is wrong. A possible interpretation might have 'contains' refer to the principle of all the particular imperatives of each type—the principle of which each is an instance; in this sense a hypothetical imperative would 'contain' the Hypothetical Imperative, and similarly a categorical imperative would contain the Categorical Imperative—as its principle. Although particular and governing imperatives do stand in these relations, this is not a possible line of interpretation of this text, since on this account we _would_ know what a _hypothetical_ imperative contains as readily as we do a categorical imperative.

There _is_, however, a distinguishing feature of each type of imperative which gives the contrast Kant would draw; it turns on what he might mean by giving an imperative's 'condition'. If we ask for the grounds of an imperative's _validity_--the conditions under which an imperative is in force for an individual--the answers we give for hypothetical and categorical imperatives are different in the required way. When we think of a hypothetical imperative, we do _not_ know whether it is valid for a particular agent until we know what ends the agent has adopted. An agent's ends are the _condition_ of a hypothetical imperative's validity, and when we know the condition (the agent's ends) we know what the imperative contains: a directive _to_ the end (whatever it is) the agent has adopted. But when we conceive a _categorical_ imperative, we know its validity is independent of the ends an agent happens to have. For a categorical imperative (considered generally) to be in force the only condition of _volition_ that must be met is that the subject _have_ _a_ _will_: the subject must be one whose reason can be practical. No contingent condition of his will needs to be given before we know a categorical imperative is valid--i.e., the validity of a categorical imperative is not dependent on what an agent <u>wants</u>. (Recall, "A categorical imperative...declares an action to be objectively necessary in itself without reference to some purpose" (G 82;415).) While it is of course true that I cannot be commanded to keep a promise I have not made, if I <u>have</u> made a promise, the validity of a categorical imperative requiring that I keep it is unaffected by what I now <u>want</u> to do. Whereas, as we know, if I have in the past adopted an end (in the ordinary sense), the pursuit of which calls for present action, the validity of a hypothetical imperative requiring that action <u>is</u> affected by what I now want to do (i.e., the present condition of my will). That is, if I now want to abandon that end, it is not true that I ought to do what the imperative enjoins. The bindingness of a promise is not diminished by my now wanting not to do what was promised. <u>If</u>, that is, promises are governed by categorical imperatives, then the logic of such imperatives prohibits abandoning 'at will' commitments we make under their authority.

We must be clear about what this analysis commits us to. It does not follow that because the validity of any categorical imperative is independent of contingent conditions of volition, <u>every</u> particular categorical imperative is valid for <u>any</u> being so long as it has a will (is rational). <u>Two</u> conditions must be met for a categorical imperative to be valid for a subject. The first is the one we have been examining-- that the subject have a will. The second pertains to the agent's circumstances: his nature, his capacities, his past actions, etc.--what one might call (if the moral connections were made) obligation <u>creating</u>

conditions. These, as we shall see in what follows, play a central role in Kant's derivation, from the Categorical Imperative, of duties suited to the conditions of __human__ (rational) beings. This derivation is complex, and is not necessary for the general point to be intuitively clear. __What__ obligations a given individual has depend on his circumstances—which include things about him as a being of a certain sort, his capacities and commitments, etc. If obligations are expressed in categorical imperatives, the categorical imperatives valid for an individual will likewise depend on his circumstances. However, and this is the point of the passage we are considering, when the second condition is met (in ways yet to be determined) the validity of an appropriate categorical imperative does __not__ depend on the contingent conditions of the agent's will. What an agent would will is not one of the conditions determining whether he is subject to a categorical imperative. In short, hypothetical imperatives are dependent on an agent's purposes as a condition of their validity; categorical imperatives are not. Both depend on the agent's having a will.

We seem to have some idea now of why Kant says we do not know what a hypothetical imperative __contains__ until its __condition__ is given—a hypothetical imperative says, 'You ought to do such and such, __on the condition__ that you will a certain end.' And we understand the difference in the conditions of the two kinds of imperative. But we must move on in the passage to see the implications of this difference for what a categorical imperative (überhaupt) contains, and why Kant says "if I conceive a categorical imperative, I know at once what it contains":

> For since besides the law this imperative contains only
> the necessity that our maxim should conform to this law,

while the law, as we have seen, contains no condition to
limit it, (there remains nothing over to which the maxim
has to conform except the universality of a law as such;
and it is this conformity alone that the imperative properly asserts to be necessary.)

All imperatives contain a law (or principle) and all imperatives
require that an agent's maxim conform to this law (or principle). But
whereas in the case of hypothetical imperatives the principle contains a
condition to limit it (If you will x...)—which is why we cannot know
what a hypothetical imperative contains until we know its condition—
categorical imperatives are limited by no such condition. A categorical
imperative, then, requires that an agent's maxim conform to its principle, and the principle applies regardless of the condition of the
agent's will. A categorical imperative therefore contains an 'unconditioned principle'; this is what we know 'at once' simply by examining
the concept of a categorical imperative.

Let us look at this distinction in yet another way. Every hypothetical imperative is an objective principle of willing: this is the
ground of what it is to be an imperative. It is hypothetical because it
is an instance of a general principle, the Hypothetical Imperative, a
principle that applies universally to rational agents who pursue ends.
In any of its instances, however, it applies to an agent only if his
will is in a particular and contingent condition. Thus no hypothetical
imperative declares an action to be unconditionally necessary, the
necessity of its requirement being 'valid only under a subjective and
contingent condition—namely if this or that man counts this or that as
his end' (to borrow the phrasing of Kant's description of counsels of
prudence at G 84;416). In direct contrast to this are the categorical

imperatives, each of which, as an imperative, is also an objective principle of willing (in imperative form appropriate to an imperfectly rational will). But they are _categorical_ because they must be obeyed "even against inclination", i.e. regardless of what an agent can or does will. "A categorical imperative is limited by no condition and can quite precisely be called a command, as being absolutely, although practically, necessary" (G 84;416). We know by this that any instance of a categorical imperative—if otherwise appropriate to the circumstances of the agent—will contain the requirement that the agent act according to its principle, and that this requirement is not valid _only_ under a subjective and contingent condition, but rather is valid for _all_ subjective and contingent conditions of the will—that is, it is _unconditionally valid_. And since, Kant claims, "only _law_ carries with it the concept of the unconditioned, and yet objective and so universally valid necessity" (G 84;416), the principle of a categorical imperative is properly called _a law_. Thus we can see how Kant is able to draw from the concept of a categorical imperative in general the conclusion that 'besides the law this imperative contains only the necessity that our maixm should conform to this law, while the law...contains no condition to limit it'. What the _content_ of any particular categorical imperative can be is the conclusion of a different argument: the demonstration that this imperative is a _moral_ imperative, and that it in some sense generates what we call 'duties'.

The principle contained in a categorical imperative is called a _law_ in the above reconstruction because Kant takes it as given (G 84;416) that only a law can be a principle of unconditional validity. This

connection is sufficient for the purpose of following transitions in the
passage we have just finished examining. It is inadequate, however, for
the last steps in the argument to the Formula of Universal Law, since
they depend on our understanding what it could be for a practical principle to be a law. We shall therefore have to investigate this identification; it should both enable the reconstruction of the last section
of the argument, and deepen our conception of what will be the moral imperative. The penultimate stage of the argument spells out what follows
if the principle of an imperative is a law:

> ...there remains nothing over to which the maxim has to
> conform except the universality of a law as such; and it
> is this conformity alone that the imperative properly
> asserts to be necessary.

We are immediately reminded by this that a hypothetical imperative
requires the conformity of an agent's maxim to its principle on the condition that the agent's will is committed to the end served by the imperative. This last is what 'remains over' to qualify the injunction of
such an imperative. For categorical imperatives the requirement that
the maxim conform to its principle is unconditional--nothing remains
over to which the maxim (expressing an agent's volition) must conform as
a condition on the validity of the imperative for an agent. But this
does not yet tell us why Kant says that nothing remains over except the
necessity of the maxim's conforming to the universality of law as such.
The use of 'universal' to qualify 'law' may seem redundant, as Kant
holds, and it is reasonable in any case to presume, that anything which
is a law is universal in its application: law is universal law. That
is, if categorical imperatives contain laws, then they apply to everything

such a law governs--not, of course, to everything there is. Laws of gases apply to all gases; they are universal laws of gases; they do not apply to solids. Imperatives are formulae derived from objective principles of willing; if the principle of an imperative is said to be a law, then it would be reasonable to conclude that imperatives apply to all beings who possess a will; they contain universal laws of rational willing; they do not apply to animals or inanimate objects. A more generous reading would see the introduction of 'universal' as a means of highlighting this very aspect of categorical imperatives which has just been given as the feature distinguishing them from hypothetical imperatives: the conditions of their application are independent of any feature of volition distinguishing rational beings from each other. That is, the maxims of a rational being are to conform to the principle of a categorical imperative regardless of the ends that rational being wants to pursue. Categorical imperatives apply to all rational beings without regard to their subjective differences. They are valid for an agent simply qua rational being, and thus are valid for rational agents universally. (I am taking validity, here, to concern the principle of an imperative, and thus talking about the validity of categorical imperatives for both perfectly and imperfectly rational beings. Strictly speaking, the principles of these imperatives merely describe the willing of a perfectly rational being, and are not properly said to 'necessitate' it, even though such a will necessarily acts according to the principle found in the imperative.) If we look forward to the expected connection with moral principles, we might describe what it means to say a categorical imperative contains a 'universal law' by saying that it

contains a law that applies impersonally and impartially--that it is
universally applicable to everyone in the same objective situation. In
sum, that categorical imperatives contain universal law reminds us that
they apply to all rational beings (as imperatives only to imperfectly
rational beings)--we know that they are concerned with the will of rational beings since that is what it is to be an imperative at all.
Also, we know from this that they apply to all rational beings unconditionally: that is, the will of a rational being is constrained to act
in a specified way irrespective of what he desires, wants, etc.

The form of a categorical imperative will therefore be something
like, 'Anyone in circumstances $\underline{C}$ ought to do $\underline{X}$'.[5] Every categorical imperative will therefore contain two elements: an action specified and a
command to perform that action which is universally valid. (Note: the
'action specified' need not be an act, in the ordinary sense of a causal
intervention, but may include requirements that certain specified ends
be adopted--e.g. the imperatives of beneficence and talents.) The command (the imperative) will be universal in form. Not surprisingly,
then, all categorical imperatives should have the same form, while directing agents to different acts; each act is required in the same way--
without regard to the agent's ends. We should expect to be able to
identify the formal feature in virtue of which an imperative is categorical; and we can: its command is universal and unconditional--it
commands as a law.

At this point we should digress briefly to consider whether it is
true that only categorical imperatives are laws. Strictly speaking, I
believe, Kant was wrong in claiming this, as the Hypothetical Imperative,

the principle of all hypothetical imperatives, also satisfies the criteria of being a practical law. Its major qualifying feature is that it
is in force universally, governing the willing of all rational agents.
(I assume there are no rational agents without ends.) It is also unconditional in the sense that it applies whenever an agent adopts an end;
it therefore cannot be evaded by abandoning some end, and it is not in
force only on condition that an agent have some specified end. Its authority is over the adoption of any end whatsoever. If it were possible
not ever to adopt an end, a being would be outside its authority, but at
the price of his rationality (or, the possibility of its exercise).[6]
That the Hypothetical Imperative is a law was not acknowledged by Kant
probably because he was somewhat over-anxious in driving home the distinction between it and the Categorical Imperative. As we saw earlier,
there is no question that we do know what the Hypothetical Imperative
commands as soon as we consider it--it commands that we take the available means to the ends we have adopted. But apart from the value of
keeping these things straight, there is yet something of significance to
be learned from this exercise. There is a distinction that is properly
drawn along these lines between categorical and hypothetical imperatives:
categorical imperatives have the force of law while hypothetical imperatives do not. That is, while the governing principles of both types of
imperatives are themselves laws, the only particular imperatives which
are also laws are those whose authority is derived from the Categorical
Imperative. The difference Kant wants is therefore to be seen at the
level of the particular imperatives: hypothetical imperatives are not
universal in application; the force of their command is end-dependent;

they do not have the unconditional force of law. Particular categorical imperatives, on the other hand, will be valid irrespective of the ends that particular rational beings happen to have; their command has the force of law. Both Imperatives apply unconditionally to all rational beings; of the particular imperatives, only the categorical are in force without regard to the subjective state of an individual's willing. This much follows from the conception of a categorical imperative überhaupt.

But we are still not clear as to why Kant says a categorical imperative requires of a maxim that it conform only to the universality of law as such, even though we _are_ clear about what it means to say the imperative contains a law, and the law is unconditional; we know, as a result, why Kant calls the law 'universal'. We may be helped in this task if we recall that imperatives were initially defined (G 81;414) as "formulae expressing the relation of objective laws of willing to the subjective imperfection of the will of this or that rational being—for example, of the human will." Objective laws of willing describe how rational beings would will if they were perfectly rational or if reason had complete dominance over their volition. We might then describe hypothetical imperatives as formulae expressing conditioned objective principles, in contrast to categorical imperatives which contain (or express) unconditioned objective principles—ones which "every rational agent irrespective of his particular desires for particular ends would necessarily obey if reason had complete control."[7] Or, to borrow Wolff's description of this difference:

> Every principle of practical reason states the conditions
> under which the adoption of a policy is rational. A hypo-
> thetical principle of practical reason asserts that the

adoption of a policy is rational under conditions which
are not necessarily or universally met by all rational
agents as such. A categorical principle of practical reason asserts that the adoption of a policy is rational
under conditions which are necessarily and universally met
by all rational agents as such.[8]

A categorical imperative therefore must contain a description of what

(or how) a rational being would will on wholly rational grounds (grounds

shared by all rational beings). Its principle can in no way be based on

subjective ends--features of volition not shared by all rational beings.

If there are ends in these unconditioned principles, they must be objec-

tive ends--ends it would be rational for all rational agents to have.

Now for imperfectly rational agents, such as human beings, objective

principles/laws appear as imperatives, requiring that maxims of action

conform to their dictates or their principle. What a categorical imper-

ative must require is that the maxim of my action be one it would be

rational (or, perhaps, not irrational) for any agent in my objective

situation[9] to act on, for reasons other than what I want, or in terms of

my subjective ends, etc. This is what it would be for my maxim to con-

form to an unconditioned principle of willing. The maxim of my action

would not support an end that was _merely_ subjective; I would not, there-

fore, be acting on that maxim in a way contingent on its being a rule

through which I might expect to serve some purpose I happen to have.[10]

If the imperative commands that I act on a maxim that is rational for me

on grounds valid for all rational beings, then it is in effect command-

ing that I act on a _universally_ _valid_ _maxim_--that the maxim of my action

conform to 'law'. Not that my maxim should conform to _a_ law, specified

in advance, but that my maxim be _law-like_: not merely a subjective principle tailored to my interests, and so 'valid' only as I (or any other agent) have such interests. In requiring that a maxim be 'law-like' we are interpreting what Kant meant in talking of the 'form' of a law--i.e., its universality. Thus we see how the requirement emerges that a maxim have the form of a law, the form of universality, and thus what it is about the categorical imperative that leads Kant to say it requires of a maxim that it conform to the universality of law as such and that this conformity alone is what is represented as necessary by the imperative. If my maxim is to agree with a categorical imperative, then whatever its specific content may be, the maxim must have the form of a universal law: it must not depend for its validity on any merely contingent or subjective end.

From this interpretation we can see easily enough how Kant derives the Formula of Universal Law: Act only on that maxim through which you can at the same time will it should become a universal law. The maxim of your action, while necessarily specific to your action, must contain nothing which would prevent that maxim from serving as an unconditioned practical principle: as a universal law for all rational beings. (It is not that all rational beings ought to act on your maxim, but that there should be nothing in your maxim that derives from the subjective condition of your will such that the maxim is not fit for the will of any rational being. What such a maxim would look like and whether it is possible are the obvious questions, but they need not be answered in or-der to see what the Formula of Universal Law says and how it emerges from the analysis of the concept of a categorical imperative.)

The insistence that you be able 'at the same time to will that your

maxim become a universal law' is, I believe, intended by Kant to characterize an agent's attitude toward his action when its maxim conforms to
the conditions of a categorical imperative: If it is an action whose
maxim is universal in form, you perform the action according to that
(universal in form) maxim because it is universal. You act on the maxim
because it is a maxim all rational beings could act on.

There is, of course, another interpretation of this passage to a
weaker requirement: A willed action has a maxim. The maxim is an expression of an agent's own willing. But suppose (counterfactually) an
agent could, through his will, make it the case that his maxim became a
maxim of action for all rational beings. Then a maxim that could be
willed as a universal law would be one suitable for all rational beings--
that is, you could will your maxim as a universal law for all rational
beings if any rational being acting on your maxim would be acting rationally. (It is no accident that this reading of the passage suggests the
Formula of the Law of Nature.)[11]

The two possible readings point to a central question of interpretation of what the Categorical Imperative requires: is it sufficient that
you be able to will that the maxim of your action become a universal
law, or must you act on your maxim knowing that it can be willed a universal law (and act on the maxim because you know that)? I believe that
only those maxims which satisfy the stronger condition are to be said to
conform to the universality of a law as such, and thus to the Categorical
Imperative. This conclusion is compatible with the dual role of the
Categorical Imperative: as a criterion of the formal objectivity of
maxims (willing) and as a test (available to the agent and to third

parties) for the (moral) adequacy of proposed actions. (The test for actions works through the Formula of the Law of Nature and is applied to the maxim of the action in question.)

In opposition to this, it is commonly said that there are two tests connected to the Categorical Imperative: one for what is morally right or wrong, the other for what is morally worthy or lacking in moral worth. One test appears to be concerned with actions, the other with volition-- although this appearance is deceiving. Some of the debate on this question has looked to determine whether Kant provides, in the Formula of Universal Law, or some other formula of the Categorical Imperative, a test for the moral rightness (etc.) of actions that functions independently of considerations of the agent's motives. Even if Murphy is right in his assertion that Kant must have a notion of moral right that does not depend on the presence of a moral motive, since, he says, "Kant makes it a necessary and sufficient condition of a morally good will that it is a will that acts in accordance with duty for the sake of duty",[12] it does not follow from this that the Formula of Universal Law (or any other Formula) can test for moral rightness without considering motives. We should recall the use that must be made of the motive in specifying the maxim of an action. In addition, it is not obvious that 'morally right' action done from, say, wholly selfish motives, is a morally serious category in Kant's ethics. Although we must not try to settle this issue prematurely, the direction of a possible solution may already be evident in the introduction of the maxim of the action: in acting on a maxim an agent acts according to a conception of a rule.

It might be useful to pose the question in a slightly different way before we go on. If acting according to duty (from <u>any</u> motive and with respect to <u>any</u> end) is to be a moral category for actions, and it is to be ascertained through the application of one of the formulae of the Categorical Imperative to the <u>maxim</u> of an action, then we are led to an unlikely conclusion. Suppose someone keeps a promise because it would be to his advantage (and only for that reason); is it likely Kant would want to say he was acting on a maxim that conforms to the universality of a law as such? or, even, on a maxim that could be willed a universal law? Could the <u>maxim</u> of such an action have any moral content? Think of the analogy that can be drawn with hypothetical imperatives: could one be said to act on a prudential maxim with a prudentially indifferent motive? It is important that we be careful here. <u>Of</u> course, if I keep my promise, from whatever motive, something better has happened than if I had not (we might well suppose); and better, no doubt, from a moral point of view. But why think that if I was merely acting in my interest that <u>I</u> was acting morally (or well, etc.)--i.e., on a maxim that conforms to the universality of a law? Similarly, if I do in fact (suppose by accident) further my interests, so much the better for me. But <u>I</u> have not acted prudentially, and the maxim of my action does not conform to the Hypothetical Imperative. We must keep in mind that action is always represented in Kant's ethical theory as <u>willed action</u>. We will return to these matters in a more systematic fashion in chapters five and six.

In summary, we will continue this discussion on the assumption that the Categorical Imperative as such, as a principle of pure practical willing, is a requirement on volition--on the <u>way</u> an agent wills. That many maxims are not but <u>could</u> be willed as the Categorical Imperative requires is what permits the Categorical Imperative (in its Formula of the Law of Nature variant) to be used as a more general test for actions, although, as we have already seen, the Categorical Imperative may not assess actions without regard to maxims, and so _some_ features of willing. It is _this_ use of the Categorical Imperative that makes the weaker interpretation of its formal requirement tempting. We should resist this, as it would cast the Categorical Imperative as something other than a principle _of rational willing_. In support of the strong interpretation of what the Categorical Imperative requires we might remember that _as_ a principle of pure practical reason the Categorical Imperative is intended to describe how it is we are acting _when_ we are acting morally.

In chapter five we will take up the Formula of the Law of Nature and the general problem of determining which of our maxims _could_ be willed as universal law. In the rest of this chapter we will be concerned only with maxims (descriptions of willings) as they do (or do not) in fact conform to the universality of a law as such: maxims, even maxims with ordinary ends, willed by an agent only as (and with the conception that) they could be universal laws for all rational beings. This is what the Categorical Imperative sets as a norm of rational willing, and it is this requirement that we look to understand.

We have seen how the Formula of Universal Law comes from the analysis of the concept of a categorical imperative as such. We need now to explain why Kant says, "There is...only a single categorical imperative" and it is the Formula of Universal Law. I think this must be explained straightforwardly. The very concept of a categorical imperative contains only the assertion that the maxim of an action must conform to the universality of a law as such. This is the unique feature constitutive of an imperative being categorical, and so must be found in every categorical imperative. As the Formula of Universal Law is the expression of this categoricality, it must in some sense be contained in each categorical imperative as that in virtue of which the imperative is categorical. Following the precedent set with hypothetical imperatives, we should call this formula the "principle" of all categorical imperatives. And, if our previous conclusions are sound, we have shown that there is a single principle for all categorical imperatives, and it is the Formula of Universal Law. What remains to be explained is why Kant calls this principle itself a categorical imperative, and, indeed, why he says it is the only categorical imperative. If a principle that is unconditioned in its application to rational beings is called a categorical imperative, then it is fitting to give this name to the principle of all such imperatives: It is what each categorical imperative requires of an agent's will, without condition. It is therefore what is required of an agent unconditionally. But if this explains the appropriateness of calling the principle a categorical imperative, it may yet seem puzzling when Kant appears to assert that it is the only categorical imperative. The puzzlement dissolves when it is realized that the relationship Kant has established between the Formula of Universal Law and all particular categorical imperatives is that between a formula (in the ordinary sense) and its possible instances. As each categorical imperative is but an instance of this one constitutive formula, there is plausible sense made in saying that there is only one categorical imperative—i.e., as one formula with many instances. (We shall continue the convention set in chapter three and call the one categorical imperative--expressed in the Formula of Universal Law--the Categorical Imperative. It is accordingly the principle of all categorical imperatives--i.e. all applications of the one principle.) The Formula by itself enjoins no action until the appropriate variables are given. What they are, or, to put this in other words, how the formula is to be applied, is the subject of the next chapter.

There is one thing that ought already to be clear about the operation of the Categorical Imperative that cuts against accusations that the ethical theory that issues from imperatives must be rigoristic-- i.e., full of exceptionless commands of the form 'You must keep promises', 'You must always tell the truth', etc. If the Categorical Imperative represents as necessary merely the conformity of an agent's maxim to the universality of law, then that fact alone cannot yield an injunction against promise-breaking, or any other specific moral obligation. The very nature of the Categorical Imperative paradoxically insures that the content of morality (the actual ethical rules, etc.) cannot be a priori. The Categorical Imperative does not work by spewing forth objective principles which then stand as a code to which an agent's maxims and actions must conform (if he is rational). As we said earlier, it does not require that the agent follow laws, but rather that the maxim on which the agent acts be law-like: i.e., universally valid, etc. It is not necessary in virtue of the Categorical Imperative alone that promises be kept or that we not bear false witness. If it is necessary that we do these things, it will be for some other reason(s), having to do with what kind of maxims we can have 'through which we can at the same time will that they should become universal laws'. The content of these maxims—the actions required—we might well suppose will depend on the _kind_ of being acting, _and_ on what such a being proposes to do for what reason—that is, on what the maxim of his proposed action is. This is an area of Kant-interpretation in which we must exercise extreme caution, as the theory is much more flexible and deep than either the use Kant sometimes makes of it (as in "On an Alleged Right to Lie") or the history of its interpretation would lead us to believe. We shall proceed as before on the working assumption that it is best to suppose the theory _is_ adequate to our most important requirements and therefore exercise all possible ingenuity to show that it is before we abandon all or part of it as unsatisfactory. Accordingly, we shall digress yet again; this time our purpose will not be peripheral to the main argument. Throughout this account we have been using the notion of the _maxim_ of an action. Although there have been suggestions as we went along concerning the ways this notion would help us through interpretive difficulties, we did not focus on the fact that the Categorical Imperative places a requirement on _maxims_, and what could be made of that fact simply on the basis of the understanding of what a maxim is that we have already developed.

What the Categorical Imperative requires of an agent's maxims is their conformity to the universality of a law as such. Leaving aside questions about the conditions in which it is appropriate to require this, or what kinds of actions issue from maxims satisfying the requirement, etc., we need now to be concerned with the more general question of what <u>kind</u> of thing is being required and what it is about maxims that makes them the suitable object of such stringent and abstract regulation. Let us, briefly, go back to the beginning. The feature constitutive of rational agency is the will. To have a will is to be able to act according to a conception of a rule (principle) or law. The degree to which one is acting rationally is the degree to which one is acting according to a (conception) of a principle. An action--or volition--that is rational is one that is conceived according to a principle. This is the point we must not lose sight of. The willed action of a rational being is not action according to a law or principle, but action according to a <u>conception</u> of law or principle. A conception of law, obviously, is not itself a law. Perfectly rational beings, one might say, are those who act according to a conception of a law (or principle) that always and necessarily <u>is</u> an objective law (or principle) of willing. An imperfectly rational being, therefore, can be described as one who <u>may</u> have and act on a conception of a law (or principle) that is not possible <u>as</u> an objective law (or principle) of willing. In a sense, such a being acts <u>only</u> on a conception. This limit on the willing of imperfectly rational beings is at the same time the ground of the possibility of imperatives in general, and, if the connection between categorical imperatives and moral principles can be made out, it is the ground of the possibility of morality itself. (It should be remembered that the concept of morality entails that of obligation, which according to Kant is possible only for a being with an imperfectly rational will.)

The <u>maxim</u> of an action is a formal expression of the principle that can be imputed to an agent as the one he does (or could be said to)

conceive as the principle of his willing an action. It is the principle
of his volition. It contains a conception of—what he takes to be—a
principle. The incompatibility here is only apparent: the maxim (the
subjective maxim) is a principle—indeed, it is the principle on which
the agent acts. It is not necessarily an objective maxim, however, and
therefore the principle on which the agent acts may not be an objective
principle (or an instance of an objective principle) of willing. As he
is a rational being, his subjective maxim contains his conception of the
objective principle of willing that applies to his case. It is what the
agent takes to be the rational thing to do: As such his willing is on a
principle, but not necessarily on a rational principle—his conception
may not in fact be in accord with the rule governing the kind of action
he intends. Thus it is possible for a rational agent to act irrationally on a principle. Indeed, the voluntary intentional acts of a
rational agent are virtually always according to a principle the agent
conceives to be appropriate to his situation (i.e. conceives as objective). This is only to say—voluntary intentional acts have and are
performed according to maxims. And, I believe, this entails the presumption that a rational agent would act rationally: that is, according
to his conception of what reason requires. Agents are presumed to act
on principles they take to be objective. Accordingly, they may be in
error about what is objective or they may be self-deceiving—as Kant
thinks they are when they make exceptions for themselves from moral
principles they know, but at the same time will not acknowledge, do not
permit exceptions (G 92;424). When they fail in these ways, the maxims
of their actions are not objective—they have not acted according to a

principle it would be rational for any agent in their situation to act on.

Following this line, we may extend our understanding of imperatives in general, seeing them now as requiring an agent to regard his action in the manner specified in the principle of each type of imperative. Imperatives command that we perform only those actions we are able to conceive of in the manner they dictate. An agent's conception of his action is found by looking at his maxim of acting, as it contains the description—in the form of a principle—of what he takes himself to be doing.[13] So if the agent's conception of his action is in his maxim, an imperative calls for actions that have maxims which meet the criteria of adequacy for a maxim set out in the imperative's principle. That is how imperatives can require us to perform actions it is possible to conceive of according to a predetermined principle.

Everything in this summary account characterizes all types of imperatives and their relations (through their principles) to maxims and actions. Our question now is what illumination this discussion of maxims sheds on categorical imperatives and what they require of maxims when they command their conformity to the universality of a law as such. At most, we are now in a position to say, they can require that an agent act in a way (according to a principle) he conceives of as conforming to the universality of a law. As we have interpreted it, this amounts to the requirement that the agent act on a maxim which is not contingent on his subjective ends—that is, the maxim of his action must have a principle which is not, or is not merely, hypothetical. An action that conforms to a categorical imperative will then be one which has a maxim of

categorical or universal form. The (subjective) maxim that is brought
to the imperative for assessment will be based on the agent's own conception of his action--his interpretation of what he is doing. The accuracy of the maxim is therefore limited by an agent's opacity to himself and his possible refusal to acknowledge what it is that he is doing
(or for what end). The possibility that the agent is __wrong__ about what
the maxim of his action is may pose problems for the Categorical Imperative's claim to be an adequate test of moral right and wrong. If a subject brings the wrong maxim to the imperative and it passes the test,
what further constraint, if any, does the theory impose, __if__, as we are
supposing, the agent has not intentionally distorted the maxim of his
action? The testing procedure provided by, for example, the Formula of
the Law of Nature, does not bear on the formulation of a maxim, but
gives a procedure for determining whether the maxim the agent brings to
the test conforms 'to the universality of a law as such'. This problem
arises because the agent can only produce a maxim according to his conception of his action--how he thinks it is appropriately described and
therefore what principle it seems to him he is acting on. We will look
to see the import of these difficulties in chapter six, after we have
seen what kind of test the Formula of the Law of Nature provides. Now
we want to see the consequences for what kind of norm the Categorical
Imperative could be given the essential subjectivity of maxim formulation. The aspect of a maxim's subjectivity that concerns us here is not
the fact that it may be a misrepresentation of an action-as-willed, but
that the very concept of a maxim imposes conditions on what a categorical
imperative could be.

The Categorical Imperative requires that the maxim of an action conform to the universality of a law as such. If a maxim is in accord with the Categorical Imperative, then it is the maxim of an action that conforms to the universality of a law as such. That is, such a maxim has the formal property of being a valid rule of action for any rational being situated similarly to the agent whose maxim it is. The validity of the maxim is not contingent on the agent's happening to have some subjective end (an end such that the agent acts on this maxim only as it promotes that end). Now, acting on a maxim is acting according to a conception of a rule (or law or principle). Then we can conclude, what the Categorical Imperative dictates is not just that the maxim of your action—the rule you have a conception of—be one which is universal in form, but that your conception of the rule embodied in the maxim be that it is universal in form. Your conception of the rule on which you act (your maxim in acting) must be a conception of a rule which is not dependent in its application (to your will) on any contingent subjective end. This is so because a maxim, by definition, includes the agent's conception of his rule of action, and the Categorical Imperative requires that the rule conform to the universality of a law as such, which amounts to the rule not containing contingent subjective ends. So if the maxim is not contingent on subjective ends, and acting on a maxim is acting according to a conception of a rule, if the maxim of an action does conform to the universality of a law as such, the agent must conceive of his action as being one whose principle is not valid for him only on a contingent and subjective basis.

When an agent's maxim satisfies the conditions of the Categorical

Imperative, he acts (or intends to act) on its principle for some reason other than its serving to promote his merely subjective ends; that is what it means to act on a maxim—a conception of a rule—that is not contingent <u>as</u> a principle of action on any subjective end. Having such a maxim, it would then seem, expresses a <u>commitment</u> the agent has in acting: he is committed to acting without regard to his merely subjective interests in the circumstances of action described in the condition clause of the maxim. For example, if, 'To do <u>x</u> when I have promised to do it' is a maxim satisfying the Categorical Imperative, then an agent who does or intends to act on this maxim, has, by virtue of having <u>this</u> maxim, committed himself to the action described in it, without any condition attached that the action (also) serve his own purposes. This, of course, is just what makes acting on this kind of maxim different from acting on a maxim such as 'To do <u>x</u> when I have promised to do it but only if it also promotes some (other) end of mine'. The condition that needs to be satisfied in order for the principle of the maxim to apply in the first maxim does not depend on the presence of any contingent subjective features of the agent. The commitment to act on a maxim that conforms to the Hypothetical Imperative, however, is always conditional on the contingent subjective state of the agent—that is, whether or not he continues his commitment to acting for the end—the object he would promote in acting on this (hypothetical) maxim. What it is that would lead an agent to act on a 'categorical' maxim, and, indeed, whether it is possible for an imperfectly rational being to make a complete commitment to a practical principle that obliges him to act and yet is indifferent to his ends, except as they occur in maxims which for <u>other</u>

reasons are permitted by the Categorical Imperative, are both questions concerned with the ultimate ground (in a rational being) of a categorical imperative. In this essay we will not be able to consider if or how these questions might be answered. Nor will we take up the issues with which they are naturally associated: the "incentives of pure practical reason" (CrPrR 74;72), or, the moral motive, and the question of the very possibility of a categorical imperative. Instead we will follow Kant's procedure in the second chapter of the Groundwork and set aside the question of whether a categorical imperative is possible (and, if it is, why one would be moved to take it as one's principle of action), in order to consider, as he does, what such an imperative would be like, if it were possible.

Before we end this discussion, we should acknowledge a possible consequence of our account that was mentioned earlier and then left without further comment. If the Categorical Imperative, as such, requires an agent to have a particular conception of his action, and if that conception is embodied in a maxim, and if you cannot specify a maxim without considering the motive, then the Categorical Imperative may not be able to assess actions independently of an agent's conception of, or the maxim of, his action. One might hope that a remedy for this is to be found in the Formula of the Law of Nature, or, if not there, then in the First Principle of Justice (which looks to 'external' features of action). In chapters five and six it will be argued that neither of these principles can assess actions without looking at the agent's maxim. They do provide a weaker requirement than the one we have been considering here: that maxims be such that they could be

willed a universal law (and be so conceived and acted on by agents).
They do not provide a maxim-free requirement. Whether we judge this to
be a flaw in Kant's moral theory will depend, to a great extent, on
whether we think it possible for a theory such as Kant's to evaluate
actions in any way other than as they are willed. It is to be hoped
that the account of the concept of a categorical imperative in this
chapter has laid the foundation for understanding the possible scope of
Kant's moral theory. We will be looking later on to see if the apparent
limits of the theory might be connected to its virtues.

One last caution before we go on: Kant frequently asserts that all
action is purposive—toward or for some end. Indeed, as we have argued,
an action can be comprehended for purposes of rational assessment in
maxims only as it is described in terms of the end for which it was
undertaken. Then, it would follow, if all action is purposive, maxims
of action must include the ends an agent acts for in acting on the rule
embodied in his maxim. That is, since the maxim of an action contains
the description of an action-as-willed, and the willing of an action is
always with respect to some purpose or end, then the maxim must include
(or reflect in an essential way) that purpose or end. This may seem to
pose a serious problem, for in our account of categorical imperatives we
have given as a definition of their categoricality that they require
maxims to contain principles which are not contingent in their application on an agent's subjective ends or purposes. It is important to see
why this requirement does not conflict with the idea of the purposiveness of all action. It must be recalled that according to our interpretation of the passage setting out what a categorical imperative requires

of a maxim, contingent subjective ends were ruled out, not ends as such.
Of course it does not follow that there are ends which are not contingent and subjective, but there is also no good reason to suppose a
priori that there can be none. One possible set of candidates are the
obligatory ends--ends we are obliged, on the authority of the Categorical
Imperative, to adopt. But even if there are obligatory ends, they will
not provide the complete answer since the Categorical Imperative requires actions and maxims that do not contain obligatory ends (in the
sense of the account of those ends found in the Doctrine of Virtue).
Moreover, obligatory ends, such as the development of talents and beneficence, are not obligatory for all rational beings, and so, possibly,
also not objective.[14] The solution, I believe, is to be found in the
argument for the Formula of Humanity and the doctrine of the end-in-
itself--an end which Kant offers as an objective end for all rational
beings. It is the sort of end, he says, "which depends on motives valid
for every rational being" (G 95;427). An objective end is an end a
rational being would adopt if he were wholly rational. 'Rational nature
as an end-in-itself' is to function as the non-contingent non-subjective
end of maxims that conform to the Categorical Imperative by serving as a
"limiting condition" on the ends and maxims an agent may have. It is
beyond the scope of this essay to show that this is the role of the concept of the end-in-itself. For our purposes, all we need to know is
that there is no concpetual barrier to there being an end which is not
merely subjective, and thus nothing impossible in accommodating Kant's
claim for the essential purposiveness of action to the constraints of
the Categorical Imperative. As I will try to show on another occasion,

this end (the end-in-itself) is the ground, in the agent, of the Categorical Imperative's possibility—as a conception of the self to which the Categorical Imperative gives expression. It is through this role that rational nature as an end-in-itself can be an end that limits all other willing.

With our present understanding of what is contained in the concept of a categorical imperative and how it is that this concept is expressed in the Formula of Universal Law, we are ready to move on to the problem of how the Formula is to be applied, and how it is to be established that it is the formula of a _moral_ principle.

Notes

1. It will be useful if we now list all the formulations of the Categorical Imperative that will be used in this essay. There are three primary formulations, each designated by a number. Each of the primary formulae has subsidiary principles of application; only the principles of application of the Formula of Universal Law will be given. They will be designated with a letter following the primary formula's number.

F1. Formula of Universal Law: Act only on that maxim through which you can at the same time will that it should become a universal law (G 88;421).

F1a. Formula of the Law of Nature: Act as if the maxim of your action were to become through your will a universal law of nature (G 89; 421).

F1b. Formula of the Typic: Ask yourself whether if the action you propose should take place by a law of nature of which you yourself were a part, you could regard it as possible through your will (CrPrR 72;70)

F2. Formula of Humanity: Act in such a way that you always treat humanity, whether in your own person or in the person of any other, never simply as a means, but always at the same time as an end (G.96;429).

F3. Formula of Autonomy: So act that your will can regard itself at the same time as making universal law through its maxim (G 101;434).

In the Metaphysics of Morals two additional principles are offered, one in the Doctrine of Justice, the other in the Doctrine of Virtue:

F4. First Principle of Justice: Any action is right if, according to its maxim, the freedom of choice of any person can coexist with the freedom of every other person according to universal law (DJ 35; 230).

F5. First Principle of Virtue: Act according to a maxim of ends which it can be a universal law for everyone to have (DV 55;394).

2. We may, indeed, be required to act for obligatory ends: ends we are obliged (by the Categorical Imperative) to adopt and are not free to abandon.

3. Here we see directly the point of challenge to Foot's claim (in "Morality as a System of Hypothetical Imperatives") that all imperatives of morality are hypothetical—i.e., they do depend for their validity on a given agent's commitments or what he happens to want. It is then clear why it is thought that if there are such things as categorical imperatives it is possible to charge an agent with irrationality even when he is doing (however efficiently) what he wants. And if it can be shown that categorical imperatives are moral imperatives, then it would be

possible to give sense to the claim that immoral action is irrational action. We will see later on that this is not to say every morally wrong or faulty action is an irrational action.

4. Kant's language may be misleading here given the conventions we have adopted. What he refers to as 'imperatives of duty' we are calling categorical imperatives (in part to highlight that they must be <u>shown</u> to be moral imperatives); the unique and single categorical imperative--expressed in the Formula of Universal Law--is the principle of all categorical imperatives--the Categorical Imperative.

5. See chapter six for discussion of the permissible range of variation for this formula.

6. One should not be tempted, I think, by even the theoretical possibility that an agent could evade the Hypothetical Imperative by acting only on categorical imperatives. As we shall be seeing later on in the next chapters, the two systems of imperatives are not mutually exclusive, and while categorical imperatives have primary authority, the prudential mode of rationality is often necessary for carrying out their directives.

7. H.J. Paton, The <u>Categorical</u> <u>Imperative</u>, p. 133.

8. R.P. Wolff, <u>The</u> <u>Autonomy</u> <u>of</u> <u>Reason</u>, p. 132.

9. An agent's 'objective' situation refers to his circumstances of action described in a way that eliminates irrelevant particulars (the kind of description we argued entered into the <u>maxim</u> of an action).

10. This may seem to rule out acting for ordinary self-interested ends, but it does not. The issue for a maxim of such an action will depend on the <u>way</u> the agent conceives of his action: whether the agent acts for an ordinary end <u>only</u> <u>as</u> the maxim of that action satisfies the requirements of the Categorical Imperative. In acting that way, an agent acting on a permissible maxim is not acting for a <u>merely</u> subjective end, nor is he acting in a way that is contingent on the action serving his purposes. The arguments supporting this view of permissible actions will be found in chapters five and six.

11. For the sake of clarity, this needs some further specification. If, for example, we took the maxim 'Having promised to grade my students' papers before their exams, I will therefore do so', then surely it would not be rational for someone who had made no such promise, or who had no students, etc., to act on that maxim. This is, of course, true, but it misses the point of what it is to say either that a maxim has the form of a universal law or that a maxim can be willed as a universal law. 'If I want to remain in my students' good favor, I will grade their papers on time as I promised I would' could not be or be willed as a universal law, not because not every rational being has students, etc., but because the imperative suited to this maxim is binding on a contingent condition of volition--that agents have the end of keeping their students' favor, <u>and</u> that they will not abandon this end.

Such a maxim does not have the form of and cannot be willed a universal law because as an objective principle, it would only be addressed to agents with a specific subjective end. Whereas a maxim that can be willed as a universal law has no such dependency as a potential objective principle. It must always be kept in mind that maxims, imperatives, and objective principles have to do with <u>willing</u>, so if the features of any of these are bound to the subjective condition of a will, it cannot possibly be universal. To return to the first example--if we suppose that promises involve categorical imperatives, whether or not a given agent has students or has made a promise, the <u>form</u> of volition embodied in that maxim is universal in that the imperative to which it conforms is in force without regard to what an agent wants to do--given that a promise has been made (and other things are equal). <u>That</u> condition, while a matter of fact, is not a contingent feature of the volition. And, moreover, once a promise has been made, it binds as a promise, and cannot be abandoned as one can abandon an end that no longer seems suited to one's interests. This is so whether or not it is also true in any particular case that the promise ought to be kept. (It should be clear that all of the remarks in this note apply to both readings of the Formula of Universal Law.)

12. J.G. Murphy, "Kant's Concept of a Right Action", p. 472.

13. All of the qualifications and cautions in determining the maxim of an action that were set out in chapter two are taken for granted here. For example, I am assuming that when we talk of what an agent 'takes himself to be doing in acting', that we read this construction as referring to the sense of his action determined according to his <u>motive in acting</u>, and not by what he might say about his action, etc.

14. I say 'possibly not objective' to leave open the question of there being ends one might have as a member of a species of rational beings, which while not objective in the universal sense, should not be labeled subjective either. We will return to this in our discussion of the third and fourth examples of the <u>Groundwork</u>.

Chapter Five: <u>The</u> <u>Categorical</u> <u>Imperative</u> (The Formula of the Law of Nature)

Having extracted the Formula of Universal Law from his analysis of
the concept of a categorical imperative, Kant continues his argument as
follows:

> Now if all imperatives of duty can be derived from this
> one imperative as their principle, then even although we
> leave it unsettled whether what we call duty may not be an
> empty concept, we shall still be able to show at least
> what we understand by it and what the concept means. (G
> 88;421)

That is, continuing to leave the question of the possibility of a categorical imperative aside, Kant would now demonstrate that this principle
of rational willing is the source of so-called moral principles. Indeed,
he would show that 'imperatives of duty can be <u>derived</u> <u>from</u> the one
Categorical Imperative as their principle'. The point of this exercise,
he explains, is that whether or not the possibility of a categorical imperative can be established, if it can be shown that imperatives of duty
<u>are</u> categorical imperatives, then we can use the concept of a categorical
imperative to explain our concept of duty. There are then two things at
stake in the 'derivation of duties'. The first is to show that so-
called imperatives of duty can be 'derived from' the Formula of Universal Law, and that they <u>are</u> categorical imperatives. The second is to
show that it is <u>our</u> notion of <u>duty</u> that is captured in this derivation.
Moreover, we might hope that if the derivation of duties is successful,
we would have an account of what the real moral content is of the things
we are said to have a duty to do.

We need not spend much time considering what Kant might have meant in talking about imperatives of duty being _derived_ from the Categorical Imperative. If we look at the relations we already know to obtain, what he means is perfectly clear. We know that the Categorical Imperative (expressed in the Formula of Universal Law) is a principle/law of rational willing, and that whatever is a categorical imperative will have it as its principle. That is, an imperative will be _categorical_ if it is an instance of the Formula--if it satisfies its formal criteria of willing. And if it can be shown that imperatives of duty are categorical imperatives, then they too will have the Categorical Imperative as their principle. This is all we really need to produce a satisfactory reading of "all imperatives of duty can be derived from this one imperative as their principle". Kant's use of "derived" must not be read to suggest that imperatives of duty are to follow directly from the very formula of the Categorical Imperative, or that they are somehow implied by it. No such thing is possible: nothing about promises or lying or beneficence could follow from the universal law requirement on willing alone. The relation of derivation that obtains between imperatives of duty (if they are categorical imperatives) and the Categorical Imperative is most clearly seen when you ask where a particular imperative gets its authority. If an imperative of duty is a categorical imperative it will get its authority from the Categorical Imperative--_as its principle_--i.e. it will have categorical authority if it is an instantiation of the principle of all categorical imperatives. Its authority--its status as an imperative--is _derived from_ the Categorical Imperative as its principle.

One would reasonably expect the argument to continue with a

demonstration that imperatives of duty are categorical imperatives, by, for example, showing that they require of an agent that his willing not be based on contingent subjective ends, etc. Instead, we find Kant introducing a new formulation of the Categorical Imperative (the Formula of the Law of Nature) and then presenting four examples which are to show that certain maxims of action are not compatible with this new formula either because they cannot be conceived as a universal law of nature without contradiction or they cannot be willed a universal law of nature without the will contradicting itself. We need to explain why the argument takes this turn and how Kant in fact determines that imperatives of duty are categorical imperatives through these examples. There can be no doubt that Kant believes he has provided the necessary demonstration; he says, after concluding the fourth example, "These are some of the many actual duties—or at least of what we take to be such—whose derivation from the single principle cited above leaps to the eye" (G 91;423-4). This surely overstates the case. But it is also quite clearly what he would contend, as he goes on to say, in concluding the passage from which we have just quoted, that the four examples represent the two possible types of duty (narrow and wide) and that as a result (of this fact and the arguments in the four examples) it is easily seen "that by these examples all duties—so far as the type of obligation is concerned (not the object of dutiful action)—are fully set out in their dependence on our single principle" (G 91;424). We must, I believe, take this and the previously quoted passage as our cue in determining a satisfactory reading of this section of the Groundwork.

Let me suggest a reading of these passages which will return us to

the point of introduction of the imperatives of duty as possible categorical imperatives ready to proceed with the argument as it is set out
in the Groundwork. Two things are asserted in these passages: (1) the
four examples are said to be some of the duties which can readily be
shown to be derived from the Categorical Imperative,[1] and (2), that
these same examples show all duties in their dependence on the Categorical Imperative. From this we might reasonably conclude that something
about the way Kant argues for (1) must yield (2), and the 'way' is not
hard to reconstruct. If all duties did divide into types, and if the
connection of representative duties of each type to the Categorical Imperative were set out, and if these demonstrations did not employ in any
essential way features of the representative duties that were not shared
by all others of their type, but instead worked from features constitutive of the type, then arguments establishing (1) would also establish
(2). The apparent typology of duties in the four examples is perfect-
imperfect (or narrow-wide) and duties to self—duties to others. But as
the arguments in the examples do not turn on any interesting or essential features of these divisions, it is reasonable to assume that for
the purposes of the Groundwork they are not the primary division of
types of duty, but merely provide a conventional and familiar order of
presentation. Indeed, Kant introduces the examples with just this emphasis:

> We will now enumerate a few duties, following their cus-
> tomary division into duties towards self and duties
> towards others and into perfect and imperfect duties.*
> (G 89;421)
>
> *It should be noted that I reserve my division of duties
> entirely for a future Metaphysics of Morals and that my

> present division is therefore put forward as arbitrary
> (merely for the purpose of arranging my examples). (G 89n;
> 421n)

and I see no reason not to take him at his word. Moreover, there is a
division of duties employed in the arguments of the examples that is not
conventional or arbitrary: the two-fold classification of rational
willing through what I will call (following Nell) the contradiction in
conception and the contradiction in will tests. That is, an action is
opposed to duty if the maxim of that action either cannot be conceived
as a universal law of nature without contradiction or cannot be willed a
universal law of nature without the will contradicting itself (G 91;424).
While it is premature to say much about these two tests (we have yet to
introduce or explain the Formula of the Law of Nature) or to indicate
what kind of division of duties they provide, there can be no doubt that
Kant believes they divide all duties between them and that they are the
principles of division which matter to the Groundwork.

We can now begin to see, at least formally, how in the transition
to the four examples Kant did intend a demonstration that imperatives of
duty (so-called) are categorical imperatives. If his division of duties
is exhaustive (of what we would call duties), and if he can show how and
that imperatives of duty are derived from the Categorical Imperative as
they are types of duty, he will have shown that imperatives of duty (in
general) are categorical imperatives. The sense of this will become
clearer as we see what Kant's actual procedure of derivation is.

To the degree that all of this is persuasive concerning Kant's intentions, one might well be surprised at the argument of the examples
which involves testing maxims, and not, as we might well have supposed,

derivations of duties. Indeed, as most recent commentaries on the
Groundwork have been at pains to point out,[2] the arguments of the examples do not show that we, e.g., have a duty never to commit suicide or a
duty not to make deceitful promises (whatever Kant himself may have felt
about these matters). What they show is that given a maxim (of suicide
or deception), if it is tested according to the principle of application
of the Categorical Imperative (i.e. the Formula of the Law of Nature),
then that particular maxim either does or does not pass the test. That
is, the supposed failure of a suicide-for-self-love maxim tells us
nothing about the permissibility of suicide on some other maxim, and so
nothing, it seems, about whether or not we have general duties concerning suicide. The examples do not seem to provide derivations of duties.

That commentators feel called upon to remind readers that "it is one
thing...to show that an action is wrong when it is performed according
to a certain maxim, and quite another thing to show that any action of
that kind is wrong",[3] or, "one could only rule out an act by showing
that every possible policy enjoining it conflicted with the Categorical
Imperative",[4] is related, I believe, to a basic set of misunderstandings
of Kant's intentions with the examples which this reminder signals without correcting. It would be wise to proceed by setting aside all pre-
conceptions about what a derivation of imperatives of duties would be
like. So that we will not be without guidance, we might return to the
presumption that the account of hypothetical imperatives which precedes
this section is intended by Kant to be helpful in understanding the more
difficult and less intuitive arguments concerning categorical imperatives.

Let us suppose we have some cluster of imperatives we think may be imperatives of prudence; what should we do if we want to show that these imperatives are hypothetical? Or, how do you tell if an imperative is a hypothetical imperative? Quite simply. You look to see whether the imperative conforms to the principle of all hypothetical imperatives--the Hypothetical Imperative. So, if we are to learn from this how to work with categorical imperatives, it looks as though we are back where we started, and we should expect Kant to take a supposed categorical imperative of duty--e.g. 'One ought never to lie'--and show that it conforms to the Categorical Imperative. But our analysis of hypothetical imperatives as they are standardly employed in practical judgment should have warned us that we have already gone astray. The hypothetical imperative appropriate to a given agent's subjective maxim is constructed given what the agent wills--given his maxim. The imperative is not derived separately and then applied to the agent's maxim; you do not know what imperative to apply--the imperative, so to speak, does not exist, until the maxim is given. The existence of pre-established technical imperatives in the sciences (rules, procedures, tests, etc.) does not really counter this claim, for the point of the imperatives in the "practical part" of all sciences is that the ends an agent pursues within the science are given; they are part of the science itself. The form of such an imperative might be 'To produce reaction q you must combine r and s'. In the ordinary cases, no given hypothetical imperative applies to an agent unless he has happened to adopt the end contained in that imperative. In principle, of course, one might attempt to produce a list of hypothetical imperatives for all possible ends of action, but there would be as many such imperatives as there are possible ends, and which imperative applied to an agent would still depend on what he had as his maxim of action. So the manner of employment of these imperatives we determined to be as follows: Given an agent's subjective maxim and so his end, we construct an objective maxim or hypothetical imperative by determining (with the aid of information about his empirical situation-- abilities, knowledge, resources, etc.) what action or kind of action would yield his end as its effect. Having constructed this imperative according to the form dictated by the Hypothetical Imperative, we know it is hypothetical. If we want to know whether the agent's maxim con- forms to the Hypothetical Imperative we see if his subjective maxim is the objective maxim for his end, etc. The movement in practical judg- ment is _from_ a subjective maxim with its end _to_ an imperative (deter- mined according to that end) which is the norm _for_ _that_ _maxim_. There is every reason to expect the same or a similar structure for categorical imperatives. That is, we should expect to _begin_ with an agent's maxim and to proceed by employing the principle of categorical imperatives to determine whether that subjective maxim is also objective. With hypo- thetical imperatives an objective maxim (of an agent) is a possible maxim for all rational beings with the same end (as is in the agent's maxim). An objective maxim which conforms to the Categorical Imperative we would expect to be a possible maxim for all rational beings regardless of their subjective contingent ends. Now this begins to suggest the procedure of the four examples.[5] If our sense of the role of hypotheti- cal imperatives in the _Groundwork_ is correct, we should expect the dir- ection the argument actually (formally) takes.

That the examples present candidate maxims which are all opposed to

duty (to the Categorical Imperative) should also occasion no surprise.
A partial function of this section of the Groundwork which introduces
categorical imperatives is to provide criteria for distinguishing categorical from hypothetical imperatives. If they are distinct--if categorical imperatives are not just a special class of hypothetical imperatives
(as Foot, for example, concludes they are), one should be able to produce cases of maxims which satisfy the norm provided by hypothetical imperatives but which fail to satisfy that of categorical ones. And, indeed, the maxims of the four examples are precisely maxims which do conform to the norm of prudential rationality. If, in addition, they are
not compatible with categorical requirements (which the argument of the
examples is to establish), then a major step will have been taken in the
demonstration that so-called imperatives of duty are not hypothetical.
This of course cannot show that there are any non-hypothetical impera-
tives--i.e., that the human will can be (rationally) constrained independently of what we would, in the ordinary sense, say an agent wants--
independently of his subjective ends. But, as we have noted before, the
point of this part of the Groundwork is to show first that coherent
sense can be given to the concept of a categorical imperative (in general) and then, that so-called imperatives of duty are instances of
categorical and not hypothetical imperatives: or, if there are such
things as duties, they, or their principles, are not heteronomous. The
examples provide the argument for the latter--and, in addition, show the
way in which the Categorical Imperative is to be employed as a principle
of practical judgment.

Given this preparatory structural sketch, one can already begin to

see how the moral argument must be shaped. For example, the very notion of a 'duty', as it functions in the argument of the examples, cannot
be that of a moral rule or general principle which stands as an authority
directing an agent to particular actions: e.g., 'Keep your promises!'
The entire picture of moral judgment and the 'derivation of duties' is
different. We start with an agent who has a definite course of action
in mind and ask whether it is morally all right for an agent to do what
he already wants to do. This suggests that the sense in which imperatives of duty are universally binding needs considerable interpretation
if imperatives of duty are to be generated from agents' maxims of action.
Moreover, I believe we will find that even if Kant himself is guilty of
a charge of moral rigorism, it is already arguable that it was not his
moral theory which forced that position on him. We will be able to make
better sense of these and related matters when we have shown in greater
detail how the actual argument proceeds. The project of the examples as
we now understand it is to provide a derivation of imperatives of duty
from the Categorical Imperative (as their principle)—to show that imperatives of duty are categorical imperatives--by showing that they require of an agent that his willing (his maxim) must, in a way not yet
specified, conform to the universality of a law as such. We will try to
show that the contradiction in conception and will tests are designed to
and do perform this task.[6] It is time, then, to introduce these tests
and the Formula of the Law of Nature which is their source.[7]

Let me state explicitly what I intend to accomplish in the rest of
this chapter. Without getting involved overmuch in problems arising

from the first Critique, I will try to develop a plausible case for the introduction of the Formula of the Law of Nature as a necessary supplement to the Formula of Universal Law. In doing this, it is to be hoped that the ground will be prepared for discussing the relations between Kant's so-called 'universalization principle' and the familiar moral question, 'What if everyone did that?' (hereafter referred to as WIEDT).[3] Kant's principle, I believe, can be seen as providing an explanation of the moral force of the WIEDT question and for why the appeal to an imagined universalization of an action or maxim is often taken to be the hallmark of essentially moral thought. With regard to the examples themselves, I will not have much to say about either the suicide or the deceitful promise example. The suicide example in the Groundwork seems an unfortunate choice for Kant to have made for a wide variety of reasons; this is especially so given the much more interesting argument in the Doctrine of Virtue, where suicide is considered as a duty of omission governed by an obligatory end of perfection. Moreover, under the more plausible Doctrine of Virtue interpretation, suicide would fall into the talents and beneficence test group (the 'contradiction in will' test) rather than being grouped with the deceitful promise (and the 'contradiction in conception' test) as it is in the Groundwork. It therefore hardly seems worthwhile to bear down on the suicide argument in the Groundwork. For quite different reasons I will also not spend much time on the argument of the deceitful promise example. There are two quite interesting accounts of this argument available,[9] and although I believe one version is closer to Kant's intentions (which I will discuss shortly), they are both illuminating. I do not go on in great detail about this argument since I simply do not have a better interpretation to offer. That is, I will discuss what the so-called 'contradiction in conception' test is and attempt to determine the source of its authority, but I will not give independent consideration to its proper method of employment. The examples and arguments I intend to examine closely fall under the 'contradiction in will' test--the duties of developing talents and beneficence. My interest in these two _is_ focused on the question of the employment of the Formula of the Law of Nature because: 1) when suitably reconstructed they reveal the introduction into the heart of Kant's ethical theory of what I call the 'conditions of human rationality' which are important both as examples of how empirical features of human existence are allowed to condition the austerity of a 'principle of pure practical reason', and because they bring into sharp relief a new sense of the significance of Kant's insistence that 'reason' is the foundation of morality; and 2) out of this understanding of the 'contradiction in will' test we can begin to see a reason why the WIEDT question might well be present as a touchstone of even ordinary moral consciousness--or, at least, why a version of it might be. That is, Kant is able to provide, I will contend, a theoretically sound and intuitively persuasive account of _why_ the imagined consequences of others behaving as I intend to should be part of my effort to understand my own intended action--from the moral point of view, as we call it.

Now let us turn to the question of why the Formula of the Law of Nature is introduced: in what respect does the Formula of Universal Law need supplementation by another formula, and how does the Formula of the

Law of Nature meet that need. (In what follows I assume the reader is familiar with this section of the Groundwork and that I need not be as fastidious as I have been with earlier sections in trying to keep to the order of the text itself as the order of interpretation.) Standardly, and with good reason, the motivation for introducing the Formula of the Law of Nature is found in the doctrine of the first Critique as it is brought to bear on the problem of moral judgment in the section of the second Critique called "Of the Typic of Pure Practical Judgment". For example:

> The difficulty about our concept of the unconditioned and absolute law of morality is that it is an Idea of reason: and therefore ex hypothesi it can have no corresponding object in sensuous experience. The actions which we to bring to bear under the moral law are--from one point of view--mere events subject to the law of nature and not to the law of freedom. They cannot be adequate to the Idea of an unconditioned law, and we have no schema, transcendental or otherwise, whereby we can exhibit an object for such an Idea of Reason.[10]

> With pure practical judgment the problem is...difficult, since the law is a law of reason, not of the understanding, and no intuition can be adequate to it. We can never be sure, in any experience, whether the full terms of the moral law have been observed.... Similarly, the morally good is not a natural property of an act standing in causal or other categorical relations.[11]

These remarks clearly have their source in the following passage:

> The judgment of pure practical reason...is subject to the same difficulties as that of the pure theoretical, though the latter had a means of escape. It could escape because in its theoretical use everything depended upon intuitions to which pure concepts of the understanding could be applied, and such intuitions (though only objects of the senses), as a priori and hence concerning the connection of the manifold in intuitions, could be given a priori in conformity to the concepts of the understanding, i.e., as schemata. The morally good, on the contrary, is something which, by its object is supersensuous; nothing

corresponding to it can be found in sensuous intuition; consequently, judgment under laws of the pure practical reason seems to be subject to special difficulties, which result from the fact that a law of freedom is to be applied to actions which are events occurring in the world of sense and thus, to this extent, belonging to nature. (CrPrR 70-71;68-69)

The idea is: the Categorical is or embodies a law of freedom (or, a law of pure practical reason), which is, by definition, outside the conditions of experience and therefore of understanding and judgment, etc. It therefore requires some mediating principle in order that it be possible to employ the Categorical Imperative in matters of judgment. This task of mediation (or 'symbolic representation' to modify Paton's phrase) is performed in the Groundwork by the Formula of the Law of Nature and, in the second Critique, by the Typic of pure practical judgment.[12]

This account is, for what it is, unobjectionable. Since, however, the Groundwork was intended by Kant to stand independently of the arguments and conclusions of the first Critique, it would seem to be a reasonable enterprise to try for an account of the transition from the Formula of Universal Law to the Formula of the Law of Nature that was not wholly dependent on some of the more unlikely principles of Kantian metaphysics. Moreover, when Kant talks in the Groundwork about the difficulties there are in finding an action done purely from duty (or, in strict conformity to the Categorical Imperative) the difficulties he cites are empirical, not logical or metaphysical (e.g., the inadequacy of introspection to determine purity of motive). Nor, in this part of the Groundwork, does Kant introduce any esoteric doctrine of the will which could be seen as calling for the account of the second Critique.

For these reasons, and for the sake of the moral theory of the Ground-work, I would try to evade theoretical problems that result from Kant's metaphysics, and instead look to the account we already have of the Formula of Universal Law (F1) for an explanation of the conditions calling for the introduction of the Formula of the Law of Nature (F1a).[13]

We might pause, in order to get purchase on this problem, and ask why there is no analogous difficulty in judgment concerning the application of the Hypothetical Imperative. It too, after all, is a practical law; and we might even be tempted to conjecture with Wolff[14] that it is not possible to 'prove' a bit of behavior is prudentially rational action--or, at least, that we can no more determine that an agent has elected a prudential end (has chosen to act from a conception of a desired state of affairs) than we can for an agent's supposed adoption of a moral end or maxim. However this question is resolved, there do not seem to be great problems in judging whether a maxim conforms to the Hypothetical Imperative, and it is quite clear why not. Questions of judgment here concern causes and effects: what you need to know is whether a proposed action is (or is likely to be) the cause of a desired end (as its effect). As Beck puts it,[15] "The criteria of successful technique or a satisfactory mode of life are to be found in experience." There seem, then, to be two ways a maxim can be evaluated by the Hypothetical Imperative: 1) that a proposed action will in fact produce the desired end as an effect, and 2) that the willing is prudential--an agent conceives himself to be acting for the end he has adopted as his purpose. According to Wolff's interpretation it is not possible to tell whether the willing is in accordance with the Hypothetical Imperative, whereas determining the adequacy of the action to the end is a relatively straightforward matter of ordinary empirical judgment. We might well expect an analogous division of tasks under the Categorical Imperative.[16] That is, we would expect all imperatives to regulate action in two ways: 1) providing criteria of adequacy for a proposed action, and 2) providing a norm of volition which requires that the action be conceived (through its maxim) as conforming to the form of the governing type of imperative. And, we also would have good reason to expect, given all of this, that the problem with the Categorical Imperative (and therefore F1) will come in making judgments of the first sort, as there do not seem to be special problems for the Categorical Imperative in the second category of judgment that are not also found with the Hypothetical Imperative. (It is not to be expected that we will come to different conclusions than those of Beck and Paton or the second Critique; our ambition is to reach the same end by a different and hopefully more attractive path.)

Now, there is no problem in making 'hypothetical' (prudential) judgments of type one, we said, because in those cases, given a willed end, what we must judge is whether the proposed action (in the maxim) is a possible means to that end: we are to judge what it is rational to do, given an end that is a possible effect of action. It is a norm of rational willing we know how to apply. The Categorical Imperative, with its formula F1, also provides a norm of rational willing; the question is, why should we have difficulty in knowing how to apply it. The Hypothetical Imperative ('Who wills the end...wills the means') directs us to ask whether the act-end relation in our maxim is a means-end relation—which we can do. According to Kant's account of the Categorical

Imperative we are to determine whether our maxim conforms to the universality of a law as such by asking whether it is a maxim 'through which
you can at the same time will that it should become a universal law'
(for all rational beings). What we must not know how to do is determine
whether our maxim is possible as a universal law for rational beings.
We should now look to see why not.

First of all, what could be meant by requiring that _my_ maxim be
possible as a universal law for all rational beings (or, for 'rational
beings in general')? How can I "act on a maxim which at the same time
contains in itself its own universal validity for every rational being"
(G 105;438)? or that "in using means to every end I ought to restrict my
maxim by the condition that it should also be universally valid as a law
for every subject" (i.e. rational being) (G 105;438)? How _could_ my
material, subjectively based maxim conform to the universality of a law
as such? Suppose we were considering a maxim of doing regular exercise
in order to maintain a level of physical fitness. Could _that_ maxim possibly conform to the universality of a law as such? or be universally
valid for every rational being? We know that the Categorical Imperative
requires that our maxims be consistent with rationality (or rational
willing) in general, but we do not know, and nothing in F1 tells us,
what _counts_ as rationality (or rational willing) for particular maxims.
Suppose there are concepts appearing in your maxim that do not necessarily _apply_ to all rational beings? E.g., borrowing, hurting, stealing,
promising, killing, etc. It does not even make sense to ask whether a
maxim of stealing is rational or even possible for rational beings who
may not have a concept of property--or, similarly, whether a maxim of

killing is rational when some rational beings might be either immortal
or invulnerable, etc. But these examples just bear witness to the fact
that we do not know how to determine whether our maxims are valid as
laws (or principles of rational willing) for all rational beings.

We can rule out in advance our account of F1 in chapter four as a
candidate for the principle of judgment of the first type. According to
F1, we said, our maxims were not to be based on merely subjective and
contingent ends (i.e., this is what we concluded Kant intended in the
requirement that a maxim conform to the universality of a law as such).
But most of our ends, and therefore most of our maxims, _are_ subjective
and contingent. If Kant is to have any kind of plausible ethical theory,
the Categorical Imperative (and so F1) should permit our acting on many
such maxims which would normally fall in the moral category of the 'permissible'. We know that Kant intended his theory to allow for such a
category as in the _Doctrine of Virtue_ (20;221) he says, "According to
the categorical imperative certain actions are permissible or impermissible, i.e. morally possible or impossible, while some of these actions or their contraries are morally necessary, i.e. obligatory." We
may reasonably conclude that our earlier account must have been of a
requirement of the second type—as it calls for the conformity of _voli-
tion_ to the principle embodied in the imperative (i.e. the universality
of a law as such). Even permissible actions can be willed _as they are_
permissible. The difficulty here is in telling _whether_ an action is
permissible. If certain actions according to subjective maxims are to
be permissible, judgment of permissibility must be a judgment of the
first type, and it must not require (as such) that an agent's _willing_

conform to the universality of law, or that (in different words) his
maxim have a universally valid form.

As these difficulties--our ignorance of the nature of 'rationality'
apart from its human embodiment and the intractability of permissible or
essentially subjective maxims--emerge naturally from thinking about using
F1 as a principle of judgment for maxims, and since, whatever else F1a
may have been intended by Kant to do, it provides a reasonable way around
these obstacles to judgment, we may take this to be the point of introducing F1a in the Groundwork and ignore the more strained metaphysical
motivation for F1a suggested by the Typic argument of the second Critique.
Neither this claim nor the interpretation I will offer of the two tests
which comprise F1a can be clearly substantiated in the text of the
Groundwork. On the other hand, the textual evidence is not sufficient
by itself to establish any interpretation conclusively. Given this fact
(which is surely known to anyone who has succumbed to the temptation to
struggle with these central passages) I have taken the following as
touchstones of interpretation: to remain as close as possible to what
Kant says he is doing,[17] to try to stay in touch with considered moral
intuition, to make use of insights we have already gained concerning
Kant's conception of maxims and imperatives as norms of volition, and to
trust an interpretation which seems revelatory of the moral content of
the F1a tests. Many interpretations do not attempt this last (and I
think most important) project; they are content if the 'right' results
follow from a principle of application similar enough to F1a.[18] Kant of
course believed that the F1a testing procedures did yield results, but
he also thought they illuminated the very structure of our moral thought

(see G 92;424), especially our efforts to rationalize actions we suspect (or ought to suspect) are really wrong.

As I can see no way to argue directly from F1 to F1a, I will instead work _from_ a sense of the problems there would be in applying F1 as a principle of judgment and what we can see Kant supplying as the content of F1a _to_ what I hope will be an adequate understanding of the latter principle _as_ a principle of moral judgment. In particular, we want to see _why_ F1a is introduced and why in the form it has—as well as looking for a plausible construal of its two tests.

Let us look again at the two principles:

> F1: Act only on that maxim through which you can at the same time will it should become a universal law.
>
> F1a: Act as if the maxim of your action were to become through your will a universal law of nature.

One of the most striking differences is at the surface: F1 is a requirement on volition; F1a is a fictive causal principle. F1a translates the requirement that we be able to will that our maxim become a universal law into a fictional model according to which we are to imagine our will producing law as a causal effect of its willing.

In our ordinary willings we adopt (or will) an end according to a maxim. The maxim can be said to describe the **way** (with respect to action) **we** will an end, embodying our intention. We might even be said to will the maxim (in a determinate willing of an end) as a principle or law for ourselves. But this does not give us much purchase on the idea of being able to will that our maxim should become a universal law (or how we might will this "through" our maxim). It is not only that we do not have the power to legislate universally, but that we cannot even imagine (for the reasons already discussed) most of our maxims serving as laws for all rational beings. (Kant takes note of this limitation later on in the Groundwork (G 99;432) where he labels a will which makes or enacts universal law an Idea of reason—which is by definition (following the doctrine of the first Critique) something outside the conditions of experience and therefore something for which the human mind can have no adequate concept.)

F1a directs us to imagine the power to legislate universally as a natural causal effect of willing. Moreover, the domain over which F1a operates is that of human beings.[19] It thereby provides the appropriate conditions for judgment, yet it still serves as a test for whether a maxim is a possible law for all rational beings. That is, if we suppose a universe of rational beings which contains all and only human beings, and if a maxim is not a possible law (or principle) in that universe, then, given Kantian assumptions about the consistency of rational principles, a maxim that is not a possible law for human rational beings could not be a law for rational beings in general.

According to F1a we are to imagine that through the willing (adopting) of an end—and so the having of a maxim—the maxim of our willing becomes a natural law for all human beings. (There are suppressed assumptions about shared language and concepts here which do not need to be spelled out for this device to be appreciated; we are looking to understand the F1a test, not to construct a formal model of it.) This gives a sense to how we might think of willing "through" a maxim. In the fictive construction provided by F1a, "through which you can at the same time will..." becomes "through your will". That is, you are to suppose that <u>as</u> <u>a</u> <u>result</u> of your willing your maxim becomes a universal law of nature. (The departure of this construction from the original F1 becomes clear when we consider the Categorical Imperative as a principle governing <u>how</u>—in addition to what—one is to will.)

If we are to imagine a maxim becoming a universal law of nature we must first know what kind of natural law we are to consider. There are two obvious candidates: a law of (human) willing and a law of (human) behavior. The idea of imagining a maxim raised to a law of behavior seems attractive because it is so straightforward and because it can look to be what Kant must mean when he talks (e.g., in the second Critique) about employing laws of nature as the "type" of a law of freedom. Moreover, we are inevitably struck by the similarity of F1a as it is used in the examples to the familiar WIEDT tests which <u>are</u> directly concerned with what happens if everyone <u>does</u> such and such a kind of thing—e.g., takes a shortcut across the park grass. It is true that the F1a tests look to what would happen if, e.g., everyone in need made deceitful promises, but we should not jump to conclude that what we must imagine is a law of behavior. We might imagine instead (and to the same effect) a law of <u>action</u>, where that is distinguished from a law of behavior by the inclusion of the volition: a law of the action-as-willed. Imagining a law of action, then, is imagining a law of willing. It is not merely the inclusiveness of this proposal that recommends it; it is also that it keeps us within the frame of thought that has been characteristic of the theory to this point, and this is not just a matter of economy. First of all, it is easier to imagine a world in which others <u>will</u> as you do than one in which while their behavior resembles yours (in the relevant respects), you have no sense of their conception of what they are doing (i.e. what _their_ maxims are). Indeed, when we look at Kant's deceitful promise example, it seems clear that it would be incoherent on a purely behavioral model. What we are to imagine there is everyone _intending_ that their false promises be taken at face value,[20] and what we need to register (for the argument) is the difference between a world in which people are incapable of _doing_ what they promised and one in which they have a different _intention_ than the one expressed in their 'promise'. As we will see later on, this distinction is essential if we are to see the first test under F1a as a contradiction in _conception_. But we need not beg the question of that test: although the notion of a law of willing seems necessary for my interpretation of the test, other interpretations which rely on behavioral considerations (e.g., imagining a world in which everyone's experience is of people making promises and then always failing to keep them) will be possible on the law of willing view as well since in imagining a natural law according to which everyone wills according to my maxim, I also imagine a world in which everyone _behaves_ (in the relevant respects) as I would, given my maxim. (We are not imagining a radically new world with F1a: since maxims ordinarily open into action, we must suppose all or most who (by natural law) had this maxim would act accordingly.) This conclusion is strengthened if we remember that maxims are not (necessarily or even ordinarily) general policies which dictate a wide range of _kinds_ of activity (e.g. "to better my interests however possible"), but maxims are maxims _of_ (intended) actions.

Two final considerations seem to me to close the question. This transition from a law of freedom (F1) to a law of human nature (F1a), understood as a law of willing, leaves room for—although it does not require—the account of the problem of judgment in the Typic and the two viewpoints of the self analysis in chapter three of the Groundwork. One could even speculate that Kant thought F1a could be employed as a rule of judgment for F1 just because he believed it possible to view the will as phenomenon (and so, as caused). The last point to note regarding the desirability of the law-of-willing interpretation is in some ways the most important: The idea behind F1 is that as a rational being I must undertake to act only on those maxims which would be adopted by all similarly situated rational beings in so far as they are rational. The translation of F1 into a test which asks us to regard our maxim as becoming a law of human willing retains the sense that we are concerned with criteria of rationality in action. The picture of full-compliance willing that comes from F1a is still a picture of willing, albeit willing which we imagine occurs as a result of our own adoption of a maxim. Without this retention of focus on rational willing it is hard to see how F1a could be a principle of application for F1 without resorting to explanations burdened with the worst of Kantian metaphysics. Such explanations are possible (see Wolff, the Typic, etc.), but it seems to me better to avoid them when we can. This is especially so if, as I believe, the law of willing interpretation of F1a will help us understand what it is about the WIEDT question that makes it an appropriate criterion of moral judgment.

Given an agent's intended action, with its maxim (M), the Categorical Imperative is introduced on the suspicion that M is not rational:

that M is <u>not</u> a maxim any agent (with the same end and in relevantly similar objective circumstances) would act on if acting rationally.[21] When judging a maxim's rationality by the Hypothetical Imperative, what the agent wants (his end) is the basis for what is judged rational. When judging according to the Categorical Imperative, what the agent wants is not the determining ground of rationality. The sense in which a maxim is not rational is determined by what Kant calls the "form" of the maxim: whether the maxim is possible as a universal law of willing.[22] What Fla captures is the agent's presumption of rationality--his inclination to believe (or convince himself) that his intended action is morally justifiable. The full-compliance model derived from imagining the agent's maxim as a natural law of human willing provides the means for testing the rationality of the maxim in question by taking literally the agent's presumption that he is acting rationally--i.e. that his maxim is one that all persons could (rationally) act on, etc. We can then see Fla's taking the maxim to be a natural law of willing as equivalent to supposing that <u>all</u> human beings (who share the end, etc.) will act on the maxim in question <u>and</u> that they will be acting rationally in doing this. It is as if everyone is taken to be wholly rational with regard to this one maxim.[23] (This is done graphically in the talents example where the volitional necessity required by Fla is represented as a natural instinct; with questions of freedom set aside, an instinct is well suited to stand in for full rationality.)[24]

We have said Fla asks of a given maxim that it be possible as a law of willing. We must now consider what such a requirement of possibility might be. A maxim might be judged 'not possible' as a law (or principle) of rational willing if it were incompatible with other known (and independently established) principles of rational willing.[25] To take an obvious example from hypothetical imperatives: the maxim, 'to embark on this project I know will not lead me to my goal' would not be 'possible' (as it stands) because it is not compatible with the Hypothetical Imperative--one of the laws of rational willing. That is, if our odd maxim were a principle (law) of rational willing (or an instance of such a principle) then the Hypothetical Imperative could not be one-- or, it would have to be possible for principles of rational willing to be mutually inconsistent. Since it is a basic tenet of Kant's philosophy that principles of reason (of practical reason) must be consistent with one another, we must reject the latter alternative as a part of any interpretation of Kant's theory. So, if the Hypothetical Imperative is a principle of rational willing, our maxim could not be. Therefore, the maxim is not a 'possible' principle of rational willing. This is the model we will try to use for F1a.

The idea for interpreting 'possible' laws or principles this way is drawn from a slightly strained analogy with standard methods of natural observation: we imagine someone formulating a test principle to describe an observed regularity, and then asking whether it is a possible principle--in the sense that if it held as a general principle or 'natural law' would it or its results be compatible with other (supposedly known) laws of nature. Of course from the fact that a conjecture is a possible natural law it does not follow that it is a natural law (if there can be more than one hypothesis describing the facts consistent with other known laws).

Applying this notion of 'possible' principles of rational willing to maxims, we would expect candidate maxims to fall into three categories: those that are possible as laws (or instances of laws) of rational willing, those that are impossible as such laws, and those that are (or are instances of) laws of rational willing. If this interpretation of F1a is correct, we can expect these to be the same as the moral categories of the permissible, the impermissible (or forbidden), and the obligatory.

Our sample maxim was judged 'not possible' as a principle of rational willing because it was not consistent with the Hypothetical Imperative (a principle we take to be given as a law of rational willing). The task for F1a is to determine whether a maxim is 'possible' when you already know it conforms to the Hypothetical Imperative.[26] If we suppose a maxim (M) has passed the Hypothetical Imperative test, there are two further ways it could fail to be 'possible' as a law/principle of rational willing: 1) we encounter some logical difficulty in imagining M as (or becoming through our will) a law/principle governing the wills of all (human) beings; 2) the maxim M as an imagined law is not consistent with other given laws of rational willing. The point of 1) is to question whether M could be a law of willing at all.[27] That is, not every trial singular principle can be cast as a universal principle without incurring logical difficulties. 'All doctors are obliged to refrain from healing' is an impossible universal principle. (Of course, the universalized maxims of most interest to a moral theory will not wear their contradictoriness on the surface.) The point of 2) ought to be clear.

According to the Groundwork's account of F1a, a maxim is to be re-jected if it can neither be "conceived a universal law of nature without contradiction" nor willed to 'be raised to the universality of a law of nature without the will contradicting itself'. It is fairly obvious that the contradiction in conception test determines 'possibility' ac-cording to our first criterion. It is less clear, but more interesting to show that the contradiction in will test is a version (variant) of the second. Our next task will be to make the case for both.

There are two extremely plausible accounts in the literature of the contradiction in conception test: one is to be found in a short article by Allen Wood ("Kant on False Promises"), the other in the recent book by Onora Nell (Acting on Principle). (John Rawls, in lectures on Kant's ethics, has offered an account rather close to Nell's; I will refer to it when Rawls' formulations of central points seem perspicuous.) I will call them the Wood and the Nell versions respectively. I will sketch each briefly and say why, although there is much that is attractive in the Nell version, I prefer Wood's as closer to Kant's intentions. I will not be concerned in any extensive way with interpretive issues here as I do not have anything new to say about how to construe the workings of the contradiction in conception test. My main purpose in discussing this test will be to show how it fits into the conception of F1a I have been sketching.

Both Rawls and Nell employ a useful technical term: the universal-ized typified counterpart (UTC) of a maxim.[28] It is the maxim univer-salized and cast in the form of a law of nature. If my maxim is 'To make a false promise when that will serve my purposes', the UTC of that maxim is 'Everyone <u>will</u> make false promises when that serves their purposes'. (The notion of a 'type' is drawn from the "Typic" of the second Critique.) They interpret F1a as instructing the agent to regard the UTC of his maxim (M) as arising through his willing of M; he is then to ask himself whether he can consistently intend the UTC to hold as a law of nature of a world to which he belongs and in which he intends to make a false promise--i.e., to act according to his maxim. The argument, according to Nell, proceeds as follows:

> In promising falsely he /the agent/ intends the normal,
> predictable result of successfully doing the act--success-
> ful deception. He intends there to be a level of general
> confidence which will lead to his promise being believed.
> But if the UTC were a law of nature, then...successful de-
> ception would be an increasingly unlikely result of false
> promising, since public confidence would diminish and
> eventually vanish. The predictable result of the UTC of
> this maxim being a law of nature in the system of nature
> to which men belong would be that there would be no
> means by which the agent could succeed in acting on his
> maxim.[29]

Or, as Rawls puts it, there is a contradiction between two intentions: the intention expressed in the UTC becoming a law of nature through the agent's willing (Rawls calls it the "legislative intention") and the agent's personal intention (expressed in his maxim). That is, the contradiction in conception test determines whether there is a contradiction between an angent's personal and his legislative intention. A maxim of false promising would be ruled out because it would not be possible to make a false promise in a world in which the UTC of a maxim of false promising were a law of nature. In the world of the agent's legislative intention he would know that people would not take his promise seriously (given the forseeable consequences of the UTC as a law

of nature), although in the world of his personal intention he does will

that his promise be taken seriously.

The appeal of Wood's account is that it focuses on the idea of a

maxim that cannot be conceived as a law of nature without contradiction:

the idea of a contradiction in conception. Wood begins by recognizing

that in the crucial passage of Kant's exposition of the false promising

example two tests are suggested:

> For the universality of a law that every one believing
> himself to be in need can make any promise he pleases with
> the intention not to keep it would make promising, and the
> very purpose of promising, itself impossible, since no one
> would believe he was being promised anything, but would
> laugh at utterances of this kind as empty shams. (G 90;
> 422)

He remarks that the line of argument the passage suggests, especially

toward the end, is the one taken up in the Nell version. But, he goes

on to argue, this is not the sort of argument Kant later indicates the

promising example was to demonstrate: i.e., a maxim which could not be

conceived or thought a universal law without contradiction. The presence

of this argument in the example is indicated by Kant's saying that two

things (promising and the purpose of promising), not just one, would be

impossible if the UTC of a false promising maxim were made a law of

nature. Wood explains this feature of the argument as follows:

> I tend to think it was because he /Kant/ was presenting
> simultaneously two arguments: (1) that M could not be
> willed to be a universal law of nature because to do so
> would be to defeat one's own purpose in adopting M, and
> (2) that M could not be thought as a universal law of na-
> ture without contradiction, because the conception of
> promising contained in M itself would involve a contra-
> diction if M were assumed to be a universal law of nature.[30]

Wood is not interested in why Kant might have done this, but I think the answer can be supplied by recalling two related facts: for practical purposes of judgment the contradiction in conception test is not necessary, the contradiction in will test being sufficient—no maxim which failed the contradiction in conception test could pass the contradiction in will test. This fact emerges in the Typic of the second Critique, where Kant wants to show how close to the ordinary WIEDT test of actions the Categorical Imperative is as a principle of moral judgment. There he gives one single principle of judgment, the Typic: "Ask yourself whether if the action you propose should take place by a law of nature of which you yourself were a part, you could regard it as possible through your will" (CrPrR 72;70). It is not surprising, then, that both tests appear in the false promising example as both tests apply. We will consider later on why, if this is so, the contradiction in conception test is introduced at all.[31]

Wood's reconstruction of the false promising argument as a version of the contradiction in conception test works with a modification of the maxim Kant presents in the example. Kant's maxim is: "Whenever I believe myself short of money, I will borrow money and promise to pay it back, though I know this will never be done." Wood's revision is this: "Whenever I find it necessary to borrow money, I will promise to repay it, although I shall not repay it unless it should be to my advantage."[32] The point of the revision is to introduce into the maxim of false promising (M) the idea of the systematic falsification of the intention naturally expressed in making a promise (see 163n). Wood argues (correctly) that such a revision is necessary if it is to be shown that

promising (or a particular kind of promising) would not be possible were
M a universal law of nature.[33] Taking the revised M, Wood reconstructs
Kant's argument:

> If M were a universal law of nature, then whenever anyone
> made a promise to repay a loan, he would have the inten-
> tion of doing so only if it were to his advantage. To
> make a promise to repay a loan, however, is to express the
> intention to repay the loan even if it were to one's ad-
> vantage not to repay it. But it is impossible in this
> system of nature for any promise to repay a loan to ex-
> press this intention, since, as a universal law of nature,
> whenever anyone makes a promise to repay a loan, he has a
> different intention. Therefore, if M is assumed to be a
> universal law of nature, it is impossible to make a pro-
> mise to repay a loan. But since M itself involves making
> promises to repay loans under certain circumstances, M
> itself is no longer compatible with the system of nature
> and therefore cannot even be thought as a universal law of
> nature.[34]

The force of this is that if M itself is not possible in a world in
which the UTC of M is a law of nature then M cannot be thought or conceived a universal law of nature without contradiction. That is, the
conception of promising contained in M would involve a contradiction if
M were assumed to be a universal law of nature. In Kant's words, "this
maxim can never rank as a universal law of nature and be self-consistent,
but must necessarily contradict itself" (G 90;422).

The Wood argument seems to me preferable. Although the Nell version does generate a contradiction (between two intentions), it does not
explain why Kant says M cannot be conceived a universal law of nature
without contradiction. The Wood explains this straightforwardly: when
you try to conceive M as a universal law you imagine a world in which
the UTC of M is a law but M itself is not possible, etc. It is possible
that the intuition behind the Nell version is closer to Wood than it

appears to be. The emphasis on the foreseeable consequences of everyone behaving a certain way may mask a contradiction in conception argument: if we interpret the maxim as including a statement of the behavior the agent deems appropriate and consistent with the concepts he employs, the UTC of the maxim in effect universalizes the behavior as well (it follows according to a law of human nature); but that behavior (if universal) would be a sign of a different concept of promising, one incompatible with the concept contained in the original maxim. To argue that this is equivalent to the Wood, indeed to give more careful argument for the Wood account, would lead us far afield into difficult questions concerning logical relations between concepts and related behavior. Since we are not trying to argue for Kant's position but rather to understand what sort of argument he might have intended, the sketch for an argument we have drawn from Wood should prove sufficient. (For much of what will be said about this and related examples, either the Wood or the Nell versions of the argument can be used, although I shall continue working with the Wood.)

Other examples Kant discusses unhappily leave the issue between the Wood and the Nell accounts undecided. In the second Critique Kant's example of giving testimony (CrPrR 45;44) gives strong support to Wood. (This is hardly surprising since Wood credits the example as the source of his interpretation of the Groundwork example of false promising.)

> When the maxim according to which I intend to give testi-
> mony is tested by practical reason, I always inquire into
> what it should be if it were to hold as a universal law of
> nature. It is obvious enough that, in this way of looking
> at it, it would oblige everyone to truthfulness. For it
> cannot hold as a universal law of nature that an assertion
> should have the force of evidence and yet be intentionally
> false. (emphasis added)

The idea here being that the concept of testimony includes the concept of an assertion that has the force of evidence—i.e., that what is asserted is asserted <u>as true</u>. Thus a maxim of false testimony, or lying, when considered as a possible universal law of nature, cannot be conceived without contradiction: the concept of testimony that would obtain were the UTC of the false testimony maxim a law of nature would not include the concept of an assertion intended to be true; but then the original maxim, in which the concept of testimony is employed in its usual sense, would not be possible. As Wood notes, it is not clear how one would show conclusively that Kant's thesis is correct. However, the claim that "it is impossible for an assertion to be a part of a system of nature one of whose laws prevents anyone asserting it from believing what he is supposed to be asserting"[35] is extremely plausible and a fair reading of the argument in the testimony example. But the difficulties of making this case aside, what is clear in this example is that Kant is <u>not</u> arguing in terms of an agent's purposes in giving testimony—unless, again, we treat the purpose of the agent to be that his words communicate their ordinary meaning.

An earlier example in the second Critique, however, leans toward the Nell interpretation. The question is asked whether I could

> make the law that every man is allowed to deny a deposit
> has been made when no one can prove the contrary. I imme-
> diately realize that taking such a principle as a law
> would annihilate itself, because its result would be that
> no one would make a deposit. (CrPrR 27;28)

The most plausible reading of this argument is that in the world of the UTC of my maxim (the world of my legislative intention, in Rawls' phrase) I would not be able to have my personal intention, since in that world 'no one would make a deposit'. That is, there would be a contradiction between my legislative and my personal intentions. While no doubt one could give a reading of this example to fit the Wood model—e.g. by recasting it as a kind of lying—there is no clear textual justification for doing so.[36] Moreover, the structure of this example fits the testing procedure of the second Critique found in the single principle of the Typic. As was suggested earlier (p. 221) this is in effect the contradiction in will test (for short: the CW test), in itself adequate to test all maxims, since no maxim which fails the contradiction in conception test (for short: the CC test) can pass the CW test.[37] If the Typic is a version of the CW test, and since it is the dominant characterization of the Categorical Imperative as a principle of moral judgment in the second Critique, it would not be surprising to find in it an example which fits the CW pattern of argument. The presence of the Typic, therefore, as the rule of judgment in the second Critique suggests that the deposit example argument is insufficient for deciding against the Wood account.

(One disquieting feature of the Nell version of the CC test should be mentioned. In looking for a strict contradiction between two intentions Nell suggests that in intending to do some act one intends the "normal and predictable results" of one's act. This modification of intention has striking results when an agent 'intends' the UTC of his maxim as a law of nature. E.g., if it would be a normal and predictable result of everyone's making deceitful promises that promises ceased to be believed, then an agent would have intended that. The contradiction with the intention in the deceitful promise maxim is obvious. The

difficulty here is that while it makes sense to say an agent intends the
consequences of his action (the intended consequences we might say), pace
the doctrine of double effect, we need to leave room for the foreseen
but unintended consequences of an action. And, it is far from clear how
"the requirement that one intend the normal and predictable results of
one's act might...loosely, but convincingly, be defended as analytic of
the notion of rationality."[38] I do not take this objection as decisive
against (something like) the Nell version of the CC test because if the
pressure for a quasi-logical contradiction is withdrawn, as it seems to
be on Rawls' account (see p. 219), then we have a satisfactory version
of this sort of CC test based on a much looser conception of contradiction between legislative and personal intention.)

Wherever one places the contradiction in the contradiction in conception test--in the conception or between two intentions--the contradiction emerges from the conception of, e.g., promising in the world of the
UTC of the false promising maxim. Following the direction of the Wood
account, we are to try to imagine a world in which the maxim of false
promising holds as a law of nature--where by a law of nature the making
of a promise cannot express its ordinary intention. We thereby discover
that our maxim cannot serve as a universal law of nature-- the concept
of promising in our maxim is such that it is not compatible with a system of nature in which promises cannot express their ordinary meaning.
In the terms we developed earlier, such a maxim is not possible as a
universal law of nature--'we encounter some logical difficulty in imagining M as a law/principle governing the wills of all human beings'.
If ordinary constraints of rationality apply to rational willing, a

rational being would also be unable to <u>will</u> such a maxim a universal law
of nature without his will contradicting itself: he would be willing
both that M should be the case and the conditions in which M would be
impossible. (We will consider shortly and in detail what a contradiction in will amounts to; the notion is introduced now simply to show
roughly that the account we have been giving fits the general requirements we have set out.)

Before turning to the CW test, it is worth noting briefly that the
CC test as Wood reads it <u>can</u> be applied to maxims other than the false-
promising and testimony maxims we have considered. Let us take a maxim
of stealing: 'To take the property of others if that is to my advantage'.[39] If this maxim were made a universal law of nature, one might
argue that in the world of its UTC the concept of property in the maxim
would not be possible: if the concept here involves something like a
property <u>right</u> which implies (other things equal) that everyone has an
obligation not to take what someone has a property right in. Such a
concept of property would simply not make sense in a world in which
everyone by a <u>law of nature</u> took what they needed. This, of course, is
not an argument, but just a sketch of the direction an argument would
go. For example, to get a contradiction in conception (to show that the
maxim in question cannot be 'conceived' or 'thought' a universal law of
nature without contradiction) we would have to expand the original maxim
to show that the 'taking' proposed in the maxim was a taking <u>for my own
property</u>, so that my maxim would not be possible in a world in which the
UTC of the maxim is a law of nature, etc. If the concept of 'taking' in
my maxim is not a concept of 'taking as property', but say, 'taking for

provisional use', it is not clear how the contradiction in conception
test will rule. We do not need to resolve such troublesome cases to see
that this version of the CC test could in principle be applied to a
variety of cases. All that I have been trying to establish in this section is: a) what sort of test the contradiction in conception test is
supposed to be, b) the plausibility of the Wood account of the test, and
c) given that account, that the contradiction in conception test does
test maxims for their 'possibility' as laws of nature, thus corroborat-
ing our discussion of the point of F1a. We will postpone discussing
what bearing a 'contradiction in conception' has on the morality of a
given act or maxim; what was needed here was just an account of a formal
criterion: that a maxim is not possible as a universal law of nature if
"the maxim cannot even be conceived as a universal law of nature without
contradiction."

The contradiction in will test has rarely aroused the interest it
deserves. The cause of this disregard, I believe, resides in the difficulty many critics have found in eliciting even a plausible sounding
argument from the examples in the Groundwork (talents and beneficence).
To the extent that an argument has been perceived, it has most often
been characterized as rather like Hare's "golden-rule" test, and subjected to criticism that the Hare test has collected, criticism Kant's
theory bears less well given his claim that the Categorical Imperative
generates normative results for, at least, all persons, if not all
rational beings. What I find striking in the CW test is not the account
of the argument (which is plausible), but the appeal made in the derivation of duties under the CW test to general features of human existence.

In what follows I will try to describe and render plausible the CW test
as it is found in the talents and beneficence examples of the Groundwork.
We will try to see what it is about certain maxims that leads Kant to
say that although it is possible for them to be conceived as universal
laws of nature without contradiction, "it is still impossible to will
that their maxim should be raised to the universality of a law of nature,
because such a will would contradict itself."[40] Moreover, I will show
that the CW test is the second criterion of 'possibility' introduced
earlier (p. 217) in that it shows a maxim could not be a 'possible' law
by showing that when the maxim is imagined as a law of (human) nature it
is not consistent with other given laws of rational willing. For the
sake of clarity, I will begin with the fourth example: beneficence.

What Kant would show in the fourth example is that the adoption of
an end of never helping anyone, gives an agent a maxim, 'To give help to
no one', which can be conceived a universal law of nature without contradiction, but which cannot be willed such a law without the will contradicting itself:

> although it is possible that a universal law of nature
> could subsist in harmony with this maxim, yet it is impos-
> sible to will that such a principle should hold everywhere
> as a law of nature. For a will which decided in this way
> would be in conflict with itself, since many a situation
> might arise in which the man needed love and sympathy from
> others and in which, by such a law of nature sprung from
> his own will, he would rob himself of all hope of the help
> he wants for himself. (G 91;423)

Reasonable interpretations of this argument[41] try to show that the willing of the maxim of non-beneficence as a law of nature yields a contradiction by arguing that in the world which would arise through the UTC
of the maxim, an agent would find that he wants help and won't be able

to get it. That is, he will want help and not be able to get it <u>because</u>
<u>of</u> <u>what</u> <u>he</u> <u>has</u> <u>willed</u>: the UTC of his maxim of non-beneficence. Nell,
for example, argues that the contradiction arises because as a rational
being an agent must will the necessary means for his ends, and "if I
will whatever means are needed to achieve whatever ends I may have, then
I must will that, should I be unable to achieve my ends by unaided
efforts, I should be given assistance." "I must will to be helped if in
need."[42] Nell concludes:

> The contradiction in will is a contradiction between a
> maxim which any agent must have to be rational, and the
> UTC of the proposed maxim of neglecting some things needed
> to help any other in need.[43]

While I am in agreement with the general line of argument taken by Nell:
that the contradiction is derived from the fact that we may have needs
we cannot meet, projects we are unable to pursue, unaided, and that the
kind of rationality expressed by the Hypothetical Imperative directs us
to find the help we need, this intuition is neither captured nor explored
in Nell's version of a "maxim which any agent must have to be rational."
<u>That</u> maxim is "To seek help when I need it", and there is no contradic-
tion to be generated between <u>it</u> and the UTC of the proposed maxim of
non-beneficence: 'To do nothing to help anyone'.[44] Nell thinks a contradiction emerges because she reads the relevant maxim of rationality
as "To <u>get</u> help (or be given assistance) when I need it", but that
cannot be a maxim of <u>my</u> action. What might do the job is a general
policy maxim of omission stating an agent's intention not to act in ways
such that he will be prevented from getting what help he needs and wants.
Where this maxim fits in and how it plays a role in establishing the

contradiction can be shown only if we go back to the general structure of F1a.

According to F1a, we are to imagine our willing of a maxim to issue in that maxim's becoming a law of (human) nature--a nature in which we are then to imagine ourselves acting. Where is the contradiction in will following from the adoption of a maxim of non-beneficence? Kant says, that an agent in the world in which the UTC of his maxim was a law might find himself in need, but that by "a law of nature sprung from his own will he would rob himself of all hope of the help he wants for himself." The operative clause here is "by a law of nature <u>sprung</u> from <u>his own will</u>"--that is the source of the contradiction. When an agent adopts an end, the Hypothetical Imperative requires of him that he adopt adequate means (as and if they are available) for the realization of his end. Surely there is included in the idea of willing the means that are indispensably necessary and in your power (G 85;417) a negative requirement that (ceteris paribus) you refrain from acts the (known) effect of which will be to make impossible your successfully reaching your end. Normally, the help others may give or withhold is not in our power; it is not the sort of thing we can will or do. In the world of F1a, however, <u>our</u> maxim of non-beneficence becomes--<u>through our will</u>--a law of nature for all human beings. That is, by a law of nature "sprung from the agent's own will", no person is able to come to the aid of another. Were we able, by our willing, to determine the will of others,[45] it would be irrational of us to will a world in which it would be impossible to be helped when in need.

If this is the claim we must ask, <u>Why</u> would it be irrational? or,

Just where is the contradiction in willing? Either it would be irrational because we necessarily have a general maxim (M1) 'Not to prevent
others bringing aid when we need/want it', and a will which had that
maxim could not also and simultaneously <u>will</u> the UTC of a maxim of non-
beneficence ("No one will/can help anyone") as a law of nature without
willing in an obviously contradictory manner, <u>or</u>, it is necessarily the
case that sometime or other an agent will need help and will <u>then</u>, if
rational, have a maxim (M2) 'Not to prevent (and indeed to encourage) the
help I now need' which will be in contradiction with his willing the UTC
of his maxim of non-beneficence as a law of nature. The latter version
of the CW has two clear problems: the delay in the occurrence of the
supposed contradiction, and the status of the claim that everyone will
at some time need <u>and</u> want (if rational) help. Even if it were arguable
that everyone will at some time need help, and if rational want it (and
in wanting it adopt a maxim of at least not preventing it, if not a
maxim of seeking it), there is no argument to a contradiction in will
arising from the willing of the UTC of the maxim of non-beneficence.
One might try to argue for a contradiction from the idea that a rational
(human) agent knows he may at some time need and want help; but even if
it is a condition of human rationality to know this, there is no contradiction in will (from the willing of the UTC of the maxim of non-beneficence) unless such knowledge is the basis for adopting a general maxim
of 'Not doing what will prevent help being available when needed'. But
this, of course, is just the first version of the argument: given the
general maxim, a contradiction in will <u>does</u> occur <u>with</u> the willing of
the UTC of the maxim of non-beneficence.[46] What remains is the question

of the supposed necessity of an agent's having the general policy maxim M1: "a maxim which any human agent must have to be rational".

Since it is conceivable that there be worlds in which no one is able to come to the aid of anyone else (Kant says the maxim of non-beneficence passes the CC test), and in such a world surely an agent would not be irrational for not adopting a maxim like M1 (there is no possible help in that world to avoid preventing), how, or in what sense, would it be irrational for a human agent to determine in _this_ world that he will not seek nor avoid preventing help being available when needed?

Wolff proposes a slightly different version of this question:

> Suppose an individual adopts as his policy /maxim/ never to set for himself an end whose achievement appears to require the cooperation of others and to forswear any ends he has adopted as soon as it turns out that such cooperation is needed. Under these circumstances, he could consistently will that his maxim of selfishness should be a universal law of nature, for he could be certain a priori that he would never find himself willing an end which that natural law obstructed.[47]

Let us, with Wolff, call such an individual a Stoic. Wolff thinks the Stoic's proposal provides a decisive argument against the CW test as applied to the maxim of non-beneficence--what Wolff calls a maxim of selfishness. And it will, unless it can be shown that the Stoic _cannot_ adopt such a policy and that he _must_ (in some sense) want help.

Suppose we consider the Stoic's end of being a Stoic, an end which requires of him that he not want help. Not, of course, that he not _need_ help; that may well be outside what he can do. But that _if_ he _does_ need help he will not for that want it. What is needed here is a slightly artificial sense of 'want' such that if I want help it would follow that if by my willing I could get someone to help me, I would so will (other things equal, to be sure). The Stoic's position is that he will never want help in this sense.[48] If this is possible then he will encounter nothing contradictory in willing that no one be able to help anyone else. To shorten the argument let us sharpen the Stoic's position to bring it into line with the conditions that obtain under F1a--let us include in the notion of his not wanting help that he also would not accept it. This is a natural enough extrapolation from our sense of wanting: accepting help is just the case where there is something you can will and do to get another's help--i.e., accept an offer. And if someone accepts help we will say he also wants it. What can be shown is that the Stoic cannot rationally forfeit accepting all help--that he cannot prevent his wanting help--which is what he must be able to do in all cases to support the claim that he can be certain a priori that he will never find himself willing an end which the natural law arising from his maxim of non-beneficence obstructed.

For purposes of argument we will characterize the Stoic's end qua Stoic as 'not to want help even if in need'. Now suppose the Stoic needs help in promoting his end of being a Stoic (his will is weakening and moral support would help). Help is offered. If he does not accept help he will not do what he must to maintain his end of not wanting (or accepting) help. And if he does not take the means to support his end, he will want (and ought to accept) help. If he does take the available means to his end, he accepts help. But then he wants help, which is what he claimed would never be the case. Nor, of course, can he abandon his end; that is, not without ceasing to be a Stoic. Thus the Stoic cannot be certain a priori that he will never find himself willing an end which the natural law arising from his maxim of non-beneficence obstructed. That is, given this fact about what he may need, the Stoic, like the rest of us, is constrained by the Hypothetical Imperative to adopt a general maxim of 'Not doing what will prevent help being available when wanted', and so would incur a contradiction in will with his willing the UTC of a maxim of non-beneficence a law of nature.

The force of the Stoic objection comes from the appearance that all that separates him from us is his willingness to forego ends (e.g. his own continued existence when that requires the help of others) which we could (or would) not. It is not so much that he might have escaped having an obligation the rest of us had, but that a maxim obligatory for us would not have been obligatory for the Stoic because of a subjective difference in will. If that were the case, the logic of the CW test would be undermined: it could not test for a maxim's conformity to the Categorical Imperative. With this, I think we can see the point of the 'refutation' of the Stoic's position. The refutation might have seemed rather slim—a cheap shot⁀ there's just this one end that the Stoic cannot give up (and maintain his Stoicism) and the argument turns on the possibility (however remote) that he might need help in achieving this end (without which his position is vulnerable to the argument of the CW test) and then is unable, if rational, to avoid wanting help, or accepting it if offered. The very narrowness of the grounds of the refutation shows its point. It is not that it is likely that the Stoic will have ends for the sake of which rationality requires that he accept (or want) help, for we will grant that if the question were one of risk, it might well be rational for him to risk living in a world where no one was able to bring aid. The point is rather that the Stoic is unable to escape an essential and necessary condition of human rationality: that we are what Kant calls 'dependent beings', always potentially vulnerable to having ends which we will not be able to satisfy independently of help from others, ends which we cannot forswear. It is not the frequency of this condition that is at issue, but the inescapability of the condition of will that makes its occurrence possible. The refutation of the Stoic's position was to show that he is as subject to this condition as the rest of us. It is this necessary feature of human existence, this condition of human rationality and action, that acts as a constraint on what one can rationally will (or will without contradiction). It is this condition of human volition that makes it impossible for any person to will (without contradiction) a maxim of non-beneficence as a universal law of nature because a person cannot (logically cannot) guard against the eventuality of his needing help, which in the world he would will in virtue of his maxim of non-beneficence he would necessarily be denied. Through the agent's own willing he would prevent his getting the help he must also will that he not prevent himself from having when he wants it.

To put this result another way, the maxim of non-beneficence is not a possible law/principle of human willing because it is shown to be incompatible with the requirements of the Hypothetical Imperative—a 'known' principle of rational willing. It is not possible that they both be laws of willing—human willing. This last is important to note; it is not clear whether the maxim of non-beneficence is also not possible for all rational beings—for example, beings who were monads or who were simply self-sufficient. Since the argument to show that we have a duty to adopt a maxim of beneficence ('To do some of what is needed to help others') depends on the fact that we are the kind of rational being that may always come to need and want the help of others, the argument would not hold for rational beings who were not of the same kind. On the other hand, it does not follow from this that such rational beings would not have an obligation to help other beings who could be helped. The argument simply does not apply—which is to be expected given that the domain of applicability of F1a is restricted to human beings.

The argument of the talents example makes similar use of the 'conditions of human rationality'. Here I think the Nell reconstruction of the argument is again plausible, but not really adequate:

> Rational beings have ends; they also will some sufficient means to these ends, and so the development of some talents is a part of the means to ends of any sort. So rational agents must make it an end to develop at least some of their own talents.[49]

A rational agent, then, who willed 'To neglect everything needed in order to develop my talents' as a universal law of nature (its UTC, that is) would have willed in a contradictory manner. This following Kant: "For as a rational being he necessarily wills that all his powers should be developed, since they serve him and are given him for all sorts of ends" (G 90;423).

The standard sort of objection to this argument is suggested in Kant's exposition of the talents example: suppose you lived in the South Sea Islands, had few needs, and sufficient 'talents' already developed to act for any end you would adopt. In that case, why wouldn't it be rational for you to will the non-development of your talents? Why couldn't you, without your will contradicting itself, will the UTC of a

maxim of neglecting talents as a universal law of nature? The answer
suggested by the example in the Groundwork and taken up by Nell is that
'as a rational being you necessarily will the development of your
talents'. But since it is obviously possible for a human being to will
the non-development of his talents, this can only mean that if an agent
were wholly rational (or determined by the rational part), then he would
necessarily will the development of his talents. A contradiction in
will, on this model, would have to be between the maxim of the will
"from the point of view of a will wholly in accord with reason" and the
UTC of the agent's maxim. (As Nell points out, on this view there would
be a contradiction as well with the agent's original maxim.)[50] Apart
from the fact that this does not yield a contradiction in willing, this
construction just begs the question of what a will wholly in accord with
reason would will. It is one thing to say that a perfectly rational
will would will in accordance with the principle of the Hypothetical Imperative (for that is said to be analytic of the concept of 'willing an
end'); it is quite another to offer as a substantive principle just the
principle the argument is to show an agent ought (if rational) to will.

If, however, we reject this view of the example's argument, it is
not clear where we should go to reconstruct it adequately. At one time
I thought the argument had to have the sort of structure Nell suggests,
and I took as the motivating idea the view that in so far as one is a
rational being, one in some sense wants to express that rationality as
fully as possible. Since developing talents facilitates such expression,
it would on this account be irrational to will the implanation of an
'instinct' preventing such development. Although I do think it is part

of Kant's view that moral action is expressive of rationality, as an argument for the talents example it begs that question. What has to be shown is _that_ it is irrational not to want to develop one's talents, and this neither my nor Nell's argument succeeds in doing.

One other strategy would be to consider the CW test as operating a-temporally: that is, it would have the agent suppose that in adopting his maxim he would create a world in which he would never have been able to develop talents of any sort. This would surely be irrational in that it would prevent him from enjoying talents already developed and needed for various ends. But the a-temporal device is artificial, and, more importantly, fails to speak to the case of an agent who chooses at some point in his life to rest on his talents.

In the _Doctrine of Virtue_ Kant remarks of someone who decides his talents are sufficient to his needs and who would adopt a maxim of neglect of talents:

> Even supposing that the native scope of his powers is sufficient for his natural needs, his reason must first show him, by principles, that this meager scope of his powers is _sufficient_. (DV 111;444)

It seems fair to read this passage as saying that in so far as an agent is rational he must demonstrate the sufficiency of his capacities to his needs such that _if_ he determined they were _not_ sufficient, he would then decide to develop them. What this suggests (and it can only be a suggestion) is that to investigate the sufficiency of one's talents entails (if the agent is rational) that one be prepared to find them not sufficient—that one have a maxim of the form, 'To develop the talents I discover I need' as a general policy maxim partially guiding the investigation.

This insight leads us to argue the talents example in rather strict parallel to the beneficence example: In so far as it is true of us that we often have and may always will ends and purposes to which our present capacities/talents are inadequate, then it will be irrational for us to will the non-development of our talents: we cannot will that a law of nature obtain according to which we <u>could</u> <u>not</u> develop talents without our will contradicting itself. This is so, again, because given the conditions of rationality that obtain for any human agent--that his talents are always incomplete with respect to possible ends (a further characterization of a human being's <u>dependency</u>, as Kant calls it)-- rationality dictates that he be <u>prepared</u> to develop talents when that is what is necessary to advance an end. Here too, then, what we have called 'the conditions of human rationality' act as a constraint on what a human agent can <u>rationally</u> will.[51]

In both the talents and beneficence examples the contradiction in will was found between the UTC of the agent's maxim, willed by him as a universal law of nature, and a general maxim which the Hypothetical Imperative requires an agent to adopt in response to the 'conditions of human rationality'. To avoid any possible confusion, it should be noted explicitly that the employment of the Hypothetical Imperative <u>in</u> the CW test does not in any way undermine the claim that the Categorical Imperative (through F1a) shows some maxims to be irrational which have already satisfied the Hypothetical Imperative: it is not <u>prudentially</u> irrational to have either a maxim of neglect of one's talents or a maxim of non-beneficence. What the agent is shown in the fiction of the CW test is that he will be prevented from having--by his own willing--what he <u>also</u>

wills that he not prevent himself from having.[52] We might still worry
that F1a is compromised by relying on the Hypothetical Imperative in the
sense that the CW argument depends on what an agent wants or could come
to need. But the very statement of this worry indicates why it is
groundless, for it is not what an agent in fact wants that enters the
argument, but what the agent would rationally want given the conditions
of human rationality. The Hypothetical Imperative is present in the
argument to show that a maxim is not possible as a law of human willing
if such a maxim when cast as a universal law of willing is not compatible with a known law (or the dictates of a known law) of willing (i.e.,
the Hypothetical Imperative) as it applies to the human will. The
serious source of concern in this argument should not be the Hypothetical Imperative, but the use of the so-called 'conditions of human
rationality'.

Let us be clear about the nature of that concern. It is surely not
that Kant employs the wrong set of conditions—i.e., the form of the argument is correct but Kant is simply mistaken about the nature of human
rationality. Nor, I think, is the concern appropriately directed at the
claim that there are any such conditions, for it is far from implausible
to claim (although how one would argue this is not clear) that part of
what it is to be a human being is to be, e.g., mortal, vulnerable, not
self-sufficient; we are beings for whom happiness is "a problem imposed
on us by our finite nature as a being of needs" (CrPrR 24;25); we set,
adopt, form conceptions of ends, and do so without knowing that we will
be able to promote the ends we give ourselves. It is not clear in what
way one could even try to dispute the claim that these are some of the

conditions that constrain and affect the actions and willings of human beings. The objection to their employment in arguments designed to show in what respects maxims contrary to duty violate the canon of rationality set by the Categorical Imperative can only be that they are 'subjective'-- not features we possess simply in virtue of our being rational. But if this is the worry, it is based on a misunderstanding of the role of F1a as a principle of judgment through which the Categorical Imperative is to be applied by human beings. Early in chapter two of the Groundwork Kant explains the relevant distinction:

> We can, if we like, distinguish pure moral philosophy (metaphysics) from applied (applied, that is, to human nature)--just as pure mathematics is distinguished from applied mathematics and pure logic from applied logic. By this terminology we are at once reminded that moral principles are not grounded on the peculiarities of human nature, but must be established a priori by themselves; and yet that from such principles it must be possible to derive practical rules for human nature as well, just as it is for every kind of rational nature. (G 78n;410n) (emphasis added)53

If, as I have assumed throughout this section, F1a is not, strictly speaking, a formulation of the Categorical Imperative, but a principle of judgment designed to demonstrate for human beings which of their maxims are contrary to duty, then it should not be either surprising or a source of concern to find features definitive of human nature in the procedure of application of this principle of human judgment. Moreover, when we realize that F1a cannot and is not intended to serve as the determining ground of the will (in acting according to the moral law), whatever the status of the 'conditions of human rationality', they do not introduce the kind of subjectivity of volition precluded by the Categorical Imperative. We see this clearly in the discussion of the application of the principle of the Typic:

> Now everyone knows very well that if he secretly permits
> himself to deceive, it does not follow that everyone else
> will do so, or that if, unnoticed by others, he is lacking
> in compassion, it does not mean that everyone else will
> immediately take the same attitude toward him. This com-
> parison of the maxims of his actions with a universal
> natural law, therefore, is not the determining ground of
> his will. But such a law is still the type for the esti-
> mation of maxims according to moral principles. If the
> maxim of action is not so constituted as to stand the test
> of being made the form of a natural law in general, it is
> morally impossible /though it may still be possible in
> nature/.... We are therefore allowed to use the nature of
> the sensuous world as the type of an intelligible nature,
> so long as we do not carry over the latter intuitions and
> what depends on them but only apply it to the form of law-
> fulness in general.... For laws as such are all equiva-
> lent, regardless of whence they derive their determining
> ground. (CrPrR 72-3;70-71) (emphasis added)

Given all of this we might ask why do the 'conditions of rationality' not appear in the CC test as well? On the Nell version of the CC
test they do; they enter into the projection of the consequences of the
UTC of a maxim becoming a universal law of nature. On the Wood account,
they can be seen, for example, in the performative logic of promising
utterances. Of course, the Wood argument would apply to any community
of rational beings who had the same concept of promising as we do, but
then, the argument against the maxim of non-beneficence would work for
any dependent rational being with ends.

What we see here is the working out of "applied" moral philosophy.
The Categorical Imperative presents a condition of pure practical rationality. It is, in Kant's over-worked but little understood phrase, a
form of rationality: a form which will get its content, its "material",
from the maxims of different "kinds" of rational beings. We see why the
variation is by 'kinds' and not by individuals most clearly in the

argument falling under the CW test which (as we have reconstructed it) shows <u>that</u> <u>there</u> <u>are</u> conditions of rationality for human beings that do not depend on whether some particular agent happens to have adopted a particular subjective end, etc.

F1a not only provides a method of judgment for maxims, it shows maxims to be contrary to duty in a way that reflects the Categorical Imperative's claim to be a principle of pure practical rationality. Let us interpret the two tests of F1a in the light of what they show about the rationality of an agent's maxim. What the agent is shown when his maxim fails the CC test is that the <u>rationality</u> of his proposed action/ maxim is contingent on the fact that others do not act as the agent intends to act. That is, a condition of the <u>rationality</u> of the proposed deceitful-promise maxim is the fact that there is a practice of promising- that others (characteristically) do make promises that are not deceitful. An agent discovers through applying the CC test to his maxim that the rationality of his proposed project is not dependent merely on his selection of a causally efficacious 'means'--or, more precisely, that what he takes to be the criteria for adequate means are incomplete; the means, for example, of employing a deceitful-promise to repay in order to borrow money would not satisfy the Hypothetical Imperative in a world in which promises would not or could not be believed--that is, in the world in which the UTC of the deceitful-promise maxim was a law of nature. The actions of others are therefore conditions for <u>and</u> <u>con-</u> <u>straints</u> <u>on</u> what is rational for a human agent. The CC test shows an agent that the rationality of his calculation of means includes an assessment of what other agents characteristically do, and then rules out maxims which depend for their rationality on others not acting in the manner proposed. One may not act in a way that requires for its 'rationality' that others act differently. This is part of the sense of rationality introduced by the concept of a categorical imperative—a concept of rationality different from and of a higher order than the concept of rationality provided by the Hypothetical Imperative.

A similar interpretation of the CW test gives us another part of the conception of rationality generated by F1a. If through the CC test I discover that for some maxims contrary to duty their rationality depends on others not acting in the same way, through the CW test I discover that my proposed maxim (if it is contrary to duty) is one that I cannot <u>rationally</u> will/want everyone (including myself) to act on.[54] That is, for a contrary to duty maxim M, it shows that it is a general condition of the exercise of my rationality[55]—of my will—that everyone not act on M.

In short, what the tests under F1a show is that the nature of human rationality (in general and with regard to particular actions) is not strictly an individual matter. They argue for a logical interdependence of agents—logical in that it follows from the 'logic' or nature of a human rational will—which is to act as a constraint on the maxims of individuals. The full expression of this idea is to be found in Kant's doctrine of the Kingdom of Ends.

We have now set out the procedures of judgment the contradiction in conception and the contradiction in will tests provide. The CC test asks of a maxim whether it can, without contradiction, be raised to the status of a law of willing; the CW test asks of a maxim which poses no conceptual problem as a universal law of willing whether it is compatible, as such a law, with the Hypothetical Imperative--a _known_ law of human willing. The procedure of imaginative willing in the CW test uses only hypothetical or prudential rationality in its argument to show some maxims (some ends that agents would adopt) are contrary to duty--i.e., contrary to categorical or moral rationality. Categorical rationality is introduced and explicated through the _structure_ of the tests; the only form of rationality appealed to in the _argument_ is hypothetical, so no questions about the appeal to 'rational willing' are begged. Categorical rationality emerges as a formal condition which prudentially adequate maxims must satisfy. Thus the general program of the derivation of duties from the Categorical Imperative (F1) as their principle has been realized through the Formula of the Law of Nature (F1a).

Notes

1. The qualifying clause in this sentence--"These are some of the many actual duties--or at least of what we take to be such--whose derivation... leaps to the eye"--needs some interpretation. It cannot mean that the four duties of the examples may not be duties in fact and yet still be derived from the Categorical Imperative. What is most likely is that the qualification refers back to the unanswered question of the possibility of a categorical imperative--that is, there may be no such things as categorical imperatives of duty.

2. See, for example, A. Wood, "Kant on False Promises", R.P. Wolff, The Autonomy of Reason.

3. A. Wood, "Kant on False Promises", p. 614.

4. R.P. Wolff, The Autonomy of Reason, p. 163.

5. One obvious objection to this claim for parallel structure follows from the defining feature of hypothetical imperatives: one does not know whether any given imperative applies until one knows the agent's willed end. One might conclude that this is the source of the necessity of beginning with an agent's maxim. By contrast, categorical impera- tives have been said to apply independently of any such consideration of agents' ends. It will have to be shown, therefore, that this differ- ence between types of imperatives does not affect the supposed formal parallel: i.e., that it is a natural method of employing categorical imperatives that the suggested parallel with hypothetical imperatives merely enables us to discover.

6. Of course they also provide a sketch for procedures of moral judg- ment. It should become clear as we go along that this is not a different task.

7. I am assuming that it is no longer necessary to establish that the Formula of the Law of Nature is the source of the two tests. See T.C. Williams, The Concept of the Categorical Imperative, p. 47ff. E.g., when, after the four examples, Kant summarizes his results, he gives as the general canon for all moral judgment of action that "we must be able to will that a maxim of our action should become a universal law" (G 91; 424). This is a restatement of the Formula of Universal Law. However, when he states what the canon of judgment is, in the sense that it is to be employed, he speaks of actions whose maxims cannot be conceived as universal laws of nature and other actions where it is "impossible to will that their maxim should be rasied to the universality of a law of nature" (Ibid.). It is clear from this that the two tests belong to the Formula of the Law of Nature, and that it provides the principle of ap- plication here for the Formula of Universal Law.

8. See chapter six, pp. 294-298.

9. See p. 218ff. where these are set out.

10. H.J. Paton, The Categorical Imperative, p. 159.

11. L.W. Beck, A Commentary on Kant's "Critique of Practical Reason", pp. 156-157.

12. Strictly speaking the Typic and the Formula of the Law of Nature (F1a) are not the same, although they in fact perform the same task in moral judgment. The Typic is really the 'contradiction in will' test under F1a. This poses no major problem since it is fair to presume that a maxim which failed the contradiction in conception test would also fail the contradiction in will test—if, as will be argued later, what is provided by these tests are criteria of rational willing. I will therefore not hesitate to use the arguments and examples of the Typic to clarify and explicate F1a.

13. To avoid tedious repetition, in what follows the Formula of Universal Law will be referred to as F1, the Formula of the Law of Nature as F1a. See chapter four, note 1.

14. R.P. Wolff, The Autonomy of Reason, p. 145.

15. L.W. Beck, A Commentary on Kant's "Critique of Practical Reason", p. 156.

16. I should emphasize that I do not agree with Wolff's claim that we cannot tell whether 'willing' is prudential or categorical. First of all, whatever the limits of introspection, we can often tell the nature of an agent's willing as, for example, he shows pleasure and satisfaction in the success of his projects, frustration and disappointment at their failure; similarly we attend to a variety of moral responses— doing what one 'has' to; living up to responsibilities; resisting temptations. Also, I do not think Wolff's account fits what Kant says in the second chapter of the Groundwork, where the heart of the moral theory lies. What Wolff's claim does show is that both types of imperative have the same features in this respect: if there are reasons for supposing we cannot tell whether anyone (including ourselves) does act on the Categorical Imperative, those same reasons apply to actions falling under the Hypothetical Imperative. (This supposes that the moral motive is not, in any special way, 'noumenal'.)

17. Failure to do this is at the root of the difficulty with Nell's otherwise plausible account of the two tests. We will see shortly how this approach unnecessarily limits both the applicability and the moral interest of F1a.

18. Nell's reconstruction of the F1a tests is a prime example of this tendency. See Acting on Principle, chapter five.

19. Although this restriction of domain is neither argued nor explicit, it is clearly assumed by Kant in the examples of F1a's application.

20. In promising to do something you express (by the promise) an intention to do what you promised. In making a deceitful promise, you want the same intention to be expressed by your 'promise' but that intention is not yours.

21. This is the formal paraphrase of an agent's asking of a proposed action, 'Is it right?' The Categorical Imperative is always brought in on <u>this</u> question. Why that should be so will be taken up later (p. 276ff.) as it is revelatory of what kind of moral test the Categorical Imperative provides and so what kind of principle the Categorical Imperative is.

22. The suggestion of two sense of rationality as applied to action is not inadvertent: much of the motivation of this thesis is to investigate the nature of this second possible 'moral' sense of rationality. See p. 244 ff. where we try to state what this sense of rationality might be.

23. "For, in fact, the moral law ideally transfers us into a nature in which reason would bring forth the highest good were it accompanied by sufficient physical capacities; and it determines our will to impart to the sensuous world the form of a system of rational beings. The least attention to ourselves shows that this idea really stands as a model for the determination of our will" (CrPrR 45;44). The point of this passage is, of course, elsewhere; its relevance to the present discussion should nonetheless be evident.

24. This should occasion no surprise when we remember that the Holy Will can do nothing but what is good. It is by nature, and necessarily, rational.

25. I say law or principle of <u>rational</u> willing as a reminder of what a principle or law of willing is, not as a specification of some kind of law of willing. Imperatives, we must remember, are formulae which express in 'ought' form principles of (practical) reason which serve as commands for imperfectly rational wills. See G 80–81;412–414 and chapter one of this thesis.

26. It is important to set the task this way since in Kant's employment of F1a all four examples concern maxims which are prudentially adequate. Or, as Kant puts it in his review of the argument of chapter two (G 105; 438), "in using means to every end I ought to restrict my maxim by the condition that it should also be universally valid as a law for every subject." At one time I thought Kant used prudential maxims in the examples primarily to emphasize the possible conflict between prudential and moral maxims; or, later, that he wanted to portray the natural movement of ordinary moral thought from the prudential to the moral through our awareness of possible transgressions of duty. I am now inclined to believe that the movement from the prudential to the moral in the examples reflects an essential structural feature of the system: (as I will show later) the Categorical Imperative may be able to test only maxims which already satisfy prudential norms. That is, F1a may not be able to give a ruling on a prudentially <u>irrational</u> maxim. (The significance of this increases if, as I believe, F1a is a necessary part of the principles

of application of the <u>other</u> formulations of the Categorical Imperative.)
The fact--that maxims to be assessed by F1a must be ones which are prudentially satisfactory--if substantiated, would suggest there is much
more than a formal hierarchy of principles of rationality at work in
Kant's ethical theory.

27. This does presume that the Categorical Imperative is a distinct law
of rational willing. As Kant says, we must do this if only to understand what is at issue in claiming the Categorical Imperative is possible:
that there might be such a law.

28. O. Nell, <u>Acting on Principle</u>, p. 62.

29. <u>Ibid</u>., p. 78.

30. A. Wood, "Kant on False Promises", p. 616.

31. I should mention that even if Wood is right about the presence of
two tests in the false promising example, it does not follow that the
Nell version of the contradiction in conception test is actually the
contradiction in will test. Both Rawls and Nell have a reading of the
contradiction in will test that distinguishes it from <u>their</u> versions of
the contradiction in conception test. In fact, I think the Rawls-Nell
version of the former is closer to what Kant intended than the Wood
sketch (615); it is their reading of the contradiction in conception
test that I find unsatisfactory.

32. A. Wood, "Kant on False Promises", p. 618.

33. As the Nell version of the argument depends on the predictable results of the UTC of M becoming a universal law of nature--"public con-
fidence ⟨in promises⟩ would diminish and eventually vanish" (Nell, 78)--
the revision of M proposed by Wood would give the Nell argument greater
plausibility. As the argument is stated, not all promises to repay
loans would be false promises in the world of the UTC of Kant's false
promising maxim, and so it is not obvious that it would (in that world)
be impossible to make such a promise and be believed. This problem does
not arise with Wood's version of the false promising maxim. Moreover,
taking into account the considerations presented in chapter two concerning the identification of the correct maxim of an action, the Wood maxim
may well be closer to Kant's intentions than his own maxim which emphasizes the circumstances in which this false promise was entertained. In
any case, Wood's revision is arguably close to Kant's intention, and the
<u>systematic</u> falsification of promises to repay loans that it introduces
makes things considerably easier for Kant's argument.

34. A. Wood, "Kant on False Promises", p. 616.

35. <u>Ibid</u>., p. 617.

36. Stanley Cavell suggests such a reading of the example (<u>Must We Mean
What We Say?</u>, p. 28n): "The difference between your <u>depositing</u> and

simply <u>handing over</u> some money has in part to do what what you mean or intend to be doing.... We may...think of the actions of depositing and accepting a deposit as complicated 'utterances': you intend that what you do shall be understood." That the example <u>can</u> be read this way is evidence for the suitability of the Wood version of the test; it does not argue for such a reading of the example in the second Critique passage.

37. As before, I am assuming a certain obviousness for these claims, as they cannot be substantiated until we have a satisfactory interpretation of the CW test. Even a superficial reading of the relevant passages shows the CW test to be a finer filter than the CC test.

38. O. Nell, <u>Acting on Principle</u>, p. 70n.

39. Once again, we are postponing until later discussion of problems concerning the selection of a maxim to be brought to F1a. This will be discussed in chapter six in conjunction with the standard criticisms of F1a in this vein--e.g. the tailoring criticism; at the same time we will consider a class of maxims Nell argues the CC test cannot manage: maxims of the form 'To receive presents, but not to give them', what Nell calls maxims of 'non-reciprocal' acts.

40. The oddness of 'their maxim' in the quotation comes from the fact that Kant describes the tests as ones which reveal what <u>actions</u> are our duties by requiring that they not be actions which are so constituted that 'their maxims' can neither be conceived nor willed a universal law of nature without contradiction.

41. See, for example, O. Nell, <u>Acting on Principle</u>, pp. 86-88, R.P. Wolff, <u>The Autonomy of Reason</u>, pp. 169-171.

42. O. Nell, <u>Acting on Principle</u>, p. 87.

43. <u>Ibid</u>. The statement of the contradiction is less clear than it need be. Nell does not mean that everyone will neglect some of what is needed to help others in need (that would not produce the contradiction), but that everyone will neglect some of what is needed by <u>anyone</u> in need. I do not see why she shifts away from the original version of the proposed maxim, 'To neglect <u>everything</u> needed to help the needy'.

44. Unless one argued that it was not possible to seek help where there was no help to be had. As we shall see, this is, in a sense, exactly right. But it does not seem to be what Nell has in mind, or, in any case, what she says.

45. It should be remembered that we in fact cannot, logically cannot, determine the will of another agent: "no one can have an end without <u>himself</u> making the object of choice into an end" (DV 43;384, see also DV 38;380). I can of course affect your choices of ends by giving you information, attaching risks to certain choices, etc. Extremes of this sort of activity may look like I am <u>trying</u> to determine your will, but,

according to Kant, in the strict sense, the will cannot be <u>determined</u> to adopt an end by the actions or volitions of another agent. Under the fiction of F1a, however, I <u>am</u> to imagine that the willing of my maxim of action is conjoined with my willing of that maxim <u>as</u> a law of human nature--as a law of willing for all human beings.

46. Two assumptions in use here should be made explicit. There could be a kind of contradiction in willing that came from an agent's failing to have a coherent maxim: what he would do is not possible, or the means he chooses do not match his end, or the end chosen is in some way itself irrational. There is no reason to think any of these could be what Kant had in mind for the CW test. The general scheme of F1a suggests that the source of the contradiction is in the willing of the UTC of a maxim as a law of nature. Under the fiction of F1a the willed UTC of a maxim itself has the status of a maxim (it <u>is</u> to be taken as the expression of a volition). Given this, it seems reasonable to assume that the CW test looks for a contradiction between two willings--willed simultaneously (by the convention of F1a--which thereby avoids confusion with a change of mind)--willings which could be presented by the maxims which express them. So we will expect to find a contradiction in will expressed in two simultaneously adopted contradictory maxims--one of which is the willed UTC of the maxim to be tested by F1a.

The second assumption concerns the volitional status of a general policy maxim like M1. General policy maxims were discussed briefly in chapter two where I was concerned to show that they were not characteristically maxims <u>of</u> actions. There I appealed to the idea (most clearly expressed in <u>Religion</u>, 20-26) that more general maxims stand in hierarchical relations--in the sense of the more general serving as the motivational ground for the less general, or for the maxim of action itself. For an agent to have a general policy maxim involves, in some sense, a continuity of willing. That is, if the general maxim expresses a standing commitment (and not merely a passing effort) such that it influences and directs the adoption of other more particular maxims, the maxim is the expression of sustained and continued willing. Thus it is possible to talk about a contradiction between a general policy maxim and the willed UTC of a maxim <u>as</u> a contradiction in will.

47. R.P. Wolff, <u>The Autonomy of Reason</u>, pp. 170-171.

48. The awkwardness in stating this argument comes from trying to avoid the error discussed on p. 230--that the contradiction comes from my being unable to <u>will</u> that others help when I am in need in the world of the UTC of a non-beneficence maxim. If the help others might give is a necessary means to an end of mine, it is not the sort of means I can will. The restricted notion of 'want' I introduce here is intended to avoid the error while retaining some relation to the agent's will.

49. O. Nell, <u>Acting on Principle</u>, p. 88.

50. <u>Ibid</u>.

51. <u>This</u> reconstruction of the talents argument requires the introduction of the ŮTC of a maxim of neglecting all one's talents to show the contradiction in will. It is not irrational (in the prudential sense) to risk unpreparedness with a neglect of talents maxim. What is irrational is to will in such a way that one would be prevented (by, e.g., an "instinct") from developing new skills should the need arise. This irrationality is demonstrated only when the 'neglect of talents' maxim becomes a law of nature 'through the will' of a human agent--under the fiction of F1a.

52. That is, what he wills given that his willing conforms to the Hypothetical Imperative.

53. In the <u>Doctrine of Virtue</u> Kant expresses the same idea: "Just as a metaphysics of nature must also contain principles for applying those universal first principles of nature as such to objects of experience, so a metaphysics of morals cannot dispense with principles of application; and we shall often have to take as our object the particular <u>nature</u> of man, which is known only by experience, to show in it the implications of the universal moral principles" (DV 14;216).

54. The sense of 'rationally will' here is just that of the CW test: what can be willed a universal law of nature without the will contradicting itself. The parenthetical 'including myself' is introduced to capture the argument for duties to the self (e.g., 'to develop some of my talents') as well as duties to others in the same formulation.

55. If the account of the Categorical Imperative we have given is at all persuasive, this use of 'rationality', without explicit reference to <u>a</u> norm of rational willing, should not seem strained or ambiguous. Part of what is being argued here is that although there are different norms of rational willing, the Hypothetical and Categorical Imperatives do <u>not</u> subtend two radically different notions of rationality. The Categorical Imperative extends and deepens the concept of practical rationality known through the Hypothetical Imperative.

Chapter Six: The Categorical Imperative—Remaining Considerations

In this chapter we will take up a broad range of issues related to
the Categorical Imperative and its embodiment in F1 and F1a: for example, the solution to the problem of permissible maxims, tailoring of
maxims and other supposed counterexamples, the proper conditions of employment of the Categorical Imperative, what sorts of moral results we
might anticipate, an examination of the bearing of F1a on the WIEDT[1] tag,
and some consideration of how to introduce the notion of the 'subjective
determining ground' of a maxim into this account of moral judgment. In
what follows we will talk about the CC and CW tests as testing whether a
given maxim can be rationally willed: a maxim that cannot be rationally
willed is one such that hidden in the logic of its volition (or of human
volition in general) is the condition that it not be a principle others
act on. A maxim that cannot be rationally willed is not "morally possible" (CrPrR 72;70) and is forbidden; its contrary is obligatory. If a
maxim and its contrary can be rationally willed, both it and its contrary are permissible.[2]

We will first look to see what we can make of the status of morally
permissible maxims under F1a. The problem posed by these maxims was
that they were essentially subjective in a way that made it seem impossible for them to satisfy the requirements of the Categorical Imperative.
How could 'To exercise regularly in order to keep fit' be willed a universal law for all rational beings? Our hope was that through F1a we
could show that such a maxim was 'possible' as a law of willing—i.e.,
not impossible. So we will show that we have made proper room for such

maxims if we can show that according to F1a it is not irrational to will such maxims as universal laws of nature. Using the exercise maxim as an exemplar of a large class of permissible maxims, if the exercise maxim failed the CC test, either we would expect to find a logical difficulty in conceiving of it as a universal law of nature (the Wood version), or the world in which the UTC of the exercise maxim was a law of nature would be one in which the agent could not succeed in acting on his maxim (the Nell version). But clearly there is no logical problem in imagining the maxim as a law of nature, and if 'Everyone will exercise regularly in order to keep fit' was a law of nature, the agent could readily succeed in the world of that law in his efforts to keep fit by exercising. If the maxim failed the CW test it would not be possible to will its UTC a law of human willing without the will contradicting itself: that is, given the conditions of human nature, it would be rational to have a maxim which was incompatible with willing the UTC of the exercise maxim. But there seems to be no such condition and no such maxim: the UTC of the exercise maxim is not incompatible with any known law of rational willing. It is not itself a law of human willing either, for, as can be readily shown, a maxim of doing nothing that will promote fitness is also possible as a universal law of nature, and if a maxim and its (loosely speaking) contrary are both possible laws of human willing, then neither of them is such a law—neither exercise nor refraining from exercise is required of us as rational human beings.

Nothing in the above discussion depends on the fact that the exercise maxim does not involve an action that affects other people. Imagine maxims like 'To spend some of my leisure time with friends'.

Such maxims can easily be shown 'possible' using the same sort of considerations as with the exercise maxim. The kinds of maxims one might reasonably worry about not being shown permissible by F1a are either maxims which would be physically impossible if a universal law—e.g., 'To go to the Boston Museum of Fine Arts every Thursday at eleven', or maxims like 'To do my Christmas shopping in the January sales in order to save money' which ought to be permissible but do not seem to be according to F1a (especially if the CC test is taken to be the Nell version), or what Nell calls "maxims of nonreciprocal action":[3] 'To buy clockwork trains but not sell them', 'To give presents but not receive them', 'To give cigarettes but not accept them', etc. The problem with all of these, I will argue, is not to be found in the account of permissibility or F1a, but in the selection of the maxim to be tested. Let us then delay their resolution until we have re-introduced the account of maxims developed in chapter two.

In chapter two it was argued that there is a maxim of an action—of an action-as-willed. It contains a privileged description of the action picked out by the motive (or the end, if end and motive are correlative). To use an example of Kant's as a reminder: two individuals may both perform apparently identical acts of avarice but according to different maxims:

> The maxim of greedy avarice (prodigality) is to get and keep all the means to good living with the purpose of enjoying them. —The maxim of miserly avarice, on the other hand, is to get and keep all the means to good living, but without regard to this enjoyment (i.e. in such a way that one's end is only to possess the means, not to use them). (DV 97;432)

Knowledge of the motive or end is necessary to determine what action the agent is performing. Assessment of actions by imperatives is done through assessment of their maxims. Thus the accuracy of the maxim brought to the imperative is essential to the correct assessment of the proposed action. Extraneous detail is pared from the description in a maxim by asking counterfactually, 'Were this feature of the description not part of the circumstances of action, would you still act as you propose?' If the answer is yes, the descriptive element is rejected as extraneous to the agent's conception of his action. Maxims that are excessively general are questioned concerning whether they are really the maxims of the action-as-willed: e.g., if 'To do what is necessary in order to succeed at my chosen profession' is offered as the maxim for my preparing a lecture on Kant's ethics, although it is possible that the maxim describes what I am doing in preparing the lecture, it would only be so in quite special circumstances. Normally what I am doing is acting on a maxim such as 'To work up lecture material in advance in order to teach a satisfactory class'. It was suggested in chapter two[4] that the more general maxims may stand (in the normal case) to the maxim of action as part of a general hierarchical structure of motivation. That is, more general maxims may be said to function as the maxims which govern the selection of ends.

The standard maxim-related objection to F1a—the tailoring of maxims with sufficient detail so they will pass the CC and CW tests—was dealt with in detail in chapter two.[5] There it was argued that since an action has a maxim, an agent does not have the option to bring any maxim he pleases to the Categorical Imperative. Of course he may insist on tailoring his maxim, but it is no objection to a moral theory that it has a principle of judgment which can be employed dishonestly. (We will discuss unintentional errors in maxim selection later.)

The apparent problem with a maxim such as 'To go to the BMFA every Thursday at eleven' is that if the UTC of this maxim were a law of nature then everyone would go to the BMFA on Thursdays at eleven, which, of course, not everyone can do. It is not possible for everyone to do anything at the same place and time. The maxim would appear to violate the CC test: either it is not possible to conceive the maxim as a universal law because of the impossibility of everyone doing what the maxim specifies (the Wood version), or it would not be consistent of me to intend both the world of the UTC of the maxim and my own maxim of going to the museum given the conditions of overcrowding that would obtain in the world where the UTC of my maxim was a law of nature (the Nell version). All of these problems stem from the choice of an implausible and incompletely specified maxim. In the first place, the 'everyone' in the UTC of the maxim is everyone with the same reason for acting—the same end— as the agent. E.g., everyone who wants to study the work of Morris Louis. But then, of course, we see that there is no problem with the maxim. But suppose the end to be less exclusive—'in order to increase my knowledge of painting' or 'in order to impress my colleagues', for examples. If these are the ends, then either the maxim is too specific (there are other ways to increase your knowledge of painting than at the BMFA, etc.) or the group involved in the universalization is so small that there is no problem with the test and the maxim is judged to be permissible. The apparent difficulty is dissolved when we see that the detail in the maxim is excessive, thereby making the maxim implausible, and the end or purpose of the action is not given, thereby omitting specification of the conditions under which the maxim will be a law of willing in the fictional world of F1a. Although maxims of action should not be excessively general, they are usually sufficiently general so that an agent must use his judgment in selecting the particulars of his proposed action. Recall the examples in chapter three[6] where the rationality of a proposed prudential maxim was shown to depend on its flexibility over variations in circumstances: a maxim contains a description of an action which indicates what kind of action the agent considers suitable to his end.

What of maxims where it is necessary to the success of the agent's project that not everyone do what he intends? For example, consider the maxim 'To do my Christmas shopping in the January sales in order to save money'. If we follow Nell's account of the CC test we seem to get a ruling that this maxim—or acts conforming to this maxim—are forbidden, since an agent cannot without contradiction intend to act on the maxim and intend its UTC to hold as a natural law. To paraphrase Nell, if I intend the UTC of my maxim to hold as a natural law I must also intend the normal and predictable results of everyone (who wants to save money) acting on my maxim, and the normal result of everyone shopping after Christmas is that stores would hold their sales later or not at all. But then I would not be able to save money on Christmas presents by buying them the week after Christmas. Nell would have to conclude that I cannot without contradiction intend to act on my maxim and intend its UTC to hold as a law of nature. Action on this maxim would be forbidden by the Categorical Imperative.

It is not clear how on Nell's account this result could be avoided. Moreover, this appears to be a maxim where the rationality of what I propose to do depends on others not doing as I do. We need to be able to distinguish this case from the ones we used earlier to demonstrate the method of the CC test (e.g., the maxim of deceitful promising) to show that the test rejects only maxims that are contrary to duty. The force of the example comes from a possible weakness in the Nell account: its dependence on the "normal and predictable results" of an action. This is why the argument is unable to distinguish between what banks would probably do if many people began attempting to steal from them, or what policies stores would probably adopt if people generally waited for sales to make their purchases, and what would happen if no one who promised to repay a loan ever intended or could intend to do so. It is possible that banks would not take "ever greater precautions to impede and discover thieves and to prevent them using or enjoying their loot";[7] it is not possible that promises to repay could be believed. This, I take it, is the force of the Wood argument. It does not depend on how good people's memory is, or how gullible they are, or on their lack of concern for money. It depends strictly on a claim about the logic of the expression of an intention in making a promise: if it is not possible for anyone to make a promise to repay with the intention to keep it, then it is not possible for a promise to express the intention to repay. It is not the probable frustration of the agent's purposes that the Wood version of the CC test shows but the conceptual impossibility of the act specified in the maxim as a universal practice. This weakness in the

Nell account is highlighted by the fact that peripheral attitudes of the agent seem to affect the ruling of the CC test. A bank robber who enjoyed challenges might find the difficulties projected in the world where the UTC of his bank robbing maxim was a natural law to be stimulating rather than a source of contradictory intentions. Nell's argument seems dependent on the rationality of risk-taking in a way that undermines the intended logical force of the FlA tests.[8] We saw the importance of avoiding arguments that depended on these subjective differences among individuals in the reconstruction of the argument for the CW test. We can conclude, then, that the Christmas shopping maxim will only be rejected on the basis of an argument which looks to the probability of my purposes being thwarted were the maxim a natural law. There is no conceptual impossibility to be found in the universal practice of everyone doing Christmas shopping the week after Christmas. Moreover, it is now clear that the rationality of what I propose does not depend on others not doing what I would do. After all, if everyone waited, 'they' might have to lower prices in general.

The problem of 'maxims of nonreciprocal action' is, I believe, a problem generated by an implausible construal of the maxim of an action. If this is so, it will be unnecessary to stipulate a second category of permissibility for those maxims and their contraries both of which fail the CC test.[9] Let me state my objection briefly: Why suppose 'To buy lettuce but not to sell it' is a plausible maxim of action in the first place? Note that there is no difficulty if an agent has two maxims of action: one 'To buy lettuce', the other 'Not to sell lettuce'. Each of these will pass the CC test—it is not necessary to fill out the details

of these ordinary maxims—and an agent who had both would not have a
pair of contradictory maxims. Of what action is 'To buy lettuce but not
to sell it' a maxim? Maxims of nonreciprocal action would seem to be
either unintended variants of tailored maxims—that is, a maxim has been
brought forward as a counterexample which is not obviously or normally a
maxim of an action, or, these maxims are _irrational_ maxims, which is not
what they are offered as and not what made them interesting counterexamples.[10] We will consider later the general question of what the
Categorical Imperative can do with irrational maxims (irrational, that
is, according to the Hypothetical Imperative). For now it seems plain
that we do not yet have a serious class of maxims where neither the maxim nor its contrary can be universalized without contradiction. If this
remains the case, no special category of permissible maxims needs to be
defined.

We encounter a more serious difficulty with agents' maxims which
(unintentionally) misrepresent the proposed action, or which are self-
deceptive, or even, simply, mistaken. That is, an agent may in all honesty bring a maxim to the Categorical Imperative which is not the maxim
of his action, _or_, the maxim he brings does not include the morally
relevant feature of what he would do. This last will be taken to include cases where the agent is unaware of, or has perhaps forgotten or
overlooked, some moral claim or previously incurred obligation. For example, I may bring to the Categorical Imperative a permissible maxim of
going to the movies when what I will also be doing (although I do not
now realize it) is breaking a promise made yesterday and subsequently
forgotten. Or, I may violate someone's rights without knowing that I am

doing so, and thus fail to assess my proposed action through the 'right' maxim. There are a number of questions here, but they fall into roughly two categories: 1) Since the Categorical Imperative—or F1 and F1a—judge maxims of action, is there any way to correct for an agent's failure to characterize his action (and so also his maxim) correctly? 2) Even if an agent correctly identifies his maxim of action—he knows what he intends to do and why—he may nevertheless be doing something 'morally wrong'. Does the Categorical Imperative provide a moral criterion for assessing actions that does not depend on the agent's maxim?

As it is not part of the project of this thesis to develop a complete and satisfactory technique for using the Categorical Imperative as a principle of judgment over a wide range of examples, some of the difficulties suggested by the above cases cannot be responded to adequately. Kant, it seems to me, grossly underestimated how difficult it is to use F1a, in part because he did not investigate the problem of an agent's specifying his maxim (it is easier to design procedures for determining which parts of a maxim do not belong than to find guidance in constructing or eliciting a maxim), and also because F1a can be hard to apply, especially if the analysis of the CC and CW tests we have given is correct. Concerning this last problem, Kant may have been aware of it and thought that the rougher and more intuitive WIEDT question might be practically sufficient. The purpose of this thesis has been to determine what kind of principle the Categorical Imperative is, and, with regard to its practical application, to indicate the general method of assessment such a principle generated. Given the limits of this enterprise, it will be satisfactory if we can suggest directions for and sketches of argument consistent with the central results we have obtained.

It is possible, for example, that F1a, or the WIEDT formulation embedded in the Typic, may be able to yield results in some cases where the agent is unaware of his motive and so his end in acting. Consider the case of someone deciding to cheat on a medical school entrance exam. Let us suppose he judges himself to be a member of a discriminated against minority group and proposes cheating as a means to neutralize the effects of discrimination. His maxim would then be 'To cheat on the exam in order to neutralize the effects of discrimination.' Let us further suppose that what is in fact the case is that he simply _very_ strongly wants to get into medical school, and raises the issue of possible discrimination as a rationalization or cover for his real motives in cheating. Here we might hope that the procedure of F1a requiring the universalization of the maxim would suggest to the agent what his motive was. That is, if he imagines that everyone cheats to neutralize the effects of discrimination and that these effects are thereby neutralized, he may discover that he would still want to cheat in order to increase _his_ chances of being admitted. He might then realize what his real motive was for deciding to cheat in the first place. This illumination, it should be clear, would not be a result of either the CC or the CW test but simply of imagining the universalized maxim becoming a law of nature which these tests require. Of course, in many other cases the masking effect of unconscious rationalization would persist through the universalization. The point of this example was not to show that F1a could always elicit hidden motives, but that it was not _necessarily_ frustrated by an agent beginning with a misconception of what he was doing.[11]

But what of cases where the agent's 'true maxim' is not revealed by bringing his supposed maxim to F1a? Here I think we find a limit of the success of the Categorical Imperative as a principle of judgment. (It is not a theoretical limit, as an action has a maxim even if the agent cannot produce it.) This will be so to the extent that it is independently possible that we may discover that the purpose for which we in fact acted was not the one for which we thought at the time we were acting. Agents then will sometimes use F1a to test maxims which are not the maxims of their actions. In such cases F1a will not be able to indicate that what they propose to do is contrary to duty, and it will be unable to do this because the agent does not adequately understand what it is that he proposes to do. (He thinks he is helping his neighbor in time of need; in fact he is currying favor. Or, someone thinks he is just making a shrewd business deal when he is not and what he is in fact doing is ruining a rival. And so on.) One could be better or worse at understanding the nature of one's actions, their motives and ends. We might even have an obligation to become more knowledgeable about the sources of our projects and critically aware of temptations to self-deception. But as F1a tests maxims and human agents do not always know exactly what principle they are acting on, it is limited, as a testing procedure, by the maxim the agent honestly believes he intends to act on. In principle there is no action F1a cannot rule on correctly; every action has a maxim. In practice the accuracy of F1a is not much better than the accuracy of an agent's conception of his action.

The seriousness of this practical problem will depend on how often and in what sorts of circumstances agents are likely to be badly wrong

about what they are doing. It is a difficulty shared by any moral theory with a principle of judgment that has the rightness and wrongness of
actions depend on the agent's intention. Nell is wrong when she concludes that Kant's moral theory, because it assesses maxims, incorporates all the errors an agent makes in its determination of right and
wrong.[12] It is only the agent, or others who judge his actions, who
will be unable in some cases to escape making erroneous judgments. It
is possible to talk of an erroneous judgment within the theory just because there is a possible determinate answer from F1a when the correct
maxim of action is used. These difficulties would be less pressing if
there were an independent method of assessing the morality of actions in
Kant's theory—a method that did not depend on the maxim of an action.
Then even if the agent deceived himself about what he was doing, or acted out of ignorance or bias, there would be a practical means of showing
his action to be right or wrong—regardless of the agent's conception of
his action. Before we assess the gravity of the problem we have been
discussing we should turn to our second question and ask whether the
Categorical Imperative provides a moral criterion for judging actions
that does not depend on the agent's maxim.

The principle one might look to for this is the First Principle of
Justice in the Doctrine of Justice[13] which regulates "external" acts and
which is distinguished from the First Principle of Virtue by generating
just that system of duties which can be enforced by legal sanctions and
so can be fulfilled independently of our attitude of will, and so, it
would seem, of our maxim. It is not clear, however, that the First
Principle of Justice (F4) can be employed without the use of maxims.

There is even some confusion in the formulations of F4: on the same page F4 is defined once with the maxim as its object of assessment: "Any action is right if, according to its maxim, the freedom of choice of any person can coexist with the freedom of every other person according to universal law" (DJ 35;230), and then it is defined without mention of maxims: "Act externally in such a way that the free use of your will is compatible with the freedom (free choice) of everyone according to universal law" (DJ 35; 231). If F4 can assess an action only through its maxim, we are no better off than with F1 of F1a, and the same uncertainties will prevail concerning the outcome of its employment owing to ignorance, opacity of motive, etc., affecting the maxim. If the second version of F4 ("Act externally...") looks attractive because it contains no mention of the maxim of an action, we must remember that the idea of a maxim of an action is a solution to a problem that a principle of judgment which does not use the maxim will still have. That is, to use Nell's phrase, how does the second version of F4 solve the problem of the 'relevant description' of an action? An 'external' action might affect the freedom of others in numerous ways—some permissible, others forbidden. How is one to choose the 'correct' description of the action? It does not, of course, follow from this that there is no other way than through the maxim to solve the problem. What is true, however, is that Kant has no other way. Moreover, we have assumed for purposes of argument that the second version of F4 does not require a maxim to judge an action—because it makes no mention of the maxim—but there is good reason to be cautious about making this assumption. The important theoretical distinction for Kant in the <u>Doctrine of Justice</u> is between

'inner' and 'external' actions: only external actions affect the freedom ('outer freedom', that is) of other persons. And to the extent that
actions do affect the freedom of action of others, they do so, it would
appear, without regard to their maxims. But again, we must not be
hasty. Two things need to be emphasized. First, Kant's caution about
maxims in the context of justice is that the moral concept of justice
"does not take into consideration the matter of the will, that is, the
end that a person intends to accomplish by means of the object that he
wills" (DJ 34;230). The purpose for which we act is irrelevant to the
effect of our action on the freedom of others. The purpose is 'inner.'
As is the motive: duties of justice do not require the agent to have
any particular motive in acting, so long as his action is in conformity
to the Universal Principle of Justice. None of this caution yields the
conclusion that the maxim is irrelevant to the assessment of actions
under the law of justice. Second, the law of justice requires that we
act in such a way that the use of our will is compatible with the freedom of everyone according to universal law. If this is interpreted that
everyone must be able to will as I do—that is, that F4 is equivalent to
the CC test—to determine that this is the case for any action surely
calls for the maxim, as 'freedom according to universal law' applies to
maxims and not actions alone: "freedom" here is "free choice."

It is not in order here to investigate whether in the Doctrine of
Justice Kant is able to develop concepts such as 'right' or 'harm' that
can be applied to cases without looking to the maxim of an action. What
I have been arguing is that the Universal Principle of Justice is not
such a principle. Speculatively, one might suspect, given our under-

standing of the Categorical Imperative, that no principle which has its
authority in the Categorical Imperative could be indifferent to willing
and therefore to maxims. I am inclined to agree with Paton's description of the problem of the Doctrine of Justice—"how to combine the
arbitrary and often incompatible ends of individuals within a framework
of law which aims at liberty"[14] and which uses coercion as its legitimate means. That seems to me right and suited to the rest of Kant's
project, but I am in no position to begin an argument for such an understanding. Given the limits of the Law of Justice we have discussed, the
general question is not pertinent to our problem. We will conclude,
then, that Kant does not appear to have a method, based on the Categorical Imperative, for assessing the moral rightness and wrongness of actions that operates without the maxim of an action. The last question
on this subject must be, is this a serious problem?

If actions are to be assessed as they can be willed a universal
law, then we must have the maxim of the action for it contains the expression of the willing that stands behind the action. We should recall
that this is a practical as well as a theoretical requirement: it is
surely as important to distinguish false promises made without regard to
the obligations incurred in promising from false promises made as the
only available means to save a life as it is to distinguish the 'rightness' of maxims from the 'rightness' of the actions agents perform. It
is possible that no single theory can do both. If this is so, the practical guidance offered by judicious and honest employment of F1a might
well, because of the subtlety it allows and at times requires, recommend
it over less fallible principles. But this will depend on the degree

and nature of its fallibility, and it is to this issue we were to turn.

In considering this issue we must be cautious that we do not introduce moral criteria from other sorts of moral conceptions. It will not
be an objection to the theory to point out that an agent while walking
according to a bird-watching maxim is nonetheless violating property
rights (he thinks he is still in the public bird-sanctuary). If we have
some intuition that says this is a wrong (because a violation of rights),
although an unintentional wrong, and the Categorical Imperative does not
allow us to make this judgment, I do not see why the intuition should be
held inviolable. After all, the rulings of the Categorical Imperative
might well be thought to be prior to concepts of rights. This is not to
say that if an agent (in a world where things are commonly owned) fails
to consider whether the bicycle leaning against the fence might belong
to someone before he acts on a maxim of bicycle riding the Categorical
Imperative has nothing to say, or permits our saying anything. This is
a very different sort of issue. Consider an example Nell uses to show
the limits of the applicability of the Categorical Imperative where the
question is whether success of execution is made irrelevant to judgments
of right by the Categorical Imperative.[15] We suppose someone fully intends to return a borrowed object to another, and he has a maxim of doing so which is in all respects adequate. But on the occasion of return
he is tripped and the object breaks. Nell thinks, correctly, that the
Categorical Imperative would judge the action on its maxim to be morally
right, whereas, in fact, "assessments of right and wrong are not thought
to take account of intentions which (for whatever reason) are not imple-
mented."[16] Again, there is no reason to be committed to such thoughts;

perhaps good intentions (with adequate care in execution) are sufficient for judgments of right. But leaving such an issue aside, why suppose the Categorical Imperative must be indifferent to such questions? Suppose we considered instead the maxim our unlucky agent had in _response_ to this accident. It is at least plausible to suppose that some maxims (offers to repay or replace, apologies, etc.) would pass the F1a tests while others might not (indifference, an unwillingness to discuss what should be done, etc.). I am not at all sure that 'what we think' is not better captured this way. We will return to this sort of example when we consider the general role of consequences in Kant's moral theory.

There is no need to take up again the question of an agent whose maxim is formulated under conditions of self-deception. He will not be able to assess his action correctly using F1a, but it would be odd if he could, given that he does not (or cannot) acknowledge what he is doing. Since, however, his action _has a maxim_, there is an answer, in theory, to the question of the permissibility of his proposed action.

Examples of this sort that might be more pressing involve the possibility that an agent may simply be unaware of some morally relevant feature of the circumstances in which he is acting or of the action itself. It is not clear what we are to suppose here. Is the agent to be unaware that his action involves hurting or killing someone? This seems flatly implausible in an otherwise normal agent. What conditions are we to imagine obtain so that someone does not know he is causing pain—not that pain is an unforeseen consequence, but that what he is doing is causing pain? Perhaps the case is too strange. What of someone who does not know he is betraying a trust? Again, we must be careful that

we get the case right: it is not that the agent never knew he was not
to speak (that is not to betray a trust), nor that he had forgotten that
he was to say nothing (that is a different issue). We may ask, if you
have a trust, how likely is it that you betray it without knowing it?
If it is a question of failing to exercise adequate caution, that is the
question of whether the Categorical Imperative can require that we se-
cure the means for what we are committed to do. The answer, I believe,
is that it does, and we will look at this in some detail shortly. Suppose you exercise reasonable caution, but a highly trained secret agent
is introduced into your household who manages to piece together the elements of the secret from nuances of utterance that you had every reason
to believe were meaningless. This seems like the case where you are
tripped while returning the china vase.

To give some order to this question, there seem to be four ways you
might do something wrong without knowing that you are doing it—and so
not have the relevant features of your action in the maxim to be assessed by the Categorical Imperative. You might forget and do something
you had promised not to do, or say something you had promised not to say.
You might be negligent in taking required precautions. Exceptional and
unappreciated circumstances might make an apparently harmless act harmful. In the first two cases, the maxim of your act would not reflect
the moral wrong, and we will have to see whether the Categorical Imperative has means to deal with them. The third kind of case we have already
worked through. The remaining case involves an agent incorrectly assessing the permissibility of his action. But here, although the agent
acts wrongly without knowing that he does, the maxim of his action would

reflect the moral wrong—i.e., this is a case of error in moral judgment, and so is not a problem for the Categorical Imperative. What we do not have, if we are dealing with normal agents, are cases where an agent does not know he is doing something wrong where the wrong is, in a manner of speaking, in plain sight. For example, an agent who plunges a dagger into someone's heart to get a good look at his ventricles, without its occurring to him that in so doing he may be harming or killing the person. Less exaggeratedly—while I may not know who owns the bicycle leaning against the fence, it would be more than ingenuous of me to claim that it had not occurred to me that it was owned.[17] Therefore, if the Categorical Imperative can manage cases of negligence and forgetting, the problems generated by having maxims as the object of moral assessment will be reduced to tolerable proportions.

When an agent has incurred an obligation—promised to repay a debt on the 15th, for example—he can be said to have adopted an end of 'repaying the debt on the 15th'. In virtue of having adopted that end he has a general or guiding maxim of doing what is necessary (ceteris paribus) to succeed in repaying the debt on the 15th. That is, he must take steps to insure that this will be done. Formally this follows from his having adopted an end: it is irrational not to intend some sufficient means to an end which is aimed at. Here the Hypothetical Imperative works in conjunction with the Categorical Imperative. Among the things that an agent with this end ought to do is not forget that he has made the promise. He must also make a serious effort to have the money available by the 15th. If he fails to take these minimally sufficient means to his end we will say either that he had not really adopted the end, or that he is acting irrationally, or that his will is weak. It is not necessary to develop the psychological apparatus to discriminate cases in order for the point at issue to be clear. The grounds for the charge of irrationality stemming from failure to take appropriate means to an adopted end were discussed in chapter three. That the end in this case is moral makes no formal difference. The two other options have not been discussed before, and will only be sketched in minimal detail here. If someone who has purportedly adopted an end of beneficence (he has a maxim 'To help some people in need') never helps or makes efforts to help anyone, we will have grounds for concluding that he does not have a beneficent end at all. Whether we would be right in concluding this was the case would depend on how, for example, he responded to questions concerning his reasons for failing to give help in conspicuous cases (walking across a bridge when someone is drowning an arm's reach away, etc.). Other things equal, to have an end is to take steps to promote it. If I say that I will protect your secret (I take that as an end for me) but pay no attention to whether what I say reveals it, it is fair to conclude that I was not sincere in my promise—that I did not make keeping your secret an end of mine. Alternatively, I may be someone who cannot keep a secret. In the face of temptation by the notoriety I will receive by telling all my resolve to be silent weakens. Once again, we will be able to see what has happened (in some cases) by what I say or do after violating the trust. Of course we may not be able to tell what has happened, but that fact poses no special difficulty for this account. To some extent what a person has willed may be unavailable to us, even with honest reports, as it may be unavailable to the agent.[18]

We may conclude that it is possible to manage negligence and forgetfulness within the ambit of the Categorical Imperative. (I am taking forgetfulness, when it is a fault, to sort conceptually with negligence, that is, with the different ways one can fail to take sufficient means to an end.) The reason it looked as though these cases were not manageable at all was that forgetting that you had an obligation, etc., simply failed to show up in the agent's maxim of action; thus an agent could act wrongly and yet find the Categorical Imperative judging his action permissible. What we see here, in short, is that we were looking at the wrong maxim. The Categorical Imperative will register the wrong in the maxim the agent has in response to his failure to do what he ought to have done. This answer is much the same as the one given for an earlier problematic case—an action thwarted by an unanticipated intervention—where we also discovered the missing moral judgment registered with respect to the maxim adopted after the action in question. That is, what may matter morally in these cases is how the agent responds to the consequences of his actions.

The conclusion to be drawn from all of this is that even if there is no way to evaluate actions without using maxims, the moral theory of the Categorical Imperative is not as limited by this as it might have initially appeared to be. The complete theory of judgment that would be generated from the Categorical Imperative might not match our intuitions in detail, but enough has been said to suggest that it would not fail to register major moral facts. It might even report them in morally illuminating ways.

From the fact that the Categorical Imperative rules on maxims we can see that its primary function as a principle of judgment is to forbid or allow proposed actions rather than to prescribe one among a number of alternative possible actions. It is not to be employed as one might employ, for example, the principle of utility. The question is not, 'What ought I to do?' but rather, 'Is what I propose to do morally right (or permissible)?' That is, does what I propose to do violate the principle of morality—the Categorical Imperative. The 'moral situation' for an agent coming to the Categorical Imperative is significantly unlike the not unreasonable caricature of the state of an agent making a moral judgment as a utilitarian: from the point of view of the Categorical Imperative the agent is not a mere locus of possible actions. Rather, the moral situation begins with the agent actively engaged—characteristically, for Kant, with the agent having a definite course of action in mind, often in the service of some interest. The agent then inquires whether or not it is (morally) all right for him to do what he already wants to do.

The theory is sensitive to an agent's conception of himself and of his projects. The Categorical Imperative will discriminate among actions as the agent has a more or less subtle understanding of what he would do and why. This means that in similar situations and with similar proposed actions the Categorical Imperative may rule differently. For example: Let us suppose that in order to save a life it may be necessary to make a deceitful promise. Consider two agents, one with the maxim 'To make a deceitful promise when that is necessary to save a life', and the other with the maxim 'To make a deceitful promise when that will aid me in what I want to do.'. I take it that the Categorical Imperative would rule the first maxim (at least) permissible and reject the second.[19] The paradox is only apparent. It looks as though we have here a case of the 'same action' being judged in one instance right and in another wrong. But the only sense in which the actions are 'the same' is behaviorally (what events the agent initiates, etc.). They are not the same actions-as-willed. As the agents' conceptions of what they are doing differ so do their maxims and so the judgment passed by F1a. The one action has as its end the saving of a life (perhaps, but not necessarily, as what I have a duty to do); the other has as its end the saving of a life as something I want to do. This sort of result may be startling, but it is not implausible for that. If deceitful promising in the service of what an agent wants is wrong, it should not be less wrong when what an agent happens to want is something we judge to be morally good or even morally necessary. Does this mean that according to Kant (or my reading of Kant) it is not morally better that a life be saved? I do not think it does mean that, but for how we are to coordinate these intuitions we must wait until we consider the general issue of the moral results we may expect from the Categorical Imperative. In any case, an agent's discovery that a maxim of making a deceitful promise to achieve what he wanted would be rejected as contrary to duty would not necessarily be the end of the agent's encounter with the Categorical Imperative. For if he felt, as we might suppose he would, that there was something distressing about the consequences of the ruling, he might be led to discover that it is not in the service of what he wants that a deceitful promise may be justified, but rather as it may lead to the saving of a life.

There is one problem in the application of the Categorical Imperative that comes from the way an agent approaches it—that is, with his maxim. Many of the maxims which an agent will bring to the Categorical Imperative will be prudential maxims, determined in content by the desires the action is intended to satisfy. These are the maxims an agent would most frequently question for their permissibility—'I want to do it, but is it right?' is what Kant imagines an agent asking (G 90;422). Suppose an agent proposed to tell a lie on the maxim, 'To tell a lie once every twenty-five years'. The UTC of that maxim would be 'Everyone will tell a lie once every twenty-five years'. Could the UTC of such a maxim become a law of nature without contradiction? Could it be willed such a law without the will contradicting itself? It seems to me the answer in both cases is that it could. The solution to this problem lies in the recognition that this aberrant maxim is also prudentially deviant. What end does this action serve? What is its point? (According to Kant, all action is purposive.) If the action has no point (not even 'because it is what I feel like doing') it need not be considered as it is not properly speaking an action and we do not in fact have a maxim. Suppose the point of the action (telling the one lie in 25 years) is to promote the agent's happiness? Then I think either we have the wrong maxim, or it is a prudentially irrational maxim, since a rational agent who saw lying as an essential part of his happiness would adopt a maxim of 'Lying only when that promotes happiness', and that maxim would be rejected by F1a. It is not important, given our general purpose here, to discuss the different ways such a maxim might be judged to have failed the test of the Hypothetical Imperative (e.g., the conception of happiness involved, the disregard for the nature or point of the particular lie, etc.). What we need the example for is simply to see that many maxims which would be judged irrational by the Hypothetical Imperative may pass F1a. The problem is, of course, that if this is the case, flatly immoral, if very odd, maxims will be judged morally permissible. Note that strictly speaking we do not have maxims which are given warrant by the Categorical Imperative—they merely pass through the mesh of F1a. So it is possible that imperfections in the testing procedure do not reflect flaws in the moral principle itself. The other way of solving the problem that is suggested by the example is to restrict the employment of F1a to maxims which are prudentially satisfactory. The principles of rationality would then operate in order— first, a maxim would be tested to see if its end was adequately served by the proposed action as a means; second, the end would be examined to see if it coordinated with other ends the agent had or intended to pursue; third, the maxim would be checked to see if it conformed to the Categorical Imperative. This would provide a complete testing procedure for the rationality of maxims, although it would not be necessary to employ the second test at all if a maxim passed the first but failed the third. Kant nowhere (to my knowledge) speaks of such a hierarchy of principles, but it is well within the scope of his apparent intentions to suggest such a structure. Rulings of F1a would be decisive, and would be made only on maxims which passed the test of technical imperatives. Certainly all the examples of maxims contrary to duty that Kant uses are maxims that are given as prudent for the agent to act on. Two questions remain: why is it that the procedures of F1a do not work on maxims which would be judged irrational by the Hypothetical Imperative? and, is it only the test of technical imperatives that maxims must pass to be suitable for judgment by F1a? These questions must—at this time—go unanswered. The most that can be offered here is a practical solution which fits the general structure of Kant's theory of volition and its norms, and which is suggestive of further lines of investigation.

We will turn now to a brief survey of the moral results we may anticipate will come from the Categorical Imperative. Although answers to many of these questions have been implicit in our discussion of the Categorical Imperative and its principle of application F1a, they should be stated explicitly. The standard charges against the Formula of the Law of Nature are expressed by Thomas Hill in a way that also indicates the appropriate response:

> If the maxims selected are too general, the test becomes rigoristic; if they are too specific, it becomes permissive. That is, the more we focus upon the very general features of acts, such as 'being a lie', the more likely we are to get simple, unqualified rules, such as 'Never lie', which a morally sensitive person could not accept. On the other hand, if we concentrate upon the details of each case, allowing maxims to be quite specific, then we can will as universal law the maxim of virtually any action which we are willing to perform.[20]

Hill at least realizes that F1a does not generate moral prescriptions except from the maxims that are brought to it. Moreover he also realizes that the rigoristic-permissive problem results from the fact that "the same act can be correctly described in a variety of ways."[21] If our argument for the maxim of an action stands, then the worry that the Categorical Imperative will produce either iron-clad injunctions or easy permissions dissipates. That is, 'Never tell lies' is not a moral injunction that F1a will generate since 'To tell lies' is not a maxim of action—or, if it _is_ a maxim of action, it is, as it stands, irrational. We need not rehearse the arguments against over-specific maxims again. Hill's maxim for generating permissive results is "'To lie, if I want, to a 25 year old, red-headed, beautiful woman, who calls me late on a Tuesday night, etc., etc.'"[22] This is either a tailored maxim, or it can be shown by the method of counterfactual questioning _not_ to be the maxim of the action in question. It is not up to the agent to choose whether his action is to be described "simply as 'a lie' or as 'answering an hysterical woman in the only way that can prevent her suicide'".[23] One or the other (or neither) will be the description of his action; the correct description will be the one which includes just those features essential to what he would do.

Two elements of our account must be emphasized. The Categorical Imperative judges maxims of action.[24] Without a maxim to test, the Categorical Imperative is mute. It cannot be the source of any lexicon of duties to which all actions must conform. As Wolff says, "the Categorical Imperative does not command any particular, substantive principle of action,"[25] it provides a method for discriminating among proposals for action. Wolff is wrong, however, in thinking the Categorical Imperative is merely a principle of volitional consistency;[26] it embodies a more substantial norm of rationality. Second, although tailored and irrelevantly detailed maxims may not be brought to the Categorical Imperative, _relevantly_ _detailed_ _maxims_ are appropriate. If I am lying because that is what I judge necessary to prevent an hysterical person's suicide—that is the conception of the action which belongs in the maxim

and which will therefore enter into the judgment rendered by F1a. It is
not _necessary_ that the Categorical Imperative rule such a maxim permissible; what I am arguing is rather that if the Categorical Imperative
rules on maxims, and the maxim of lying to save a life is a different
maxim from, say, lying to get ahead in my profession, then it is _possible_ and even reasonable that the Categorical Imperative evaluate these
importantly different maxims of lying differently.

The reasonableness of the above suggestion turns on what has been
called the problem of 'conflict of duties'. Several examples of this
form have already been introduced and it is in order to see what can be
said about them. Kant gives very little help. In the _Doctrine of Virtue_ (DV 23;223) he asserts that "a conflict of duties and obligations is
inconceivable" although

> there can, it is true, be two _grounds_ of obligation...both
> present in one agent and in the rule he lays down for himself. In this case one or the other of these grounds is
> not sufficient to oblige him...and is therefore not a
> duty.—When two such grounds conflict with each other,
> practical philosophy says, not that the stronger obligation takes precedence...but that the stronger _ground of
> obligation_ prevails. (DV 23;223)

Unhappily, Kant does not provide us with criteria for determining which
of two grounds of obligation is the stronger. "_Obligation_ is the necessity of a free action under a categorical imperative" (DV 20;221). "A
duty is an action to which we are obligated" (DV 21;222). Thus we see
why Kant insists in strictness that there can be no conflict of duties
and obligations as "two conflicting rules cannot both be necessary at
the same time" (DV 23;223). It is not clear, however, what a "ground of
obligation" is.

Suppose we turn the issue on two famous possible maxims:

Maxim 1: To tell a lie in order to save a life.
Maxim 2: To tell the truth even if in so doing I do not
prevent a death.

One way of looking at this would be to argue that both maxims would pass the CC test and that therefore both are permissible. An agent may do either. While this would not solve the problem of choice for an agent who was perplexed, it would provide a formal solution in that there would be no 'conflict of duties'—i.e., we could conclude that it is not necessary to 'tell the truth even if in so doing I fail to prevent a death', and it is also not necessary to 'tell a lie in order to save a life'. It is less clear how to go beyond this in order to use the idea of the 'stronger ground of obligation' to resolve the question of what to do.

Nell suggests[27] that a resolution might be found in looking at some of the consequences of the UTC's of these maxims. The UTC of maxim 1 (everyone lies when that is required to save a life) would not lead to a general breakdown of trust and cooperation; paradoxically, Nell suggests, the UTC of maxim 2 (as a law of nature) would lead to a breakdown of trust and cooperation, for "if we know that others will not tell a lie even to save a life, then we can hardly trust them in any situation of potential danger."[28] These would then be consequences willed by agents (with these maxims) according to the Nell version of the CC test. While no contradiction emerges when either maxim is passed through the test, Nell suggests the concept of the CC test might be extended to show that maxim 1 in fact represents the stronger ground of obligation: If the UTC of maxim 2 were willed by the agent to be a law of nature, the agent would will (Nell says 'intend') "a situation which tends towards a Hobbesian state of nature, and so tends to impede or prevent all plans of action" including that envisaged in maxim 2. "Our cooperation with others would have to be carefully limited in such a situation."[29] This diminution of trust under the UTC of maxim 2, making our projects (in general) subject to great risk, suggests that it would be rational to prefer a world in which this did not occur: the world of the UTC of maxim 1. It would not be rational to will a world in which, as a result of one's willing, uncertainty increased. This extension of the CC test—the difference in the results of universalizing maxim 1 and maxim 2—is taken as the basis for calling maxim 1 the stronger ground of obligation.

The solution is ingenious and intuitive. Its faults lie with the general difficulties of the Nell version of the CC test. This can be seen rather strikingly in the way in which considerations appropriate to the CW test are required to generate a solution: e.g., the conditions for the reasonable pursuit of our projects, given our dependence on the cooperation of others. But then, there does not seem to be much real difference between the CC and CW tests as Nell describes them, so this should occasion no surprise. It is a more serious problem that it is less than clear how we would argue within the framework of F1a that a world in which people acted on maxim 2 would also (necessarily?) be a world which lacked trust and cooperation more generally. Still, one can see the idea in the argument.

There is another possible solution to the 'grounds of obligation' question which is suggested by a remark in the Doctrine of Virtue. Kant says, "we can be obligated in different ways to one and the same duty (that is, to one and the same action which is a duty)" (DV 21;222). The idea seems to be this: suppose I have a duty to perform some action x. The 'ground' of this duty might be in a promise I had made (I have a duty to do x on the basis of having promised to do x), or, I might have a duty to do x because it is the necessary means to promoting an obligatory end (e.g., helping some one in distress). The obligatory end is then the 'ground' of the duty to do x. This is as close as I can come to finding an account in Kant that fits the sense of 'ground' in 'grounds of obligation'. That is, we can be obligated in different ways to the 'same' action which is a duty: in the first case by a promise, in the second by the obligatory end of beneficence.

In applying this analysis to our problem we would be concerned in particular with finding the ground (or grounds) of the obligation to tell the truth. We must not be deterred by Kant's notorious obsession with truth-telling, an obsession which suggests that even raising the question of more than one ground for the obligation to tell the truth is out of order. Until better reason than I know can be found to justify his claim, there is no reason not to treat truth-telling in the same manner as everything else. What we need to get away from is the idea that there is a single truth-telling duty—i.e. a duty with a single ground. Most cases of lying fall under an injunction against deceit. But what if some truth-telling duties had as their ground our duty to help others in need? To give information when it is requested, for example. If this is conceivable then the apparent strain in maxims 1 and 2 is dissolved. It looked as though we had to choose between a strict (or narrow) duty to refrain from lying and a wide duty to help others.

Since it is only in the latter case that we have choice about how (or whether) to fulfill the duty in a given instance, maxim 2 seemed the only possibility. However, if the ground of a duty to tell the truth can also be our obligatory end of beneficence, then it is not hard to see how the conflict could be resolved in favor of maxim 1. The obvious difficulty with all of this is that it is not clear how one might argue for it. Nonetheless, it seems to be a promising proposal, and one which would lead us deeper into the Kantian conception of obligation. Perhaps one could even come to argue on Kantian grounds for a difference in the obligation not to lie and the obligation to tell the truth, and then make better sense of his objections to lying. But this must remain speculation.

There are two difficulties that such a proposal, when more adequately argued, would have to answer. First, if the suggestion is indicative of a procedure for resolving conflicts of duty, it does not seem to see the problem in terms of _different_ grounds of obligation, but in terms of two grounds of the same sort, of different strength. It is not then clear in what sense the rejected ground was not "sufficient to oblige" the agent. This may be connected to a second question—whether the one example indicates any _general_ solution for conflicts of duty. I do not at this time know how to answer this. This is so in part because it is not yet clear to me what the nature of the 'conflict of duty' problem is. Perhaps we are to read Kant as saying that there are only apparent conflicts of duty, but then we need to know what happens to the "weaker" ground of obligation, which, I presume, _would_ _have_ _been_ sufficient to obligate the agent had not the 'stronger' ground of obligation been present. It may be that Kant's notion of the 'necessity' of an obligated action will block an adequate solution within his theory. If we were to work toward an understanding of the problem of 'conflicts of duty' within a Kantian framework we would have to start by examining how it is that an agent arrives at the conviction that there are two incompatible things he ought to do. This would lead into interesting territory which cannot be investigated here: among the things we would need to look for is a distinction between cases of moral perplexity—not knowing _what_ to do—and conflicts of duty—not knowing _which_ of the things we are obliged to do we ought to do.

Another area of difficulty concerning the 'results' of the Categorical Imperative as a principle of moral judgment has to do with the _consequences_ of action. Traditionally, there have been two 'problems of consequences': first is the challenge, offered most famously by Mill (_Utilitarianism_ I,4), that despite Kant's claim that it is not the consequences of acts that determine their morality, there is nonetheless an appeal to consequences in determining the moral acceptability of maxims in the CC and CW tests; the second and related challenge is that Kant's moral theory fails to count consequences as morally relevant, and is therefore a defective moral theory. We will look at the two challenges in turn; neither of them, I believe, has any force; both of them arise from misunderstandings of the moral argument Kant makes.

There _is_, of course, an appeal to consequences in the CC and CW tests. But there is no appeal to the consequences of the action in question—as Kant remarks in the discussion of the Typic:

> Now everyone knows very well that if he secretly permits
> himself to deceive, it does not follow that everyone else
> will do so, or that if, unnoticed by others, he is lacking
> in compassion, it does not mean that everyone else will im-
> mediately take the same attitude toward him. (CrPrR 72;70)

The appeal to consequences in the two tests (and the Typic) is an appeal

to the consequences of the imagined universalization of the maxim of an

action. Moreover, the question is not, 'If your maxim were a law of na-

ture would the consequences be good or bad?' but, 'Can the maxim of your

action be conceived or willed a universal law of nature without contra-

diction?' If more is needed, one should remember that F1a is not,

strictly speaking, a formulation of the Categorical Imperative: it is

the principle through which beings such as ourselves may employ the

Categorical Imperative in judging our actions and maxims.

The general claim that practical rationality is exhibited in voli-

tion, in maxims—as opposed to action and consequences—is the direct

analogue of the familiar "a good will...is good through its willing

alone" rather than good "because of what it effects or accomplishes"

(G 62;394). It does not follow that consequences are unimportant, but

that they are not the point at which either rationality or moral good-

ness are assessed. A central point in Kant's conception of a good will

is characteristically overlooked in most readings of this famous passage.

The good will does not ignore consequences: good willing is with re-

spect to an end. Indeed, Kant says, the good will calls on us to strain

"every means so far as they are in our control" to realize its proposed

end (G 62;394). What is claimed for the good will is that its success

or failure in yielding results "can neither add to, nor subtract from"

its value. Similarly, willing is not judged rational or not as the action in which it issues is successful in attaining a willed end.

Consequences do count as morally relevant in two ways, then: the consequences we intend count as they appear in our maxims of action, and we are required to take sufficient means to promote our ends—e.g., the end of keeping a promise. This last is especially relevant when we recall that there are ends (beneficence, talents, etc.) we are morally required to have: we must not be careless or negligent in our efforts to produce 'required consequences'. So the objection cannot be that consequences are ignored in the moral theory of the Categorical Imperative. The objection can only be that the <u>actual</u> consequences of an action do not determine the morality of an action. But while it is true that they do not (or do not if the agent has made appropriate efforts, not been negligent, etc.), that fact by itself is hardly grounds for an <u>objection</u>. The actual consequences do not determine the morality of an action because the morality of an action is judged by its maxim. The argument cannot be: there are two kinds of moral theory: one that does and one that does not determine the morality of an action by its actual consequences; the one that does not is therefore morally defective! Perhaps the objection is simply—the actual consequences of an action must make <u>some</u> moral difference. But if this is the objection then we can answer that they do make a moral difference, just not the difference that is 'determining the morality of an action'. We have already remarked[30] that given the actual consequences of an action there is an appropriate moral question raised concerning the agent's <u>response</u> to those consequences. If an effort to fulfill an obligation fails an agent will usually adopt a maxim in response to that failure—a maxim which will in turn be evaluated by the Categorical Imperative. An agent cannot be required to guarantee successful execution of his proposed actions; it is not within his power as an agent. (Although an agent is required to guarantee success to the extent that it is in his power.) It is not clear what maxims will be 'morally correct' to adopt in response to different sorts of failures—accidents, interventions, mistakes, natural disasters, etc., may each call for a different moral response. All that we need to see here is that the agent does not terminate his moral relation to an action once he has adopted a maxim and prepared himself to act according to its principle. It is fair to conclude, then, that the moral theory of the Categorical Imperative does not fail to consider consequences in any clearly important way. There may be reasons to prefer a moral theory that evaluates actions by their consequences, but those will be reasons of a very different sort.

Before leaving the subject of the moral results of the Categorical Imperative we should consider one last fairly common objection. The first part of this objection appeals to the fact that the concepts and descriptive elements that appear in our maxims, and which form the basis of our assessment of maxims under the F1a test, consist in part of, or are understood through contingent social and empirical facts. For example (one which I borrow from Thomas Hill), it might be thought that you could not determine the acceptability of a maxim of divorce without considering the actual social context ("Strict divorce laws may be desirable where marriages are hard to get but undesirable where marriages are easy."[31]), or perhaps an agent's conception of marriage. Some of the force of the objection is deflected when we remember that we are not to use the Categorical Imperative to determine the moral acceptability of divorce (or of strict divorce laws) in general, but to assess particular maxims of divorce. It is not clear what _moral_ question Hill thinks strict divorce laws pose—not that I think they do not pose any, but that they could pose a great number of problems. I also take it to be plain that 'marriage' does not by itself suggest a moral problem, although there are surely moral problems that attend marriages. So if the problem of strict divorce laws is not an issue for the Categorical Imperative as such, perhaps we can remotivate the objection if we acknowledge that maxims of marriage (and so divorce) will involve an agent's conception of marriage—and that conception may well be connected to contingent social beliefs and institutions (e.g., the importance of stable nuclear families). The worry, clearly, is that if an agent's judgments are determined by his conceptions and existing background institutions then the Categorical Imperative may just validate maxims which reflect the prevailing social and cultural norms which determine the agent's conception of his action. A second and related concern is that because of this, the Categorical Imperative is not morally creative; it cannot lead an agent to reassess his given moral views, and this just because it is limited to the prevailing conceptions, etc.

Neither has much force as a general criticism. There is no reason why a given society might not condone practices which when they occurred as part of maxims would be rejected by F1a. A society that tolerated deceit would provide such an example. If the point is that individuals in such a society would not be likely to judge their maxims of deceit to be morally defective, this is not a failing of the Categorical Imperative.

If a maxim of deceit were brought to the Categorical Imperative and taken through the CC test, it could not pass. The problem is, agents in such a society would not be likely to think their maxims of deceit were even morally questionable and so would not bring them to the Categorical Imperative. Agents must be alive to moral problems if they are to evaluate their actions; no moral principle can be applied mechanically to all of an agent's actions. To someone who raised the question (in this odd society), the Categorical Imperative would deliver the answer.

Similarly, since agents bring maxims to the Categorical Imperative and maxims contain an agent's conception of what he would do, as agents have sharper perceptions about the world, see more deeply into themselves and their relations with others, the Categorical Imperative would (or could) evaluate their maxims differently. Some new insights about what one was doing might thereby be validated as moral insights. An agent who was troubled by a practice (e.g., deceit) which he had always taken for granted could be directed to act differently than he was accustomed to if he looked to the Categorical Imperative for guidance. If this is possible, it is not clear in what respect the Categorical Imperative could be accused of not being morally creative—i.e., incapable of leading an agent to reassess his moral views. The only limitation inherent in the theory is that agents must have some interest in the moral status of their actions and have some idea of what about an action might be morally relevant. This hardly seems stultifying.

But let us return to the divorce (or marriage) case for a moment; looking longer at what is problematic about it may yet be illuminating. Suppose one had a conception of marriage which included notions of family stability, transmission of values, etc. What you would then have is a conception of marriage as a means to an end. In that case, it would be perfectly appropriate for the activities associated with marriage to change (for the morally valid activities to change) as the circumstances of and beliefs about the end changed. Apart from this, what do we make of the fact that marriage is the sort of thing of which an agent can have a conception? (An answer to this may provide part of the explanation for why marriage as such is not a moral relation, although, as we noted earlier, relations within a marriage certainly are moral (among other things that they are).) Different people, in otherwise similar circumstances, but with different conceptions of the moral components of marriage, would find the Categorical Imperative ruling differently on their marriage-related maxims. Is this a serious objection? If the data are accurate, we might feel compelled to conclude that this evidence shows _no_ marriage maxim as such is a morally relevant maxim. But there is no good reason to accept this conclusion unless one is wedded to aprioristic canons of consistency among moral results—i.e., resulting _actions_. Alternatively, we might recognize that the canon of rationality established by the Categorical Imperative (through F1a) puts a requirement of consistency on an agent's maxims, but of a special sort—i.e., that the rationality of his actions not be contingent on others acting differently. On this account, the conception of an action which is embodied in the maxim may be a relevant determinant of the morality of a proposed action. The important point is, this is not always the case. Maxims of deceitful promising, for example, are not subject to this variability of conception. No one who makes a deceitful promise can escape its performative logic. If the concept of promising is ours, promises just do express certain intentions, etc. Agents may have or develop different conceptions of marriage, they cannot (logically cannot) have or use different concepts of promising. (They may not have to use the concept of promising at all, but that is a different matter.) Whether or not a maxim is morally relevant depends on the nature of the relations between persons which acting on that maxim will produce. Whether or not an agent's conception of what he would do determines moral relevance depends on whether the concept is one for which it is logically possible that there be different conceptions. It would be of no small interest to investigate which concepts applying to actions fall into which category, and to find an explanation of why they sort the way they do.

The tendency of these remarks is to suggest that we should attend to the fact that not every situation will pose the same moral problem to all moral agents, and that this need not be viewed as a fault either of the agents or of the theory that reflects and supports the difference. Such attention might also lead away from our present excessive focus on moral sketpticism and on arguments to rule people in or out of 'morality'. Instead we might look to and hope to learn from differences that exist within the community of the moral.

Early on in the discussion of F1a the hope was expressed that through our examination of it we might come to better understand the moral force of the common moral injunction, 'What if everyone did that?' (WIEDT). Apart from obvious similarities with elements of the F1a tests, we had good reason to hope for some clarification since Kant says (CrPrR 72;70) that the Typic version of F1a is a statement of the rule that people do use in deciding the permissibility, etc., of their actions. That is, if this is true, and if F1a is the moral foundation of the WIEDT question (or a version of it), then as we understand F1a and its moral point, we might hope to see why one might be moved by the consideration of what it would be like 'if everyone did that'.

The WIEDT question is interpreted in a variety of ways in contemporary literature. Hare,[32] for example, thinks it might be looked at as a common sense statement of his golden-rule or role-shift test: Do not do to others what you would not consent to have done to yourself were you in their position. Kant remarks that such a principle is trivial as a standard or principle of action, because, for example, "many a man would readily agree that others should not help him if only he could be dispensed from affording help to them" (G 97n;430n). In any case, the Hare test is obviously not equivalent to F1a as it requires no more of an agent than mere consistency of judgment and is not a criterion for what an agent can 'rationally will'. (Or: it interprets rational willing as mere consistency of judgment; the difference is not essential.) As a version of the WIEDT question the Hare test is disappointing in that it fails to show that there is any special moral force in the question, as there is nothing essentially or interestingly moral in consistency as such.

Marcus Singer[33] takes the question to be the moral question, but never gives a satisfactory explanation of why it is.[34] Nor, as Nell points out,[35] does he have a satisfactory solution to the problem of the relevant description of an action: how to answer 'What if everyone did __what__?' in order to be able to ask 'What if everyone did __that__?' While we are told to look to the desirability of the consequences of everyone's doing what we would do, no explanation is given for why the response 'But not everyone __will__ do that' is inappropriate. David Lyons'[36] argument for the extensional equivalence of act and rule utilitarianism effectively disposes of this analysis of the WIEDT question, for if they __are__ extensionally equivalent—if the 'that' is filled by the 'complete causally relevant' description of an action[37]—then the WIEDT question would neither offer nor register any special moral insight.

One last interpretation of the WIEDT question should be mentioned—that of fairness.[38] The idea here is that the WIEDT question points to essential conditions of social cooperation. It is not that the consequences of everyone doing 'that' would necessarily be undesirable (they might not be), but that if everyone did what the agent proposes (evades income taxes, etc.) a state of affairs from which all (including the agent) presently benefit would not obtain. The proposed action is unfair; the agent might be said to be taking unfair advantage of the cooperation of others. Although it is not clear how one might argue from the fact of social cooperation (producing benefits for all) to a duty of fairness, we __can__ see that on this sort of account the WIEDT question does have substantive moral content. Our interpretation of the WIEDT question according to F1a resembles the argument from fairness, although its scope is not restricted to the moral requirements of social cooperation. It will not be appropriate here to consider to what extent (if any) the Kantian argument could be used to ground a duty of fairness.

As I understand Rawls' conception of fairness in <u>A Theory of Justice</u>, this may well be what he has in mind.

If we read the WIEDT question through F1a we see it directing us to acknowledge that the rationality and point of our projects may depend on other persons in ways that may not be apparent to us. F1a shows us, by asking us to consider a world arising through and shaped by our willing, that we are members of a moral community, and that we are dependent on that community in ways we logically cannot evade. The CC test, which generates duties of justice, rejects actions whose maxims, because of the conception of action they contain, are not logically compatible with a like exercise of volition by everyone else—that is, maxims which cannot be conceived as a universal law of human willing without contradiction. The CW test, which generates duties of virtue, rejects maxims which express an unwillingness to acknowledge and accept the conditions of human willing. Because we do and cannot but depend on others, we may not refuse all claims on our help. Duties of justice depend on the logic of the concepts we use—and which we <u>must</u> use—in acting. Duties of virtue are derived from the conditions of our exercise of rationality in action. Together they describe the limits of what we can rationally will. It is a requirement of rationality that in our willing we not distinguish ourselves from others in the wrong way. (When the Categorical Imperative is considered as a requirement on <u>how</u> we will, this notion recurs in the idea that the ground of our maxims not be essentially subjective.) The Categorical Imperative opposes the adoption of any maxim which has hidden in the logic of its volition the requirement that it not be a principle others act on. It is this logic of action and volition that F1a draws to the surface. This substantive norm of rational willing is the Kantian explanation of the moral force behind the WIEDT question. It explains the sense in which we may not do what not everyone can do.

It is interesting, in this regard, to look at what Kant says we are characteristically doing when we do not act morally—when our maxims are contrary to duty:

> If we now attend to ourselves whenever we transgress a duty, we find that in fact we do not will that our maxim should become a universal law—since this is impossible for us—but rather that its opposite should remain a law universally: we only take the liberty of making an <u>exception</u> to it for ourselves (or even just for this once) to the advantage of inclination.... This procedure, though in our own impartial judgment it cannot be justified, proves none the less that we in fact recognize the validity of the categorical imperative and (with all respect for it) merely permit ourselves a few exceptions which are, as we pretend, inconsiderable and apparently forced upon us. (G 91-92;424)

This is a description of the moral transgressions of a <u>moral</u> agent—one who does not act on what Kant calls an 'evil' maxim (see Religion, 24ff). The agent makes an exception of himself from a rule whose authority he generally acknowledges. He might admit, for example, that it is wrong to deceive others to advance our own interests—Kant says he might even hold that the opposite should remain a law universally. He would not think himself to be acting on such a rule of deceit but either modify the rule ('To deceive only in extenuating circumstances x and y') to release himself from its injunction, or convince himself that it could not make a difference if he just once deceived. Formally this is like tailoring a maxim; it differs from tailoring in several important ways, however. First, it is not done with the intention of 'beating' the

Categorical Imperative; second, it is self-deceptive, as the agent will not be acting on the maxim he thinks he is, and, moreover, even the maxim he thinks he is acting on might not pass F1a. The apparent authority for the action—what the agent takes to justify what he would do—are, as Kant describes them, revealing of the agent's relation to moral requirements. Either all that he is doing is permitting himself a few inconsiderable exceptions—that is, I take it, he thinks he will not do this very often, and the consequences of his action are not very serious—or, he believes this action is forced upon him—that is, circumstances being what they were he really had no choice (he would argue), he <u>had</u> to deceive. I am not entirely sure what Kant meant the import of this to be. It might be that justifications of this sort are indicative of the fact that an agent does not fully understand what morality requires of him. This interpretation seems unlikely, as Kant thinks we <u>do</u> know what is and what is not a morally relevant justification of our action. The most plausible view, I think, is that Kant is here sketching the phenomenology of moral temptation. The strength of our own interests will lead us to believe that we are specially situated when we are not; the force of our feeling will convince us that we cannot choose to act otherwise when in fact we could, and so on. It is because we are not evil, because we do acknowledge moral claims, that our transgressions take the form of self-deception. It is a telling, brief sketch. We might do well to follow its lead and investigate the most common forms of moral failing as we look to understand the nature of moral obligation.

In these last two chapters the emphasis has been entirely on Kant's account of moral right and wrong. We have examined the principle of judgment (F1a) by which we may assess our actions as obligatory, forbidden, or permissible, and we have tried to indicate why this principle which tests maxims for a principle of pure practical reason (F1: a principle we are not capable of applying) should be a moral test. That is, we have tried to show the source of its moral content. We have seen that the 'morality of actions' cannot be determined independently of consideration of an agent's motive, because it is only through the motive of an action that we may know its maxim. What we have not said is that the 'morality of an action' depends on the agent having a moral motive. If I determine that action according to a certain maxim is forbidden, then I know I am required to act on the contrary of my maxim, but there is no specification in that of the motive with which I am to act. However, we argued earlier (p. 206) that all imperatives regulate action in two ways: 1) they provide criteria of correctness for proposed actions, and 2) they provide a norm of velition—a requirement on how as well as what an agent wills. (The latter was the subject of much of the discussion of the Categorical Imperative in chapter four.) Since our ambition in this essay has been to approach an understanding of the concept of a categorical imperative, we should conclude by saying something more about the second requirement—about moral willing—than we did in chapter four and in light of our increased understanding of the Categorical Imperative as a principle of judgment. Although the two requirements are distinct—Kant warns us (CrPrR 72;70) that the comparison of a maxim of action with a universal natural law (its UTC) is not to be the determining ground of the agent's will—we will try to sketch the

shape of an account of moral motivation in line with our analysis of
F1a, without violating the terms of Kant's warning, and without entering
the abyss of Kant's moral psychology.

The Categorical Imperative is said to require of us not only that
our actions conform to its principle (our maxims must pass the test of
F1a) but also that our willing be according to the Categorical Imperative: our will must conform to the Categorical Imperative as its principle. The principle of a volition is essential to how an agent conceives himself to be acting. What the Categorical Imperative must require of our willing, then, is that in acting on maxims which satisfy
F1a we conceive of ourselves as acting on maxims which do (or could)
have the Categorical Imperative as their principle: that is, we would
have our action be according to a maxim which conforms to the Categorical Imperative—a maxim which conforms to the 'universality of a law as
such'. This formally describes the moral motive—the subjective determining ground of a will which has the Categorical Imperative as its
principle. Whatever the psychological theory we import to fill out the
formal theory, this is the sketch of moral motivation it must fit.

There is much that is difficult and obscure in Kant's theory of
moral motivation, and it would take another long essay to do justice to
such complex problems. What we can do here is try to use our analysis
of the moral content of F1a to provide some intuitive grasp of the conception of himself acting an agent would have in acting morally—with
the Categorical Imperative as the principle of his volition. An action
whose maxim has passed the tests of F1a is one whose rationality is not
contingent on the fact that not everyone does act on that maxim. It is

not a maxim which is rational for an agent just because others do not act on it. An agent might act on such a maxim without having a conception of it as satisfying this condition of rationality. An agent might have a conception of his maxim as satisfying the condition of rationality but choose to act on such maxims for extraneous reasons (a hope for salvation, etc.). Only an agent whose maxim embodies this condition of rationality as an essential part of his conception of his action would be acting on a moral motive.

Every maxim necessarily has a subjective determining ground—what we call a motive. The subjective ground of most maxims is to be found among the agent's interests, needs, wants, etc. (Kant calls it the motive of self-love; it is the motive which has as its correlative end an agent's conception of happiness). The moral motive is also a possible subjective ground of maxims. When an agent acts on a maxim which could not pass the F1a tests, the ground of that maxim is essentially subjective—that is, deriving its claim to rationality solely from the needs or interests of the agent. Its logic is that of the isolated subject. Agents who act on morally satisfactory maxims out of other than moral motives do not, from the point of view of the subjective ground of their action, act differently from agents who act on morally forbidden maxims. In acting on a moral motive, the ground of the action is not essentially subjective. That is, in acting on a moral motive the agent acknowledges himself to be a member of a moral community—a community which defines the conditions of and limits the expression of his rationality. The logic of his action is that of a rational agent among others. We might say, with Kant, that he acts as a law-making member of a Kingdom of Ends.

Notes

1. <u>What if everyone did that.</u>

2. We will consider the possibility (raised by Nell: <u>Acting on Principle</u>, pp. 68, 76) that there may be maxims such that both the maxim and its contrary <u>cannot</u> be rationally willed when we take up the question of tailored maxims and other problems connected to the specification of the maxim with which an agent comes to the Categorical Imperative. The reason for this delay is the conviction that this problem arises for Nell largely because of the nature of the maxims she imagines being brought to F1a for testing.

3. O. Nell, <u>Acting on Principle</u>, p. 76.

4. See p. 53 ff.

5. See p. 61 ff.

6. See p. 131 ff.

7. O. Nell, <u>Acting on Principle</u>, p. 71.

8. This, as such, does not constitute a decisive argument against the Nell version of the CC test. If, however, the Nell test cannot deal with these cases, that fact would weaken its claim. I hesitate to conclude that it cannot, as it is possible that the Nell test can be revised to include the agent's anticipation of his likelihood of success (and the <u>grounds</u> for such anticipation) <u>in</u> the maxim of action, and thus judge these cases correctly. What problems such a procedure might pose, and how (or if) they might be resolved need not concern us here.

9. See O. Nell, <u>Acting on Principle</u>, p. 77.

10. Or, they <u>are</u> maxims of morally suspect actions: e.g., an attempt to manipulate a market or explicitly free-ride.

11. One interesting result of this exercise is the raising of the possibility that an agent who in fact merely desired to neutralize discrimination might find his maxim passing the F1a test. We should not suppose this is so prematurely, however, for the crucial element that the CC test would look at is the cheating—i.e., what sort of act that is. What actions can be justified by what ends is a question that should not have an obvious answer.

12. O. Nell, <u>Acting on Principle</u>, p. 113.

13. Part one of the <u>Metaphysics of Morals</u>.

14. H.J. Paton's Foreword to the Gregor translation of <u>The Doctrine of Virtue</u>, p. xi.

15. O. Nell, Acting on Principle, p. 115.

16. Ibid.

17. I must confess to a certain degree of 'naturalism' in these re-marks, but this bias of mine does not really affect Kant's theory. As we will see in the next section, Kant's conception of moral judgment is parasitic on agents' having moral views—on their seeing their actions in moral categories. This is a much stronger requirement than the rather weak claims of moral relevance I have been making, but if my way of putting the argument is objectionable, it can be made in Kant's terms. I should add that in saying the method of moral judgment is parasitic on an agent's having moral views I do not mean to suggest, and will argue against, the view that Kant's theory is wedded to the moral principles moral agents happen to have.

18. I make no effort in this discussion to give an account of weakness of will within the framework of volition and maxims. Problems with this notion are notorious on most accounts of volition, and while it would be of independent interest to see what purchase we could get on the problem of akrasia using the Kantian apparatus, it is not really at issue here and unnecessary for the point at hand.

19. I recognize that the Categorical Imperative has a reputation from Kant's own employment of it that suggests no maxim of deceitful promis-ing could ever be permissible. I see no reason to suppose this is a fair assessment of the Categorical Imperative. We will take up the ar-gument for this type of example when we consider cases of supposed 'con-flict of duties'.

20. T.E. Hill, "The Kingdom of Ends", p. 311.

21. Ibid.

22. Ibid.

23. Ibid.

24. It might be thought that this is not, strictly speaking, true, since there are formulations of the Categorical Imperative which make no mention of maxims. In particular, one might point to F2: The Formula of Humanity. Two facts are pertinent here. First, Kant emphasizes that it is F1a that must be used in moral judgment. The Formula of Humanity is said to be closer to 'intuition'—showing in a more perspicuous way what is 'wrong' with a maxim judged irrational by F1a. Second, and more to the immediate point, close inspection of the Formula of Humanity re-veals, I believe, that it cannot be applied to cases without using the agent's maxim because it requires that we limit our actions by what the person affected (ourselves or another) can rationally will.

25. R.P. Wolff, The Autonomy of Reason, p. 51.

26. <u>Ibid</u>., pp. 49-51, 159.

27. O. Nell, <u>Acting on Principle</u>, pp. 134-135.

28. <u>Ibid</u>., p. 135.

29. <u>Ibid</u>.

30. See p. 275.

31. T.E. Hill, "The Kingdom of Ends", pp. 311-312.

32. R.M. Hare, <u>Freedom and Reason</u>, 137n-138n.

33. M.G. Singer, <u>Generalization in Ethics</u>.

34. There is no need for us to enter the controversy surrounding Singer's deduction of his generalization argument. Even if it were possible to reconstruct his argument, the absence of a solution to the problem of relevant description would render it uninteresting.

35. O. Nell, <u>Acting on Principle</u>, pp. 22-30.

36. D. Lyons, <u>Forms and Limits of Utilitarianism</u>.

37. See <u>Ibid</u>., pp. 55-61.

38. See, for example, Colin Strang, "What If Everyone Did That?"

Bibliography

1. Works by Immanuel Kant

Critique of Practical Reason. Translated by L.W. Beck, New York: Bobbs-Merrill, Library of Liberal Arts, 1956.

Immanuel Kant's Critique of Pure Reason. Translated by N.K. Smith. London: Macmillan, 1933.

The Doctrine of Virtue. Translated by M.J. Gregor. New York: Harper and Row, 1964.

The Groundwork of the Metaphysics of Morals. Translated by H.J. Paton. New York: Harper and Row, 1964. (Also translated by L.W. Beck, as The Foundations of the Metaphysics of Morals. New York: Bobbs-Merrill, Library of Liberal Arts, 1959.)

The Metaphysical Elements of Justice. Translated by J. Ladd. New York: Bobbs-Merrill, Library of Liberal Arts, 1965.

"Perpetual Peace", in H. Reiss (ed.), Kant's Political Writings. Cambridge: Cambridge University Press, 1971.

Religion Within the Limits of Reason Alone. Translated by T.M. Greene and H.H. Hudson. New York: Harper and Row, 1960.

2. Other Works

Anscombe, G.E.M. Intention. Oxford: Basil Blackwell, 1958.

Beck. L.W. "Apodictic Imperatives", Kant-Studien, 49(1957), 7-23.

_____. A Commentary on Kant's Critique of Practical Reason. Chicago: University of Chicago Press, 1960.

Cavell, S. Must We Mean What We Say? New York: Scribner's, 1969.

Foot, P. "Morality as a System of Hypothetical Imperatives", Philosophical Review, LXXXI (9172), 305-316.

_____. "Reasons for Action and Desires", Aristotelian Society, supp. vol. XLVI (1972), 203-210.

Hampshire, S. Freedom of the Individual. Princeton: Princeton University Press, 1975.

Hare, R.M. Freedom and Reason. Oxford: Clarendon Press, 1963.

Harrison, J. "Kant's Examples of the First Formulation of the Categorical Imperative", reprinted in R.P. Wolff.(ed.), Kant: A Collection of Critical Essays. London: Macmillan, 1968.

Hill, T.E. "The Hypothetical Imperative", Philosophical Review, LXXXII (1973), 429-450.

_____. "The Kingdom of Ends", in L.W. Beck (ed.), Proceedings of the Third International Kant Congress. Dordrecht-Holland: D. Reidel, 1972.

Lyons, D. Forms and Limits of Utilitarianism. Oxford: Clarendon Press, 1965.

MacIntyre, A. A Short History of Ethics. New York: Macmillan, 1966.

Murphy, J.G. Kant: The Philosophy of Right. London: Macmillan, 1970.

_____. "Kant's Concept of a Right Action", in L.W. Beck (ed.), Kant Studies Today. La Salle, Ill.: Open Court, 1969.

Nell, O. Acting on Principle: An Essay on Kantian Ethics. New York: Columbia University Press, 1975.

Mill, J.S. Utilitarianism. New York: Bobbs-Merrill, Library of Liberal Arts, 1957 (reprinted).

Paton, H.J. The Categorical Imperative. Philadelphia: University of Pennsylvania Press, 1971 (reprinted).

Rawls, J. A Theory of Justice. Cambridge, Mass.: Harvard University Press, 1971.

Sidgwick, H. The Methods of Ethics. New York: Dover, 1966 (reprinted).

Singer, M.G. Generalization in Ethics: An Essay in the Logic of Ethics with the Rudiments of a System of Moral Philosophy. New York: Alfred A. Knopf, 1961.

Smart, J.J.C. "Extreme and Restricted Utilitarianism", Philosophical Quarterly, 6(1956), 345-54.

Strang, C. "What if Everyone Did That?" Durham University Journal, 53(1960), 5-10.

Williams, T.C. The Concept of the Categorical Imperative: A Study of the Place of the Categorical Imperative in Kant's Ethical Theory. Oxford: Clarendon Press, 1968.

Wolff, R.P. The Autonomy of Reason: A Commentary on Kant's Groundwork

<u>of</u> <u>the</u> <u>Metaphysics</u> <u>of</u> <u>Morals</u>. New York: Harper and Row, 1973.

Wood, A.W. <u>Kant's</u> <u>Moral</u> <u>Religion</u>. Ithaca, N.Y.: Cornell University Press, 1970.

_____. "Kant on False Promises", in L.W. Beck (ed.), <u>Proceedings</u> <u>of</u> <u>the</u> <u>Third</u> <u>International</u> <u>Kant</u> <u>Congress</u>. Dordrecht—Holland: D. Reidel, 1972.

DATE DUE

HIGHSMITH   # 45220